BASEBALL HISTORY 2

BASEBALL HISTORY 2

An Annual of Original Baseball Research

**Edited by
Peter Levine**

Meckler Books
The Trade Division of
Meckler Corporation

BASEBALL HISTORY
An Annual of Original Baseball Research

Cover art reproduced from the limited edition lithograph
"Left Field Corner" by Andy Jurinko, published by Bill Goff, Inc., P.O. Box 508, Gracie
Station, New York, NY 10028.

ISBN 0-88736-342-3   65313824

Meckler Books, the Trade Division of Meckler Corporation,
  11 Ferry Lane West, Westport, CT 06880.
Meckler Ltd., Grosvenor Gardens House, Grosvenor Gardens,
  London SW1W 0BS, U.K.

Printed on acid free paper.
Printed in the United States of America.

Contents

EDITOR'S NOTE

Welcome to the second annual volume of *Baseball History,* the only book devoted to publishing the year's best original popular, scholarly, historical pieces about baseball. This year's selections include our usual mixture of essays, interviews, and personal reminiscences. Among them are Robert Barney's perceptive analysis of the cultural significance of baseball in Canada, Debra Shattuck's pathbreaking study of women's participation in America's "National Game," David Voigt's interesting attempt to understand the fans who follow it, A.D. Suehsdorf's entertaining story about "two shortstops"—Mark Koenig and Dick Bartell, and Bill Felber's gripping account of Jack Chesbro and the 1904 pennant race between the New York Highlanders and the Boston Pilgrims. Thanks to the addition of Fred Roberts as book review editor, the book review section contains the perceptive comments of such fine writers as Larry Ritter and Jules Tygiel. The "Extra Innings" section is truly extraordinary. It contains "The Dixon Cornbelt League," a short story graciously offered by W.P. Kinsella, the renowned author of *Shoeless Joe*. I hope you enjoy our efforts.

Peter Levine
East Lansing, Michigan

Diamond Rituals:
Baseball in Canadian Culture

ROBERT KNIGHT BARNEY

Late in the American Depression, 1939 to be exact, my father's daily woodcutting chores (like millions, he was jobless), complemented by my impatient stacking of the split pieces, inevitably were accompanied in summer months by an imposing New England cultural ritual—afternoon radio broadcasts of Red Sox games from Fenway Park in Boston. Jimmy Foxx was my first baseball hero. Even though I never saw him play, his feats described by Jim Britt, the play-by-play announcer, were magnified several times over by my imagination. By the summer of 1941 the nation's economic woes abated. America girded for war. My father got a real job. He celebrated his first paycheck, I remember, by taking me on an odyssey of odysseys. From our home in the Lakes Region of New Hampshire we journeyed down to Boston, Fenway Park, and a Red Sox game. In ensuing years Fenway became my cathedral; Ted Williams and Dom DiMaggio, my bishops. Right from the start, I had visions of someday becoming a major leaguer. I lived baseball, breathed it, immersed myself in its every facet. And I was not unique. There were millions of American boys just like me. We were all preoccupied with baseball. Through a genealogical process by which we are endowed with blue eyes or brown, motor skills ability, proclivity for using numbers or words, so, too, it seems, are Americans endowed with a particular love for baseball. That's the way it has been for over a hundred years, and probably will remain so for the next hundred.

So what does this have to do with baseball in Canadian culture? In effect, it has everything to do with baseball in Canada, because the enduring diamond spectacle has developed a cultural identity in Canada that approaches its American counterpart in intensity. In recent times the success of the Expos and the Blue Jays has projected baseball to a feverish pitch; indeed, the fortunes and misfortunes of the two clubs as members of the major league fraternity have roused the interest of Canadians from coast to coast in a way that few events have. And though baseball can count legions of older fans, it is a game that has

1

particular appeal to youth and young adults. Much of the success of the two decades of major league experience in Canada can be traced to the enthusiasm that young Canadians can at last exhibit growing up with a "home team." Despite this enthusiasm for the game, it is evident that most Canadians enraptured by the mystique of baseball know little about, much less have an appreciation for, the game's roots and its subsequent evolution in Canada. This essay attempts to explain those roots and, as well, comment on the extraordinary set of circumstances which baseball enjoys in contemporary Canada.

***

It is well known that baseball has been imbedded in America's cultural genes since the children of English settlers in Colonial America paused in their daily routines to muster ball and bat and play at various versions of what we know today as baseball.[1] To be sure, the rules were different then than those we know now, they even varied from locale to locale, but there were important common features that kept the game in a perspective of "sameness." Balls were tossed and struck by bats. Runners ran to bases or goals. Players were put out. Tallies scored. So it is today.

In tracing baseball's genesis in Canada, it is natural to postulate that if the game's roots were entrenched in the play of American colonial children, then the pastime must have journeyed to Canada in the cultural baggage of children arriving with their parents from the Revolutionary War-torn, politically fragmented and economically devastated American colonies. Such early immigrants to Canada were called Loyalists, but one must remember that their motivation for leaving the colonies notwithstanding, they were distinctly American in cultural context.[2] Indeed, they were descendants of several generations of American-born individuals. The first wave of these immigrant types made a beeline for lands north of the St. John River (today's New Brunswick, Nova Scotia and Prince Edward Island). By 1784 their numbers amounted to almost 30,000. Be that as it may, it is not from this first wave of American immigrants that the earliest records of baseball are found. Rather, they surface some 1,000 miles to the west, namely, in the southwestern portion of Ontario (then called Upper Canada).

By the eve of the War of 1812, Ontario had received some 60,000 American immigrants. They made up three quarters of Ontario's total population. About 35,000 of them were the result of a second wave of Loyalist migration to Canada. The remaining 25,000 were later arrivals.[3] Following the War of 1812 American immigration once again intensified along both flanks of Lake Erie. When Americans, especially those in New England and New York, looked westward for a suitable route to new settlement regions in what is today Michigan, Illinois, Wisconsin, and Minnesota, the shortcut Canadian corridor between the Niagara and Detroit Rivers did not escape their attention. A well-trod path developed between Buffalo and Detroit, over which a steady stream of Americans plied their way westward in search of new lives and better economic substance. British administrators tried to keep them out, but the task proved well nigh impossible.[4] Land speculators in Southwestern Ontario, faced with little prospect for land sales and development resulting from gradual immigration and settlement on the frontier of people from the British Isles, seized on American immigrant pocketbooks for quick sale and tenancy of their lands.[5] Thus, Southwestern Ontario, in the years following the War of 1812, came to resemble a giant filter. Thousands of Americans, it is true, permeated the filter and reached the American West. Thousands of others did not, electing instead to remain in Canada and build their homes and new lives there.[6] The resulting regional cultural manifestation was one of marked American flavor. The evidence suggests, therefore, that American immigration into Southwestern Ontario before and after the War of 1812 deposited the roots of a recreational pastime known as baseball.

The reminiscence of Adam E. Ford (see Appendix), a resident of the area as early as the 1830s, establishes the earliest documented reference to Canada's baseball legacy. Adam E. Ford was born in Oxford County, Ontario in 1831. During his youth he witnessed baseball games played by older youths and adults; later he played the game himself. After graduating in medicine from McGill University in 1855, Ford settled in St. Marys, Ontario. There he established a medical practice and became active in community civic and sport affairs. Socially and financially prominent by virtue of marriage and personal initiative, Ford's record of sport participation and organizational leadership characterized him as a man of zeal and dedication. He was an active curler, cricket player and rifle shooting enthusiast. In the 1870s he served on the managing directorates of the local race track association and lacrosse club, respectively. His sharp interest in baseball matters prompted his election as president of the St Marys Young Actives, a team composed of community youth, and the Beaver Baseball Club, the town's senior baseball organization.[7] Such energy and enthusiasm extended from his interest in sport as a youth. And he never forgot the experience of his favorite boyhood pastime—baseball. When he was 55 years old his reminiscence of baseball events in Oxford County during the 1830s, 1840s and 1850s was published in the popular American weekly, *Sporting Life*.[8] Ford's recall provides legitimate and graphic descriptions of local baseball rules and conditions as they had evolved in his boyhood locale by the 1830s. Equally important, Ford's reminiscence renders insight into baseball's circumstances well before the time of his youth. And finally, his message reflects on modifications to the game occurring during his young adult years. Combining Ford's reminiscence with known events of immigration and social development in Southwestern Ontario establishes a starting point for understanding baseball's roots in Canada.

Ford's reminiscence pointed specifically to June 4, 1838. That date documented his earliest memory of baseball in the locale of his youth—the village of Beachville, Oxford County, Ontario. We know that the 4th of June was an annual holiday in Ontario at the time. It had been since 1793, at which time King George III's birthday was legislated into statute law as Militia Muster Day.[9] On that day each year in Ontario, every community's merchants, tradesmen, and rustic hearties from the surrounding area gathered to drill at arms, indulge in sporting events, and enjoy social activities common to the occasion. It was at such a celebration day in 1838 that young Adam Ford witnessed his first

Adam Enoch Ford, circa 1886. Courtesy St. Marys District Museum, St. Marys, Ontario.

baseball. The entire proceedings and flavor of the day made quite an impression on him. Years later he wrote of them. Research on the Ford reminiscence has confirmed many of the events he described.

There are several dimensions of Ford's reminiscence that merit attention here. For instance, primary sources confirm Ford's recall that a detachment of militia viewed the baseball play as it mustered for action in support of the government's sustained campaigns against restive American settlers in Southwestern Ontario during the Rebellions of 1837-1838.[10] Further, a study of genealogical, obituary, and tombstone evidence, together with land ownership records, supports the fact that most of the players mentioned by Ford did indeed live in Oxford County and were between 15 and 24 years of age in 1838.[11] And nineteenth century maps of Beachville confirm the location of the shops behind which the game was played.[12] Finally, Ford's description of home-manufactured baseball equipment, particularly a "calfskin-covered ball of twisted yarn and a club (bat) blocked out from an oversized wagon-wheel spoke and finished on a shaving horse," coincides with other early accounts of attempts to construct homemade baseball paraphernalia.[13]

Of major interest to baseball historians, of course, is Ford's commentary on the playing field of his youth. At first glance Ford's diagram (included in

Appendix) appears quite similar to the square baseball configurations known to be in vogue in both New York state and Massachusetts by the early 1840s. On further examination, however, certain aspects of Ford's "plan" reflect parallels to Alexander Cartwright's historic 1845 field design. Both Ford's and Cartwright's field schemes possessed two features that distinguished them from the early New York and Massachusetts playing fields. The first difference involved territory for fair and foul struck balls or, as Ford described them, "fair hit" and "no hit." Such a concept proved to be an important innovation in diminishing baseball's character association with cricket. The second difference related to a "home base" common to the activities of striker (batter) and baserunner alike. Both of the foregoing innovations have ordinarily been attributed to Cartwright's genius. Ford's reminiscence of them existing in a game played on a pasture field behind Enoch Burdick's shops in Beachville, Ontario in 1838, of course, predates Cartwright's revolutionary ideas by seven years. Could knowledge of the "Canadian game" have prompted Cartwright? Or did Cartwright simply synthesize the rules of a number of baseball forms known to him by 1845?

Similar to all early forms of baseball in America, Ford's "Canadian game" featured strikers or knockers (batters), catchers, throwers or tossers (pitchers), fetchers (fielders), byes (bases), and baselines. Unlike Cartwright's scheme, earlier New York and Massachusetts forms of baseball, as well as Ford's "Canadian game," afforded the striker an easy time in getting to the first bye. After that, however, the baserunner became the object of much fun and excitement as he made his way around the bases dodging balls thrown at him while he was running between bases. The practice of "burning," "soaking," or "plugging" was commonplace until the Cartwright rules replaced the often painful experience with the far less lusty practice of tagging the baserunner.

Ford's reminiscence also addressed the internal dynamics of early baseball in

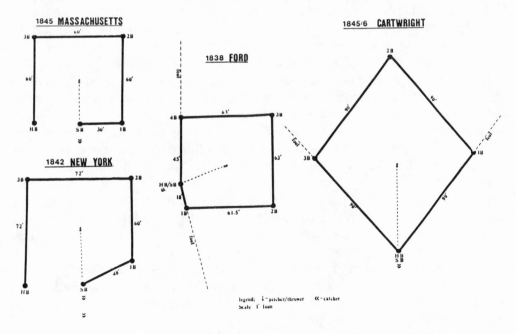

nbb/rkb 87'

5

Canada. On the relationship between pitcher and batter, Ford alluded to a "rule of honor" which abrogated the need for externally imposed authority in the form of umpires. Mutual consensus, informed by oral tradition maintained by "local old-timers," provided the basis for agreement on all matters pertaining to playing the game, including its duration and the number of players involved. Such consensus called for a game which featured between 6 and 9 innings of play, and a team composition which ranged from 7 to 12 players per side. Continuity between past and present, as described by Ford, extended beyond mere playing rules. The fame and physical prowess of former athletes, for instance, were etched into local baseball tradition. Ford's reference to "Old" Ned Dolson is a case in point.[14]

Ford recounts that the local Ontario game experienced some drastic changes as Cartwright's New York game began to penetrate Southwestern Ontario in the early 1850s.[15] The intrusion of "new ways" encroached on the old traditions of play. The differences between the two styles (the "old" local game and the "new" Cartwright game) impressed Ford, particularly the impact wrought on hitting and fielding by the introduction of a baseball containing a measure of "Indian rubber." Despite early experimentation with Cartwright's game, Oxford County ball players persisted with their regional variation of baseball for at least a decade. Familiarity, underscored by local tradition and derived local cultural meanings of the game, it seems, left little room for change. As late as 1860, for instance, matches between Beachville's sister communities Ingersoll and Woodstock involved 11 players, rather than 9, and used 4 bases, rather than 3.[16] This prompted the New York *Clipper* to refer to the type of baseball played in the region of Southwestern Ontario as the "Canadian game"—something understood to be quite distinct from the game then popularly played in New York City and its environs.[17]

By the mid-1850s, however, the portent of change to established local baseball tradition began to be noted. The advent of telegraphic communications and the development of railway networks expanded the world of heretofore isolated inland Ontario communities. When this happened it was only natural that localized baseball zeal seek the challenge of competition with teams from other communities. Mutually agreeable, transregional, written rules were essential. The so-called New York Rules, drawn up by Alexander Cartwright in 1845, modified in the late 1850s and throughout the 1860s by the National Association of Baseball Players (an American organization), provided the necessary standard for Canadian intercommunity play.[18] In 1859 the Hamilton Young American and Toronto Young Canadian Baseball Clubs competed in Canada's first intercommunity baseball game under the New York Rules.[19] By 1861 the town of Woodstock had embraced the same rules as the standard for competitive play.[20] American baseball's playing rules, originally set in place by amateur authorities, in time gave way to rules formulated by professional elements; first, the National Association of Professional Base Ball Players (NAPBBP) in 1871, and finally, in 1876, the National League of Professional Base Ball Clubs (NLPBBC). In each instance the playing rules of the professional organizations were adopted by Canadian clubs.[21]

It is well known that the New York Knickerbocker Club was the first baseball organization in America. In 1845 the Knickerbockers established a club constitution and formulated a set of rules.[22] Throughout the 1850s baseball clubs proliferated in the northeastern United States, particularly in and around New York City and in New England.[23] The first baseball club organized in Canada was the Hamilton Maple Leaf Club. In 1854, drawing on the model of American baseball club organization pioneered by the Knickerbockers, the Maple Leafs struck a constitution, formed an executive, set annual dues, and arranged for a place to play.[24] In 1856 a baseball club was organized in London, Ontario. J.K. Brown, a French millinery shop owner, became president of the first executive. Practices for the club's 22 members were held twice weekly on the military reserve grounds.[25] Woodstock's Young Canadian and Ingersoll's Rough and Ready Baseball Clubs were organized in 1860.[26] Following club organization in other Southwestern Ontario towns, among them, Dundas, Guelph, Stratford, and St. Marys, intercommunity competition blossomed.

An inevitable extension of intercommunity play was the organization of baseball tournaments. Spurred by community pride, competitive tournaments involving several team entries became popular in the late 1860s. Cash prizes, together with handsome silver ball or gold bat symbolic trophies, prompted baseball tournament appearances by teams throughout Ontario. In this respect, Woodstock was a leader in both organization and participation, an influence duly noted by a popular American sporting publication. "The Woodstonians," reported the *Clipper*, "hold a high position in the advancement of matters pertaining to the American National Game."[27] Ultimately, the zeal to play on competitive terms in regional tournaments led to the specter of professional baseball in Canada.

A natural extension of intercommunity rivalries and quest for tournament prizes and championships were efforts to acquire and retain the playing personnel which guaranteed success. Canadians emulated the American model of baseball professionalism in rapid order. There is no doubt as to which Canadian town, team, and individual was responsible for ushering in the era of bona fide professional baseball in Canada: the town was Guelph; the team was the Guelph Maple Leafs, and the individual was George Sleeman. Guelph started playing intercommunity baseball as early as 1863.[28] The Maple Leafs were organized in 1864. By 1870 they had developed to the point where they rightfully deserved the reputation of being Canada's best baseball team.[29] Their desire to test themselves with more demanding challenges led them to seek matches with American teams. In 1871 the Maple Leafs invited the Forest City Club of Cleveland, a member of the Professional Players' League in the United States, to play a match game in Guelph. Before a reported crowd of 5,000 Guelph lost the contest by a run, a deficit rationalized by a claim of conspiracy against an umpire's decision in the final inning.[30] The following year the Baltimore Club of the same American professional league visited Guelph. This time Guelph triumphed by a run.[31] Guelph's success roused American awareness of Canadian baseball expertise. "Beware of those upstarts from the North," commented an American baseball columnist.[32]

George Sleeman, wealthy brewing entrepreneur and zealous Guelph civic leader, had gained a measure of local baseball fame through success in organiz-

Woodstock's Young Canadian Baseball Nine, circa 1862. Courtesy Ye Olde Museum, Beachville, Ontario.

ing and developing his Silver Creek Brewery nine for local competition. Eventually Sleeman was invited to head up the Maple Leafs. Sleeman was quick to ensure that Guelph's premier team retain the services of its good players sought by teams in other Ontario communities (and by some American clubs, too). The aggressive Sleeman was also industrious in acquiring better personnel for playing positions not capably filled.[33] In this way the Guelph Maple Leafs were able to triumph consistently over all Canadian competitors. As well, the Maple Leafs held their own in games with professional teams from the United States, which included contests against some of the best clubs of the era—Philadelphia, New York and Boston.[34]

When the determination of other Ontario baseball clubs rose in the quest to establish a competitive balance, one can well imagine the result. Baseball professionalism spread across the province, much of the phenomenon buttressed by the importation of American players. The most determined of Guelph's challengers was the Tecumseh Baseball Club of London. A heated rivalry developed between the two cities and their representative ball clubs. London, with greater financial resources at its disposal, acquired the necessary players to bring Guelph's domination to an end.[35] By 1875 a new baseball scene evolved, one in which professionalism in both large and small context became a fact of life.

Canada has experienced more than a century of minor league professional baseball history. Exactly 90 years before the Expos became Canada's first team to make it to "the Bigs," Guelph's Maple Leafs and London's Tecumsehs were admitted to the International Association, a league which baseball history has recorded as "the first minor league."[36] In reality, it was not a *minor league* at all. Rather, it was the first of several unsuccessful attempts to challenge the National League's grasp for urban markets and the best playing personnel available.[37] In that regard, the establishment of the American League in 1901 finally produced a stable and durable competitor.

London's powerful Tecumsehs won the inaugural International Association championship in 1877.[38] Since then, minor league baseball in Canada has been an established fact. By 1912 Canadian-based teams were playing in four minor leagues.[39] During the decade 1926–1935 Canadian teams were represented in six minor leagues, three of which were composed of strictly Canadian teams (Western Canadian League, Eastern Canadian League, and the Colliery League), and three of which were American-Canadian in context (Western International League, Michigan-Ontario League, and the International League.)[40]

Spurred partly by minor league activity and partly by general interest in big league competition south of the border, Canadian interest in the diamond sport

Manager George Sleeman (center) with Guelph Maple Leafs of 1874. Courtesy Canadian Sports Hall of Fame Archives (Toronto).

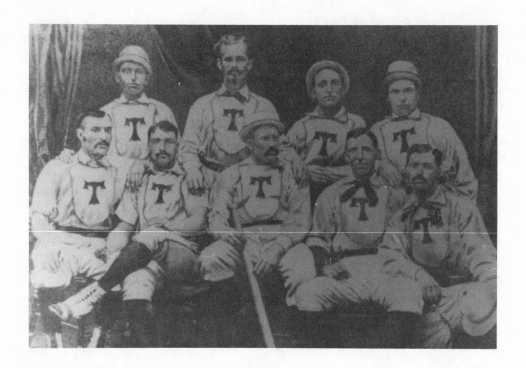

The London Tecumseh Nine, Dominion Champions, 1876. Courtesy D.B. Weldon Library Archives, The University of Western Ontario, London, Ontario.

expanded during the first half of the twentieth century. A content analysis of the newspaper coverage of sport for two different time frames demonstrates quite conclusively that baseball was a dominant activity in overall sports reporting and, at the same time, underscores the growth in popularity of the diamond sport in Canada. In the Maritime province of Nova Scotia, for example, the Halifax *Herald* allotted 37.6 percent of its 1915 sports coverage to baseball, a figure outdoing hockey, the second most reported sporting activity. Similarly, in 1915 baseball received the greatest share of newspaper attention compared to all other sports in the leading newspapers of large Canadian urban centers: 1) Toronto (*The Globe*—23.5 percent); 2) Montreal (*La Presse*—18.6 percent); and 3) Edmonton (*The Bulletin*—32.0 percent).[41] And a content analysis of the sports pages of five major urban Canadian newspapers for the decade 1926 to 1935 ranked baseball virtually even with ice hockey as the most reported and highlighted sport.[42] The sample reflected a coast-to-coast perspective (Halifax, Montreal, Toronto, Winnipeg and Vancouver). Only in Montreal, a city of indelible French infatuation with hockey, was baseball second in newspaper attention.[43] On the other hand, in Toronto and Vancouver the supremacy of baseball over hockey as the most reported and highlighted sports item was clearly evident.[44] In Halifax and Winnipeg the two sports were about evenly reported.[45] Canadian interest in baseball reflected an egalitarian following, gathering adherents from all socioeconomic classes, ethnic groups, and geographical regions. Very early in the twentieth century Canadians developed intense interest in major league teams and annual pennant races in the States. And a substantial number of their sporting heroes were American big league baseball stars, such as Cap Anson, Napoleon Lajoie, Honus Wagner, Walter Johnson, Christy Mathewson, Ty Cobb, Babe Ruth, and a host of others.

By the time that the second half of the twentieth century was under way, a rich baseball culture of significant longevity lay like a freshly plowed field ready for seeding by entrepreneurial efforts aimed at Canadian Major League membership. The first resulting success, of course, came in the form of the Montreal Expos. Montreal had joined the International League in 1898. The Royals, as they came to be called, became celebrated in baseball history as the ball club from which Jackie Robinson vaulted to the Brooklyn Dodgers of the National League, becoming the first Negro to play modern major league baseball.[46] The second success, of course, was the Toronto Blue Jay franchise. Toronto also owned a storied membership in the International League, having first become a member in 1897 under the name Maple Leafs. The Maple Leafs were still members of the Triple A International League as late as 1966.

In August 1967 America's so-called baseball bible, *The Sporting News,* published editorial comments directed toward the prospect of major league baseball in Canada:

> It is unrealistic to expect either Toronto or Montreal ever again to support minor league ball. But it is downright stupid to allow these huge markets to go by default. . . . Baseball's big leagues are big league in name only so long as major cities such as Montreal and Toronto are on the outside looking in.[47]

The Tecumseh Baseball Club of London (Ontario) vs. The Stars of Syracuse (New York) at Tecumseh's Ball Grounds, 1875. Courtesy Canadian Sports Hall of Fame Archives (Toronto).

In what must have been greeted with shock by hopeful Buffalo major league franchise seekers, Montreal joined San Diego as the new National League expansion teams in 1969. Named the Expos in honor of Montreal's hosting of the World Exposition two years earlier, Canada's first experiment with major league baseball cost Seagram's whiskey heir Charles Bronfman and a group of associates a $20 million franchise fee. John McHale was engaged as president of the club; Jim Fanning as vice president. The Expo plan for a home stadium centered on an expansion of Jarry Park *(Parc Jarry)*, at that time a small 2,000-seat venue used for amateur baseball. National League president Warren Giles, in time, approved a $4 million plan to expand and modify Jarry to accommodate 28,000 fans. The work was accomplished in four months. During Giles' first appearance at an Expo game in spruced-up Jarry, he was greeted with cries of *"Le grand patron!"*[48]

The new Expo franchise in Montreal had some dramatic effects on baseball in the city. For example, in 1968 there were 222 amateur baseball teams playing at various levels of competition. A year later, Montreal boasted 430.[49] Following the Games of the XXIst Olympiad hosted by Montreal in 1976, the Expos took up tenancy in what is perhaps baseball's most cavernous stadium, the "Big O," a magnificent architectural wonder as well as an incredibly deficient atmosphere for playing and viewing baseball. It took almost a decade for the Expos to gain membership in the ranks of baseball's better teams. In 1979, 1980, 1981, and 1982 the Expos recorded "near misses" at achieving baseball's most coveted goal—a World Series berth. In each case they were stymied in late-season play or league playoffs by teams that ended up actually winning the World Series.[50] In 1979, locked in a wild divisional title scramble with the Pittsburgh Pirates, manager Dick Williams was said to have received a note from an impassioned Expo follower expressing the country's support for the team's success. "The Pirates have a city of supporters," exclaimed the fan, but "You sir, have an entire nation behind you!"[51] The patriotic message failed to ring completely true. By then Montreal's urban rival to the west, Toronto, had a major league franchise of its own, and with it, a prospective identification with Canada's majority Anglophone population.

It was the entry of Toronto's Blue Jays into American League membership in 1977 that produced the full flowering of Canada's baseball heritage planted over 150 years ago. Drawing support from the largest population center in Canada, developing extensive exposure from print and electronic media outlets of both Canadian and American affiliation, marketed by a "baseball sharp" who "learned how" under McDonald's Golden Arches, capitalizing on a natural rivalry (the nearby Detroit Tigers), and playing in baseball's most glamorous division (the American League East), the Blue Jays very rapidly became "Canada's team." In the Jays' inaugural season they lost 107 contests and finished 45 games behind the eventual World Series champion New York Yankees. On the asset side of the ledger, however, they attracted 1,701,039 fans to their home games and recorded a profit of some $1,500,000.[52]

The huckster of Blue Jay mania was Peter Bavasi, son of the highly respected and eminently successful Buzzy Bavasi. Young Peter's first step toward following in his old man's footsteps (the elder Bavasi was, at the time, general manager of the San Diego Padres) was to accept Dad's appointment of him as director of the Padres' minor league operations.[53] When Ray Kroc bought the Padres in 1974 he made Buzzy club president. Son Peter was appointed vice president and general manager. From Kroc, the impressario of McDonalds, young Bavasi learned about "selling the sight, sound, taste, touch and smells of a product."[54] To Kroc, that meant marketing Big Macs. To Peter Bavasi, it signified the essence of marketing Blue Jay baseball. Kroc's parting message to Bavasi as young Peter left California for Hog Town (Toronto) was to "sell the sizzle if you don't have the steak ready."[55] Baseball fans are consumers. Marketing baseball is no different than getting across the "Big Mac" message.

A Bavasi strategy from the beginning was to seek public involvement in Blue Jay development. A "name the team" contest was the first order of business. The name *Blue Jays* won out. The *Toronto Island Ferries* did not, thank God![56] Next in priority was the creation of a team logo. Bavasi sought a symbol as sensational in public recognition as Kroc's golden arches had become. Although he didn't quite equal the arches, he did come up golden, as the saying goes. The cocky Blue Jay, superimposed on a baseball with a red maple leaf "stuck in its ear," became a symbol of national recognition. A saturation marketing of the logo led to its embossment on everything imaginable, from Irwin Toys, to baby bibs and frozen pizza packages. To thousands, the logo became a symbol of fond worship. Youngsters, in particular, wore the natty emblem with prideful display. Such was the mystique of baseball and the newly hatched Blue Jays.

The Jays finished dead last in each of their first three seasons, but in the process set a standard for being a well-managed, financially sound enterprise (despite the decrepit state of the Canadian dollar against its American counterpart).[57] The franchise increased in value from $7 million (its approximate purchase price) to an estimated $40 to 45 million (U.S.) in 1986.[58] Twenty-eight radio stations carried Blue Jay baseball in 1977; twice that number a decade later.[59] And all of this while playing in a venue described by many as absolutely the worst in major league baseball. This deplorable state of affairs was rectified in 1989 when the Blue Jays moved into new digs—Toronto's grandiose Skydome, a 54,000 seat edifice with retractable roof touted to be the "best baseball facility ever built."

A rich baseball history and the success of the Blue Jay phenomenon aside, a question begs comment. Are Canadians attracted to baseball because of the nature of the game itself? Or is fascination for the game generated by its development as a modern sports spectacle? Certainly, mass media attention to baseball, advanced technological developments, and startling increases in discretionary income and leisure time, have all had a dramatic impact on the ritualization of certain character components associated with the sport. One such ritualization is the growing Canadian phenomenon of bars, pubs and taverns as ersatz stadiums in which worship of particular major league teams (particularly the Blue Jays) is carried out. In dimly lit, often loud and raucous confines, legions of steadfast fans of male and female gender alike gather to drink beer, munch peanuts and popcorn, and root for the success of their favorites. The game from the stadium is seen live on a huge television screen. In effect, thousands of baseball fans across Canada experience the atmosphere, the drama, and the camaraderie that go hand in hand with watching the home team perform in the stadium. There are a few qualities missing, of course, but the absence of sunshine, green pasture-like spaces, even hot dogs, appear to be only minor irritations when compared to the greater gain. Television has made this particular ritualized behavior possible.

Another ritual notation is the annual spring rite of Canadians (particularly residents of Ontario) journeying southward to Florida in order to witness an institutionalized characteristic of baseball—spring training. "The Grapefruit Circuit" is now within the financial/time means of thousands.

But the success of baseball in Canada, indeed its modern spectacle state, is not solely due to modern television, marketing skill and entrepreneurial endeavor, technological impovement, growth in leisure time, increased affluence, nor even the advent of major league "home teams." Long before the advent of television, radio and, for that matter, the sports page, the ritualization of baseball in Canadian culture had occurred, because baseball had penetrated to every nook and cranny of Canada.

In a rich baseball atmosphere that has witnessed the rise of the sport from early nineteenth-century immigrant play to modern major league competition, Canadians have demonstrated a consistent desire for baseball—playing it, watching it, reading about it; glorying in the triumphs, bemoaning the tragedies. And although Americans may have planted the seeds for baseball's heritage in Canada, Canadians themselves have been the sport's fertilizers, harvesters and consumers. The thoughts of W.P. Kinsella, (with some license) says it all for baseball being "in the heart and mind" of Canadians:

> I don't have to tell you that the one constant through all the years has been baseball. (Canada) has been erased like a blackboard, only to be rebuilt and erased again. But baseball has marked time (while Canada) has rolled by like a procession of steamrollers. . . . It (baseball) is a living part of history, like calico dresses, stone crockery, and threshing crews eating at outdoor tables. It continually reminds us of what once was, like a (George V) penny in a handful of coins.[60]

Although Kinsella's thoughts may serve as a pleasant ending to this essay, I am reluctant to conclude without stating the firmly held belief that baseball is as much a Canadian national sporting pastime as any other sport. Americans, indeed most contemporary Canadians, might find that hard to fathom, believing as they do that Canadian interest in baseball can be pinned to the fact that two Canadian teams are now members of the major leagues. But as I have tried to demonstrate, baseball has enjoyed high profile status in every era of sporting history. Other sports during particular eras rose to challenge baseball's prominent position in Canadian sporting culture—cricket and curling prior to 1875, rowing and lacrosse in the latter part of the nineteenth century, hockey and football in the twentieth century. Baseball's future appears to be in no jeopardy. In all probability Vancouver will someday join with Toronto and Montreal as members of the major league community. More and more Canadians will ply their talents to the summer diamond sport, swelling the already considerable numbers now populating youth and adult competitive and recreational leagues.[61] An added boost to Canadian baseball interest is a long tradition of fast-pitch softball competition and the extraordinary contemporary popularity of slow-pitch softball (baseball played with a large ball on a smaller playing field), both of which draw adherents from all age groups as well as both sexes.[62] Playing ball, spectating and becoming immersed in the cultural qualities of baseball and its ersatz forms, then, is the action of millions of Canadians, young and old, male and female, rich and poor, French and English, Maritimer, Prairieite, and Westerner alike.

I began this essay with a bit of nostalgic reflection. I end it in the same manner. A half century has passed since my childhood infatuations and fantasies about baseball consumed my life. Now I live in another country, my father watches Boggs, Evans and Clemens from another world, and economic times are pretty good compared to 1939. And I have my own son now. Each spring for some time now, after the snow vanishes from the ball park in Toronto, he and I head that way to relive a cycle that has gone on unabated for far longer than any of us living today can remember. The time and place may be different, but the ritual is the same. The fact, though, my son roots for the Blue Jays. But I, eternally, for the Red Sox.

NOTES

I am indebted to Nancy B. Bouchier for her helpful research regarding material on Adam E. Ford. I also gratefully acknowledge the North American Society for Sport History in permitting specific material concerning Ford to be published in this work.

1. Several historians of sport have outlined this American Colonial phenomenon, the most comprehensive treatment of which is Robert Henderson's *Ball, Bat and Bishop: The Origin of Ball Games* (New York, 1947). See also, Jennie Holliman, *American Sports: 1785–1835* (Durham, 1931); David Quentin Voigt, *American Baseball: From Gentleman's Sport to the Commissioner System* (Norman, 1966); and Harold Seymour, *Baseball, The Early Years* (New York, 1960).

2. Not all so-called Loyalists left the American colonies simply because they were loyal to the British Crown. Substantial numbers left because they feared social and economic ostracism, or because they perceived better opportunities in Canada.

3. See, for instance, Stephen Leacock, *Canada: The Foundations of its Future,* Montreal: Privately Printed, 1941, p. 119.

4. American immigration into Southwestern Ontario after 1815 is clearly documented by the sound scholarship of Fred Landon, published in his *Western Ontario and the American Frontier* (Toronto, 1967), pp. 46–61.

5. A microcosm of the larger picture of land speculation in Southwestern Ontario between 1790 and 1825 can be found in the records of land patents granted speculators in Essex County (Windsor and its eastern environs). Between 1790 and 1825 individual speculators accounted for about 98 percent of land patents granted by the Crown. Their strategies for profits were linked to sale of lands to settlers (most of whom were Americans) or from development of their land holdings through tenancy. After 1825 the control of land in its larger context passed to the clergy, the Canada Company and to the energies of Thomas Talbot, supervisor of vast tracts of Crown land placed in his custody by the government. For a detailed explanation of the land speculator phenomenon in Essex County between 1790 and 1825 see: *The Western District,* Essex County Historical Society Papers, 1983, pp. 68–111.

6. This analogy has been described in similar context to other immigrations westward. See, for instance, my investigation of German-Americans passing through Louisville, Kentucky on their way west in the 1850s (Robert Knight Barney, "German-American Turnvereins and Socio-Politico-Economic Realities in the Antebellum and Civil War Upper and Lower South," *Stadion,* Vol. X, 1984, pp. 143–144).

7. Ford's sporting activities in St. Marys are documented in the pages of various issues of the St. Marys *Argus* between 1864 and 1879. Ford was president of the St. Marys Curling Club in the early 1870s (see *Argus,* 1 October 1874). By 1876 the Beaver Baseball Club, an organization which

had commenced play in 1868, included some 50 members, each of whom paid a one dollar fee to join (see *Argus,* 13 April 1876). For more on Ford and his adult athletic activities, see Nancy B. Bouchier and Robert Knight Barney, "A Critical Examination of a Source on Early Ontario Baseball: The Reminiscence of Adam E. Ford," *Journal of Sport History,* Vol. 15, No. 1 (Spring 1988), pp. 78–79. For the earliest activities of the St. Marys Beaver Baseball Club in intercommunity competition, see *London Free Press,* August 22, 24, 26 and 37, 1869; and *London Advertiser,* July 7, 1870.

8. *Sporting Life,* May 5, 1886. Ford's letter was posted from Denver, Colorado. He had moved there in 1880, where he continued to be energetic in both curling and baseball activities.

9. *Statutes of Upper Canada.* 33 George III ch. 1, 1793 (legislated 9 July 1793, "An Act for the Better Regulation of the Militia in this Province"), amended by 48 George III ch. 1 (16 March 1808), and 1 Victoria ch. 8 (6 March 1838). See also Majorie E. Cropp, "Beachville, the Birthplace of Oxford," *Western Ontario Historical Nuggets,* No. 14 (1967 Reprint, Beachville Centennial Committee), pp. 18, 32. According to Cropp, Militia Day activity was evident in the Beachville area by the early 1820s.

10. On the rebellion, see Colin Read, *The Rising in Western Upper Canada, 1837–1838: The Duncombe Revolt and After* (Toronto, 1982), pp. 132–148; and Brian Dawe, *Old Oxford is Wide Awake: Pioneer Settlers and Politicians in Oxford County, 1793–1853* (Woodstock, 1980), pp. 43–61. See also, Thomas Shenston, *The Oxford Gazetteer* (Ingersoll, 1852), p. 106; Herbert Milnes, *The Story of the Oxford Rifles* (Woodstock, 1974); and Cropp, *op. cit.,* p. 22.

11. The Karns, represented by family branches in both Beachville and Zorra Township, contributed four players to the 1838 game. They were: Adam (age 16 in 1838), Peter (16), Harry (16), and Daniel (18). See "Karn Family History," Unpublished Genealogical Manuscript, Oxford County Library, Woodstock, Ontario. William Dodge was 15 years of age in 1838. See "Tweedsmuir History," *West Oxford Township* (Vol. 1), Unpublished Manuscript, Oxford County Library, "Genealogy of William Dodge," p. A107. No birthdate is known for Reuben Martin, but his gravestone, on which no vital events appear, is located in the Beachville cemetery. Martin is recorded in the 1825 County Assessment Rolls. Nathaniel McNames was born in 1814, making him 24 years old in 1838 (tombstone in Beachville cemetery). George Burdick may have been related to Enoch Burdick, the owner of the pasture field in which the 1838 games was played. Enoch Burdick is listed on the Oxford County Assessment Rolls for 1812. William Ford appears to be Adam Ford's brother. See Bernie McLay, "Cruttendon Family" (especially Pfaff's addendum, pp. 6–7), unpublished genealogical Manuscript (St. Marys Museum, St. Marys, Ontario). Of "Old" Ned Dolson, I. Van Alstine, William Hutchinson, and Abel and John Williams, no vital records exist. Their family names, however, are recorded in the area. See the 1812 Oxford County Assessment Rolls; Oxford County and Woodstock Public Library Names Indexes; and *History of Zorra and Embro: Pioneer Sketches of 60 Years Ago* (Embro 1909).

12. See Cropp, *op. cit.*

13. See, for instance, Douglas Wallop, *Baseball: An Informal History* (New York, 1969), pp. 34–35; and Frank G. Menke, *Encyclopedia of Sports,* 4th Revised Edition (New York, 1969), pp. 50–51.

14. Tales of the physical prowess of Beachville area baseballers were "etched" into local tradition through the oral reminiscence of "old timers." Silas Williams, to whom Ford refers in this context, is listed on the Oxford Country and Zorra Township Assessment Rolls as early as 1812.

15. Ford entered McGill University in the autumn of 1849. He may have returned home to Oxford County for summer vacations as early as 1850. Therefore, it might be suggested that his first confrontation with Cartwright's innovative "New York Game" occurred in 1850. However, Ford's utterance "when I came home from university" might have referred to any summer holiday between 1850 and 1854, or to his permanent return after his graduation in 1855.

16. *New York Clipper,* 18 August 1860.

17. William Humber, *Cheering for the Home Team: The Story of Baseball in Canada,* Erin: The Boston Mills Press, 1983, p. 15. Here, Humber refers to a *Clipper* pronouncement, but offers no specific citation. A review of the *Clipper* for 1860 fails to reveal Humber's authority.

18. *Ibid.,* pp. 85–86.

19. Peter Leslie Lindsay, "A History of Sport in Canada, 1807–1867," Unpublished Ph.D. dissertation, University of Alberta, 1969, p. 79.

20. *Clipper*, June 22, 1861.

21. Canadian baseball clubs carefully observed rules changes made from year to year by the NAPBBP and the NLPBBC. For example, the Ingersoll *Chronicle* (March 18, 1875) reported the rule changes emanating from the NAPBBP's convention in Philadelphia. Likewise, the Woodstock *Sentinel* (November 20, 1886) described rules changes created by the National League for play in 1887. Many nineteenth-century Ontario newspapers published comments on how American rules changes would affect local play.

22. Several baseball historians have chronicled the Knickerbocker's historic contribution to the game. Among the most detailed accounts is one provided by Melvin L. Adelman, *A Sporting Time: New York City and the Rise of Modern Athletics, 1820–1870* (Urbana, 1986), pp. 121–142.

23. *Ibid.*, pp. 121–183.

24. *Lindsay, op. cit.*, p. 79.

25. *Directory for the City of London (1856–1857)*, p. 25.

26. Ingersoll *Chronicle,* July 27, 1860.

27. *Clipper,* July 17, 1869.

28. Humber, *op cit.*, p. 28.

29. *Ibid.*, pp. 28–29.

30. *Ibid.*, p. 29.

31. *Ibid.*

32. As cited by Humber, p. 29.

33. See George Sleeman Collection, Regional Collections, D.B. Weldon Library, University of Western Ontario. Sleeman's personal papers include several letters to and from ballplayers on the subject of being paid for services rendered to the Maple Leafs.

34. Cited in Humber, pp. 29–30.

35. Several writers have recorded the success of the London Tecumsehs in the 1870s. See, for instance, Humber, *op. cit.*, pp. 30–44; and Henry Roxborough, *One-Hundred-Not-Out: The Story of Nineteenth Century Canadian Sport* (Toronto, 1966), pp. 112–116. For penetrating insight from a primary source, see Tecumseh Baseball Club of London, *Tecumseh Minute Book*, June 22, 1868–May 1, 1872, Regional Collection, D.B. Weldon Library, University of Western Ontario.

36. See Humber, *op. cit.*, pp. 39–41.

37. Voigt, *op cit.*, p. 76.

38. See Humber, *op. cit.*, pp. 39–43.

39. Data on Canadian minor league growth and development has been compiled by the Canadian Baseball Hall of Fame, Toronto, Ontario. I am grateful to the Hall for its access.

40. *Ibid.*, Canadian Baseball Hall of Fame.

41. I am indebted to Alan Metcalfe for his newspaper research concerning 1915. See his *Canada Learns to Play: The Emergence of Organized Sport, 1807–1914,* (Toronto, 1987), p. 85.

42. See Evelyn Janice Waters, "A Content Analysis of the Sport Section in Selected Canadian Newspapers: 1926 to 1935," Unpublished Master's Thesis, University of Western Ontario, 1981.

43. *Ibid.*, p. 60.

44. *Ibid.*, p. 64 and p. 74.

45. *Ibid.*, p. 56 and p. 70.

46. The saga of Jackie Robinson's abbreviated career with the Montreal Royals and his subsequent promotion to the Brooklyn Dodgers is best captured in the scholarly work of Jules Tygiel, *Baseball's Great Experiment: Jack Robinson and His Legacy* (New York, 1983).

47. *The Sporting News,* August 5, 1967.

48. Quoted by Humber, *op. cit.*, p. 131. But without citation.

49. *Ibid.*, p. 134.

50. Pittsburgh Pirates (1979), Philadelphia Phillies (1980), Los Angeles Dodgers (1981), and St. Louis Cardinals (1982).

51. Quoted by Humber, *op. cit.*, p. 131. But without citation.

52. Larry Millson, *Ballpark Figures: The Blue Jays and the Business of Baseball* (Toronto, 1987), p. 137.

53. Buzzy Bavasi's first position as general manager of a ball club was in Montreal with the Royals during the 1948 and 1949 seasons. He subsequently became "Big League" as General Manager of the Brooklyn Dodgers from 1950 to 1957, Los Angeles Dodgers from 1958 to 1967, and San Diego Padres from 1968 to 1973.

54. Millson, *op. cit.*, p. 125.

55. *Ibid*.

56. *Ibid.*, p. 131.

57. *Ibid.*, pp. 134–135 and pp. 284–286. Here, Millson describes the terrifying ramifications of Blue Jay finances wrought by the disparity of the Canadian dollar against its American counterpart.

58. *Ibid.*, p. 9. According to Millson, *Fortune* magazine's assessment was less, putting the value of the Blue Jay franchise at between 36 and 40 million dollars. Roger Noll's assessment of between 40 and 45 million dollars (U.S.) was made at a time when the noted Stanford University economics professor was serving the Player's Association in a review of the financial status of all major league clubs.

59. *Ibid.*, p. 136.

60. W.P. Kinsella, *Shoeless Joe* (New York, 1982), p. 213. (Some license, in parentheses, mine.)

61. Statistics on Canadian participation in baseball at various levels in 1988 reflect a total registration figure in excess of 200,000 individuals. Roughly broken down, the data are as follows: Little League Baseball—54,000; Babe Ruth baseball (present only in the province of British Columbia)—2,500; all other levels and categories of amateur baseball—147,000. I am indebted to Joe Shea (Calgary) *Little League Baseball of Canada;* Al Elliott (Vancouver), *Babe Ruth Baseball of Canada;* and John Hamilton (Ottawa), *Canadian Federation of Amateur Baseball* for the statistical information noted above.

62. The statistics for participation in fast-pitch and slow-pitch softball for 1988 are startling. Slightly over 2,000,000 Canadians, almost 10 percent of the nation's total population, play softball, of which 210,000 are registered in league play leading to local, regional, provincial and national championships. The 210,000 figure is split almost evenly between males and females. I am indebted to Gail Gibson (Ottawa), *Softball Canada* for the participation statistics noted above. It might be of interest to readers that hockey and its ersatz forms (ringette and ball hockey) count approximately 500,000 registered players (there is little organized hockey played in Canada featuring non-registered players). For participation statistics relevant to forms of hockey, I am indebted to Dennis MacDonald (Ottawa), *Canadian Amateur Hockey Association;* Wes Clarke (Ottawa), *Ringette Canada;* and Althea Arsenault-Sharkey (Toronto), *Ontario Ball Hockey Association.* Despite the disparity between baseball and hockey in terms of participation, it must be recognized that hockey enjoys more true identity with Canada than does baseball. This is partly because Canada is "perceived" as a wintery country and because the nation's greatest sports heroes are native-born hockey players.

APPENDIX:
TRANSCRIPT OF ADAM FORD'S LETTER TO *SPORTING LIFE,*
PUBLISHED 5 MAY 1886

MUCH LIKE BASEBALL

A Game of Long-ago Which Closely Resembled Our Present National Game.
Denver, Colo., April 26. Editor *Sporting Life.*

The 4th of June, 1838 was a holiday in Canada, for the Rebellion of 1837 had
been closed by the victory of the government over the rebels, and the birthday
of His Majesty George the Fourth was set apart for general rejoicing. The chief
event of the village of Beachville in the County of Oxford, was a baseball match
between the Beachville Club and the Zorras, a club hailing from the township of
Zorra and North Oxford.

The game was played in a nice smooth pasture field just back of Enoch
Burdick's shops; I well remember a company of Scotch volunteers from Zorra
halting as they passed the grounds to take a look at the game. I remember seeing
Geo. Burdick, Reuben Martin, Adam Karn, Wm. Hutchinson, I. Van Alstine,
and, I think, Peter Karn and some others. I remember also that there were in the
Zorras "Old Ned" Dolson, Nathaniel McNames, Abel and John Williams,
Harry and Daniel Karn, and, I think, Wm. Ford and William Dodge. Were it not
for taking up too much of your valuable space I could give you the names of
many others who were there and incidents to confirm the accuracy of the day
and the game. The ball was made of double and twisted woolen yarn, a little
smaller than the regulation ball of today and covered with good honest calf skin,
sewed with waxed ends by Edward McNames, a shoemaker.

The infield was a square, the base lines of which were twenty-one yards long,
on which were placed five bags, thus:

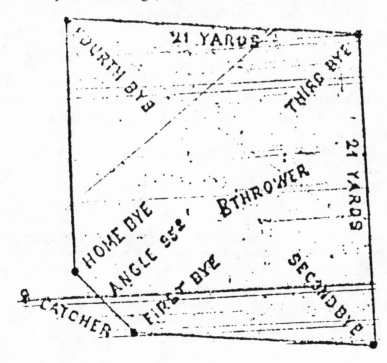

The distance from the thrower to the catcher was eighteen yards; the catcher standing three yards behind the home bye. From the home bye, or "knocker's" stone, to the first bye was six yards. The club (we had bats in cricket but we never used bats in playing base ball) was generally made of the best cedar, blocked out with an ax and finished on a shaving horse with a drawing knife. A Wagon spoke, or any nice straight stick would do.

We had fair and unfair balls. A fair ball was one thrown to the knocker at any height between the bend of his knee and the top of his head, near enough to him to be fairly within reach. All others were unfair. The strategic points for the thrower to aim at was to get near his elbow or between his club and his ear. When a man struck at a ball it was a strike, and if a man struck at the ball three times and missed it he was out if the ball was caught every time either on the fly or on the first bound. If he struck at the ball and it was not so caught by the catcher that strike did not count. If a struck ball went anywhere within lines drawn straight back between home and the fourth bye, and between home and the first bye extended into the field the striker had to run. If it went outside of that he could not, and every man on the byes must stay where he was until the ball was in the thrower's hands. Instead of calling foul the call was "no hit."

There was no rule to compel a man to strike at the ball except the rule of honor, but a man would be despised and guyed unmercifully if he would not hit at a fair ball. He was out if the ball was caught either before it struck the ground or on the first bound. Every struck ball that went within the lines mentioned above was a fair hit, every one outside of them no hit, and what you now call a foul tip was called a tick. A tick and a catch will always fetch was the rule given strikers out on foul tips. The same rule applies to forced runs that we have now. The bases were the lines between the byes and a base runner was out if hit by the ball when he was off of his bye. Three men out and the side out. And both sides out constituted a complete inning. The number of innings to be played was always a matter of agreement, but it was generally 6 to 9 innings, 7 being most frequently played and when no number was agreed upon seven was supposed to be the number. The old plan which Silas Williams and Ned Dolson (these were gray-headed men then) said was the only right way to play ball, for it was the way they used to play when they were boys, was to play away until one side made 18, or 21, and the team getting that number first won the game. A tally, of course, was a run. The tallies were always kept by cutting notches on the edge of a stick when the base runners came in. There was no set number of men to be played on each side, but the sides must be equal. The number of men on each side was a matter of agreement when the match was made. I have frequently seen games played with seven men on each side, and I never saw more than 12. They all fetched.

The object in having the first bye so near the home was to get runners on the base lines, so as to have the fun of putting them out or enjoying the mistakes of the fielders when some fleet footed fellow would dodge the ball and come in home. When I got older, I played myself, for the game never died out. I well remember when some fellows down at or near New York got up the game of base ball that had a "pitcher" and was played with a ball hard as a stick. India rubber had come into use, and they put so much into the balls to make them lively that when the ball was tossed to you like a girl playing "one-old-cat" you could knock it so far that the fielders would be chasing it yet, like dogs hunting sheep, after you had gone clear around and scored your tally. Neil McTaggert, Henry Cruttenden, Gordon Cook, Henry Taylor, James Piper, Almon Burch, Wm. Harrington and others told me of it when I came home from university. We, with "alot of good fellows more" went out and played it one day. The next day we felt as if we had been on an overland trip to the moon. I could give you pages of incidentals but space forbids. One word as to the prowess in those early days. I heard Silas Williams tell Jonathan Thornton that old Ned Dolson could catch the ball right away from the front of the club if you didn't keep him back so far that he couldn't reach it. I have played from that day to this and I don't intend to quit as long as there is another boy on the ground.

Yours, Dr. Ford

Two Shortstops

A.D. SUEHSDORF

There are interesting parallels and overlaps in their careers. Both had a season or two playing beside Charlie Gehringer at Detroit; they share an unqualified admiration for the Mechanical Man as a player and as a friend. Both had a mixed-blessing season with the Cubs. They were road-trip roommates for two seasons with the Giants. Both batted No. 2 in the lineup most of the time. Both were first-ball, fast-ball hitters. Both have a World Series lapse that sticks in the memory, vivid as instant replay, after half a century or so. Both loved the baseball years and recall them fondly. Today they are at home in California at the far end of long lives. They are Mark Koenig and Dick Bartell.

I

Koenig, now 85 (he says he was born in July 1904, not 1902, as "the Macmillan" has it) still has vestiges of the square, ruddy face, sharp nose, and thick shock of hair that marked him as a youngster. The dark slash of eyebrow which made him look glowering in photos in the twenties is no longer prominent, but his eyes still have the squint of the infielder picking a pop fly out of the sun. He has added many pounds to his playing weight of 174, many of them around the middle, and complains mildly of the afflictions of age. "I've got Heinz's disease," he says with a smile. "Fifty-seven varieties." He lives with his daughter and son-in-law in Orland, in the farming country of northern California.

As for many old players, the past glows brightly: "I played sandlot ball with the Sunset Midgets of San Francisco until I quit high school in my sophomore year to turn professional. I joined the Moose Jaw, Saskatchewan, team in the Class B Western Canada League for $200 a month Canadian." When the league folded Bob Connery, the scout who discovered Rogers Hornsby and George Pipgras, offered him $500 to sign a Yankee contract. While Connery waited for New York to confirm the bonus, however, Koenig got a telegram from the St. Paul Saints (Double A) offering $400 a month. He took it.

St. Paul farmed him to Jamestown in the Dakota League. In 1924 he moved to Des Moines and late in the season was recalled to help the Saints clinch a pennant and win the Little World Series against the Bob Grove-George Earn-shaw-Joe Boley Baltimore Orioles (IL). The Saints had Chuck Dressen at third, Johnny Neun at first, and right-hander Cliff Markle, moving downhill after a patchy career with the Reds and Yankees. Koenig was the Saints' regular shortstop in 1925 and was brought up to the Yankees in the final month of their disastrous seventh-place season. His price tag was $35,000.

In 1926 Miller Huggins settled on Koenig and Tony Lazzeri to stabilize the Yankee infield. The rookies replaced Pee Wee Wanninger, the shortstop for whom Lou Gehrig had pinch hit to start his 2,130 consecutive-game streak, and Aaron Ward, who had been the New Yorkers' regular second baseman for six years. Koenig and Lazzeri made a significant difference at bat and in the field. They outhit their predecessors by 30–35 points and, although a hair's-breadth behind them in fielding average, handled 422 more chances! The Yanks topped Cleveland by three games to start Huggins on his second string of three consecutive pennants.

Koenig batted second, behind Earle Combs and ahead of Babe Ruth.

I was never a classic No. 2 hitter. I could go to right or left field, but on that team bunts, sacrifices, hit-and-run, and so forth, weren't often needed. Earle was the greatest leadoff man I ever saw. He or I would get on base and Babe or Lou would bring us home. Ruth lofted the ball, of course. A high arc. Some of his infield pops were so high he could be on third if they ever dropped the ball. Gehrig hit with tremendous power, but Ruth could hit 'em hard, too. I remember an exhibition in Atlanta. He belted one to right field, up over an embankment, over the fence, and over a string of boxcars on a siding beyond.

Afield the Yankees were just as awesome: "Meusel had a great arm. Ruth had a good one. I never saw him drop a fly or throw to the wrong base. But on a ball hit between Bob and Earle, or between Earle and the Babe, they always yelled, 'Go get it, Earle!'"

Most of his memories are happy ones. He liked spring training. He liked the train travel—usually in two private cars. On the road he roomed with Lazzeri, though Bob Meusel was his particular friend. Other buddies were Gehrig, Benny Bengough, and Joe Dugan. "The Yankees were a class outfit. We had great fun. I never found ball players much interested in lobby talk. We played a lot of cards—poker, pinochle. After the game we liked to go out for sandwiches and beer. There was no curfew. You could come in at 4 A.M. if you wanted to, as long as you got the job done."

As a young bachelor he lived at the Ansonia Hotel, on upper Broadway. After his marriage in 1928 he lived in an apartment at 181st Street, in the Bronx. "I usually left for the park around 12, 12:30. Games started at 3 [or 3:30] and usually were over by 5:30. I never played a night game in my life.

"In my day the sportswriters never bothered us much. There was no press-room at the stadium and they were rarely in the clubhouse."

The club provided four sets of uniforms—two home, two away. The players bought their own spikes and gloves. Gloves lasted about a season. Koenig had a Spalding. "We used to throw them out onto the infield grass between innings."

He remembers no instruction in hitting or fielding. Clubs carried two coaches,

Mark Koenig. (Photo courtesy of the National Baseball Library, Cooperstown, N.Y.)

one at first base, one at third [New York's were Art Fletcher and Charley O'Leary]. "They never said much."

Koenig was a switch hitter, better left-handed than right. [In 1928 he hit left-handed exclusively.] "I never took many pitches. I don't care how powerful a pitcher is, you can't throw it by a good fast-ball hitter. And throwing at 'em doesn't bother a good hitter. You just get up more determined.

"I loved to hit against Grove. A cousin for me. [Dizzy] Dean, too. The toughest pitcher I ever faced was George Uhle [a 200-game winner at Cleveland and Detroit]. He had good speed, a good change, a terrific curve, and he was smart."

For all the pleasure of making good as a rookie, Koenig found the 1926 World Series against Rogers Hornsby's Cardinals an ordeal. In seven games he had only four hits for a meager .125 average and was charged with four errors—three of them leading to crucial St. Louis runs.

Grover Cleveland Alexander's relief stint in Game 7 has become legend, but what Koenig remembers is his bobble that started the Cards on their way to three runs, all they would need to win the game and the Series. With one out in the fourth, Jim Bottomley singled to left and Lester Bell spanked a grounder to short. "It came right into my glove," Koenig recalls, "but I was using a brand-new glove, like a damned fool, and I booted it. I blew an easy double-play ball."

A double play would have taken the Yankees out of the inning. Even a force play would have made two out. Instead, trouble loomed. Chick Hafey hit a Texas League single into short left, filling the bases. Meusel—steady, reliable Long Bob—unaccountably dropped Bob O'Farrell's easy fly, scoring Bottomley and leaving the bases loaded. Tommy Thevenow is now at bat. A .247 lifetime hitter, he is having the Series of his life and will lead both teams with a .417 average. His puny pop fly falls behind Lazzeri for a single—his tenth hit—driving in Bell and Hafey. The Cards lead 3–1. With Alex's later heroics they will win, 3–2.

"I always had small hands and short fingers," says Koenig, offering the offending digits for the visitor's examination. "And we used those little gloves. Not like those butterfly nets they have today." Regretfully: "The ball just bounced out."

Les Bell, replaying the game for Donald Honig in *October Heroes,* called it a sure hit, not an error. "Koenig went far to his right and fumbled the ball. They gave him an error on it, but there was no way he could have thrown me out, even if he had handled it cleanly. No way."[1] Fellow feeling for a fellow fielder or a hitter still arguing with the official scorer?

In 1927 it was Mark's turn. He got a $3,000 raise to $7,000 and survived a terrible training camp. In 16 exhibition games he made seven errors and batted .046 while Ray Morehart, an infielder acquired from the White Sox with catcher Johnny Grabowski, could do no wrong: .360 average and 52 chances without error. Miller Huggins said candidly that Koenig had problems to work on. For one: Gloving grounders to his left. "Many a game has been saved by a one-hand stop near second base," Hug explained, "and Koenig will have to learn to do it."[2]

In truth, Koenig was error-prone. He topped all American League shortstops for Es in both 1926 and 1927. *Babe Ruth's Own Book of Baseball,* ghosted by Christy Walsh in 1928, described Mark as "nervous, high strung," a fellow for whom the slow fall of a high pop fly was agony.[3] One that eluded his glove entirely hit him in the face. Grounders caromed off his arms and chest. Koenig confesses that for a time his Yankee nickname was "Up the Sleeves."

During that miserable spring of 1927 the sportswriters rode him hard. Covering an exhibition at Chattanooga as the teams made their way north, Richards Vidmer of the *Times* snapped that the foe would not have scored in one inning, "except for Koenig's daily error."[4] Huggins ignored the critical barrage. "Koenig played good ball for me last year," he said mildly, "and I'm confident he will come around."[5]

"Whatever he said to me he said privately, in his office," Mark remembers with affection. "He never balled a player out in front of others. A wonderful manager."

He confirmed Hug's judgment with 7 hits in 10 at-bats against the A's in the team's first two games, and overall contributed a fine season to the Yankee's spectacular one. He upped his BA to .285 and did well in double plays and total chances per game. A high point was his triple off Tom Zachary immediately ahead of Ruth's memorable No. 60 at the stadium. The Yankees won an amazing 110 games and coasted easily to the pennant, 19 ahead of the Athletics.

In the four-game World Series against the Pirates there was no stopping him: 9 hits in 18 ABs and 14 chances without an error. Lloyd Waner, another of Honig's *October Heroes,* said: "Do you know who hurt us. . . ? Mark Koenig. . . . We just couldn't keep that fellow off the bases. . . . That's what did us in . . . that fellow always being on base when the big guys came up."[6] And Combs. Between them Earle and Mark scored 11 of the Yankees' 23 runs.

II

Dick Bartell was less impressed than Lloyd Waner. He played one game for the Pirates that year and was ineligible for the Series. But he sat on the bench, watched the four straight losses, and does not recall Koenig as a standout. He denies the Pirates were shell-shocked by the Yankee onslaught. Amazed by their power, perhaps, but not overawed or psyched out.

Bartell was 19 years old. Chicago born, he had come to California as a baby and graduated in 1926 from Alameda High School, across the bay from San Francisco. He already was recognized as a hot-shot infielder and had been offered scholarships by three colleges. Instead, he joined a semi-pro team in Butte, Montana, playing twilight games before crowds of miners. His father, Harry, a one-time semi-pro second baseman whose career highlight was an unassisted triple play, was a friend of Joe Devine, then a Pittsburgh scout, and signed his underage son to a Pirate contract. "If you're going to sign with a major league club," he told Dick, "it's going to be the Pirates."

"Worst thing that ever happened to me in baseball," Bartell grouses, 60-odd years later. "I signed for $2,750 and no bonus. Two years later Devine was with the Yankees and might have signed me for New York." At which point, of course, he'd have had to beat out Mark Koenig for the shortstop job!

Assigned to New Haven (Eastern), he found that George Weiss, another minor leaguer headed for the majors, had no need for an extra infielder and was moved along to Bridgeport, where he batted .280 in 148 games and led the league in putouts, assists, and errors. Called up by the Pirates after the pennant was won, he played in a 1–0 loss to the Reds to which he contributed an unassisted double play. He also was included in the Pirates' team picture, top row, far right. Two spaces to the left is another fresh-faced rookie: Joe Cronin, who had played 12 games and would spend 1928 with Kansas City (Double A), a decision the competitive Bartell heartily approved.

Glenn Wright was the Pirates' main man at short. Hard hitting, hard throwing, and still in his twenties, "Buckshot" seemed a fixture. In 1928 Bartell, although hitting a sharp .305, saw only spot duty: 72 games at second, short, and third. He was encouraged enough to marry his high school sweetheart, Olive Loretta Jensen, and spent the winter as a liquor salesman and department store floor-walker to supplement his chinchy Pirate salary.

In December, however, the Pirates were desperate for some left-handed pitching and gave up Wright to get Jess Petty from Brooklyn. It was an odd deal. Petty was of little value. Wright, already having twinges of arm trouble, smashed his right shoulder in a winter handball game after the trade. With surgery he recovered in 1929, but thereafter was more scattergun than buckshot. Bartell, as the Pirates expected, took up the slack: .302 in 143 games, including some at second.

In the spring of 1930 he held out for more money and incurred the wrath of Barney Dreyfuss, the Pirates' seigneurial owner, whose supply of wrath was abundant. "A dreadful man," says Bartell, even today. "After I signed he punished me with fines. Once it was $50 for not covering second, although I was in the outfield for the relay, and it was [2B George] Grantham who didn't cover."

Actually, his contract had been handled by Dreyfuss' pleasant and reasonable son, Sammy. It provided that the club would pay Mr. and Mrs. Bartell's train fare—lower berths and meals—between Alameda and Pittsburgh.

> When the season ended I asked Barney for the travel money. "It's not in your contract," he says. We're in St. Louis so we don't have the contract in front of us. "Let me use your phone," I say. "I'll get you the facts." "No," he says. So I have to go down to the lobby and make my call. When I proved my point, he blew a fuse. "Well," he says, "one lower berth should do for the two of you." I never did get the train fare. Just $3.75 a day meal money—the standard rate for ball players in those days. When I kept arguing he slapped me with a fine for—get this—"insubordination in the office!"

Bartell, never one to go quietly, filed a grievance with Commissioner Landis, who sidestepped, calling it "a league matter." So on to National League President John Heydler. No, Bartell really should address the Pittsburgh board of directors. Sure.

Dreyfuss got in the last lick in November, trading Dick to the lower depths—Philadelphia—for Tommy Thevenow and right-hander Claude Willoughby. Willoughby wasn't much. His ERA for 1930 was 7.59. But Thevenow, still under 30, was coming off an excellent season: 156 games played, a .286 average, and league-leading numbers for putouts, assists, and double plays. Unfortunately, he never did that well again. At Pittsburgh he soon declined to the career-ending status of veteran utility man. What saved Barney's bacon was the discovery and rapid development of Arky Vaughan.

At Philadelphia, meanwhile, Bartell became perhaps the NL's best shortstop. Certainly he was the equal of Maranville, Boston's aging Rabbit, of Durocher at Cincinnati, Stonewall Jackson at New York, and young Jurges at Chicago. Although paired with bottom-drawer second basemen—Les Mallon, Jack Warner, Barney Friberg, Lou Chiozza, Irv Jeffries—he led the league in double plays three of his four Phillie years.

He also meshed better with his third basemen than he had with Pie Traynor, whom he found overzealous in working shortstop territory and rather less of a team player than his Hall of Fame reputation would suggest. "Cutting in front of me meant I lost sight of the ball," Dick explains. "If he couldn't make the play—and many times he couldn't—it set me up for an error. I squawked that this was messing up our defense, but if [manager] Jewel Ens didn't want to call him on it, Pie sure wasn't going to pay any attention to me!"

At moribund Philadelphia, however, he was the pepperpot of the infield, twice handling more than 900 chances a season, and leading the league three times in putouts, twice in assists—plus once in errors.

Richard William Bartell. (Photo courtesy of the National Baseball Library, Cooperstown, N.Y.)

"There are no secrets to fielding," he says. "Just get the ball clean, and get it away fast. But playing your position well can take years to learn. I never worried about my statistics. The only one players care about is their batting average."

Lifetime, Bartell's was a very respectable .284. He hit better than .300 six times. A right-hander, he swung a 30-ounce, 34-inch bat, a Mel Ott model with a thickened handle to help with wrist hits. Early on, he even tried a bottle bat. He had the good No. 2 hitter's skills: bunting, punching hits to right behind the runner, rarely striking out. In 18 years he had only 627 Ks.

Like most old timers, he remembers no instruction from managers or coaches. The only hitting help he got was from Joe Devine, the scout, who took an interest in the youngsters he signed. "He'd get me up in a hotel room and check my form while I swung a bat at a pillow."

He developed his own hitting form, gradually.

> There's no use copying a Hornsby or a Frisch. Everyone's body is different. I worked for good balance and a level swing. I tried to hit the ball out front. With two strikes I choked up on the bat, tried to protect the plate, and simply hit the ball someplace. That's not a time to wait for your pitch. You go with whatever the man throws you.

He found no cousins among the pitchers he faced. "No one was easy for me. On the other hand, I always felt I could hit any of them." In time, anyway. He remembers watching Dazzy Vance warming up his strong right arm—and flapping sleeve—and thinking, "He doesn't look so tough." Three strikeouts later, "I was choking the bat so much the bench wanted to know which end I was hitting with."

He learned not to take liberties. When he ran up in the box to bluff a bunt against Root, the next pitch hit him in the throat. "That'll teach you," said Charlie, amiably.

As for the ball parks, he liked the Polo Grounds, had trouble with variable winds at Wrigley Field, hated Sportsman's Park: "Terrible heat and a terrible infield." He recalls the sweat running off his legs and squishing in his shoes. Baker Bowl's short right-field fence was within reach, but high: "You had to hit the ball pretty good to get one over it."

Bartell's penchant was the double. He hit 442 of them in his career, which has earned him 56th place on the all-time list. Cepeda, Clemente, Stargell, Eddie Collins, Sisler, and Slaughter, plus the only other legitimate star of the sad Phillie teams of those years, Chuck Klein, are among the big guns who trail him. In April 1933, with the season barely under way, he popped four consecutive two-baggers against the Braves at Baker Bowl to tie a major-league record.

That was the year he, Bill Terry, Frank Frisch, and Pepper Martin were picked as the NL's starting infield for the first All-Star Game. Bucky Walters, who joined the Phils from Boston while still a third baseman, says, "Bartell was the greatest infielder I ever played beside."[7]

"I can't pay you what you're worth," owner Gerry Nugent told him, "but I've got to hold you. You're the key to the franchise." All too true. Dick barely squeezed over $10,000 with the Phils. He remembers a road series at Chicago when Nugent said, "Let's stay over one more day. Then we can take a day coach to Cincinnati instead of a sleeper, and I'll order box lunches." As team captain, Bartell had to square this penny pinching with the players.

III

Mark Koenig hit his peak in 1928, as Bartell was getting his first action as a regular in the Pirate infield. It was one of the Yankees' glory years and Mark contributed his share to their success. He played 132 games—125 at short—and hit a resounding .319.

He had competition. Not Roy Morehart, who was never more than a marginal

29

player, but a slick-fielding, abrasive, roughneck kid named Durocher. While acknowledging Leo's skill, Koenig admits, "I disliked him the most of all the ball players I ever met." Lippy played 29 games at short, another 66 at second.

The Yankees took their third straight pennant, again over Connie Mack's persistent, improving A's, and executed the Cardinals four in a row. Babe Ruth had such a stupendous Series—four home runs, a .625 BA—that Koenig's lapses were unimportant and barely noticed: .158 BA and two errors in 21 chances.

By 1929 Durocher had the edge. If he couldn't hit with Koenig, he had the surer glove. He was at short for 93 games, Mark for only 61, plus 37 at third, a position he never liked.

In 1930 both were gone. Leo was dealt to Cincinnati, the start of a highly successful NL career. Koenig and Waite Hoyt, who still looked like a Brooklyn schoolboy but no longer had a hop on his fast ball, were traded to Detroit for Ownie Carroll, Harry Rice, and "Yats" Wuerstling.

For the second-division Tigers, then managed by Bucky Harris, Koenig played a season and a half, mostly at shortstop, but also at second in 1931, when Charlie Gehringer missed a number of games because of an ailing right arm. Mark was uncomfortable on that side of the infield. He also had a brief and unremarkable turn at pitching. His old nemesis, George Uhle, then on the Tiger staff, suggested he give it a try. "I always had a good arm. As an infielder I threw a light ball. Gehrig, now, he threw a ball like lead. Pitching, I had pretty good stuff, an okay curve. But to be really good, you've got to start young." In two years he appeared in five games with an 0–1 record. He was rapped for 11 hits in the complete-game loss, the big one, as he recalls it 59 years later, a four-run ninth-inning homer by someone after Elias Funk's fly-ball error with two outs filled the bases.

In 1932 Billy Rogell was established as the Detroit shortfielder. The club wanted Koenig to manage at Toronto (IL). "I said no. I wanted to go home to San Francisco, so they released me to the Missions."

Early in August, with the Cubs battling Pittsburgh for first place, he was bought by Chicago for $10,000. Rookie Billy Jurges, whose flashy play had moved Woody English to third, had been shot by a distraught female admirer.[8] While his wounds were not serious, the Cubs needed infield insurance for the stretch run.

Mark obliged. In 33 games he hit .353 with 17 RBIs, "many of them," said Charlie Grimm, who had just replaced grim Rogers Hornsby as manager, "for the winning margin."[9] The Cubs went on a tear which included a string of a dozen wins, and won the pennant by four games over the Pirates.

As everyone knows, the Cubs inexplicably voted Koenig a mere one-half World Series share. It worked out to $2,212.30. They also gave him six Series tickets—"every one behind a post." After "the deal the Cubs gave me, I was kind of tickled the Yanks beat the hell out of them. [Burleigh] Grimes and [Pat] Malone each told me they thought I should have had a full share, but they weren't at the meeting when shares were voted."

Mark played only the first game, injuring his hand sliding into third on a triple off Ruffing. Jurges was sufficiently recovered to play the rest of the way. Thus,

Koenig was on the bench for Ruth's famous did-he-or-didn't-he-call-it home run at Wrigley Field. After two losses, and derision by the Yankees for being such cheapskates with Mark—Babe called the Cubs "nickel squeezers"—the Cubs were furious and the atmosphere was ugly. A three-run homer by Ruth in the first didn't help matters.

In the fifth, against Charlie Root, it is generally agreed that Ruth acknowledged the first and second strikes with gestures toward the Cub dugout. As for what happened next, Mark says, "Ruth raised his arm, but I didn't see him point to the outfield. Root always said he didn't. Grimes said he didn't. [But] it never mattered to me whether he called his shot or not. In New York, he'd come out to the Stadium and say, 'I feel good today. I think I'll hit one.' And he would!"

Koenig was the Cubs' utility man in 1933, playing 80 games and hitting .284. During the winter he was a pawn in the big trade for Chuck Klein, going to Philadelphia with outfielder Harvey Hendrick, pitcher Ted Kleinhans, and $65,000. With Bartell still in the lineup, the Phils kept Koenig only as long as it took to sell him to Cincinnati.

This was the end of the line in 1934. The Reds had been a fixture in last place since 1931 and were about to repeat. Their lineup was a patchwork of other clubs' castoffs: Jim Bottomley, Chick Hafey, Sparky Adams. And they went through three managers—Bob O'Farrell, Barney Shotten, and Chuck Dressen— while losing 99 games. Still, Mark had a respectable season, racking up 151 games playing every infield position and hitting .272.

The Reds were perhaps most famous as the first major league team to fly. Not Bottomley and Koenig, however. They insisted on taking the train.

In 1935 Mark was sold to the Giants.

IV

When Bill Terry succeeded John McGraw as the Giants' manager in 1932, he began angling for Dick Bartell. Travis Jackson, a Polo Grounds favorite, was hampered by ailing knees, and Doc Marshall and the inspirational Blondy Ryan were not long-term prospects. "Deal for Bartell," Terry told Horace Stoneham, who was now running the club for his father. "I promise you a pennant the season after we get him."[10] In November 1934 the trade was made: Bartell to New York for Ryan, third baseman Johnny Vergez, outfielder George Watkins, pitcher Johnny Pezzullo, and cash reported at $50,000. Stoneham grumbled. He didn't think Dick was worth it. A bonus for the Phils, aside from the money, was getting an everyday third baseman, which gave manager Jimmie Wilson the leeway to switch Bucky Walters to pitching.

Dick flourished in his four years in the Big Town. He was an assured professional at the top of his game and the one stable factor in the Giants' infield. As usual, he played alongside a platoon of second basemen—eight altogether. In 1935 Hughie Critz, ending an honorable career, and newcomer Koenig split second base, Travis Jackson shifted to third, and strong-minded, uncompromising Memphis Bill was at first. By 1938 Mel Ott was on third, Alex Kampouris on second, and Johnny McCarthy on first.

For all the shuffle, Dick led the league's shortstops three times in total chances/game, once in double plays, and once in assists. (He also played a 10-

inning game in 1935 without a single fielding chance.) "Terry always checked with me when he wanted to know how his pitcher was doing. Is he getting tired? Is he losing his stuff? A shortstop has the best position to see if a pitcher is laboring, if his arm is dropping or he's altering his stride—everything a pitching coach in the dugout does these days."

He also hit well, sometimes from his accustomed No. 2 spot, behind Joe Moore, sometimes as leadoff. He averaged about 30 doubles a season, and with Terry's encouragement he learned to pull down the 275-foot line in left and upped his home-run production twice to 14.

He was cocky and aggressive and lit a fire under the somewhat phlegmatic Giants. He had run-ins with pitchers who threw at him, catchers who blocked the plate, baserunners trying to thwart the double play, and front-office executives who wrote his contracts. His friend Garry Schumacher, of the *Journal-American,* dubbed him "Rowdy Richard." Today it surprises him to think he was so feisty. On the other hand, he says mildly, "I've always had a temper."

Perhaps the most equable of his teammates was his road roommate, Mark Koenig. "He was quiet and easy," Dick says. "Nicest guy you could imagine." "A good friend," says Mark, reminiscently. "Rowdier than I was, but a good friend."

"There's one thing I can't stand about you, though," he told Bartell. "It's the way you grind your teeth at night!"

Did the two veteran shortstops exchange baseball wisdom with each other? No. "We had a close relationship," Dick says, "but I guess we felt we each knew our business and weren't going to improve the other guy." Says Mark: "We just went our own way."

In 1936 Bartell helped Terry deliver on his promise of a pennant as the Giants won by five games over the Cubs and Cardinals. And he had a good Series, although the Joe McCarthy Yankees won easily in six games. He batted .381 with eight hits—three of them doubles and one a homer—scored five runs and drove in three. Koenig, in his last major league season, was utility man and pinch hitter. He had a single in his fifth World Series, and was returned to the Missions. He was not sorry to go. He found Terry a tough nut, a demanding and critical manager—"no Huggins, that's for sure."

Bartell, who admired Bill's aggressiveness and dogged will to win, which were rather like his own, continued to thrive. In 1937 he made the NL All-Star team for the second time as the Giants repeated both as pennant winners and Series losers to their crosstown rivals. After a third-place finish in 1938, he was traded to the Cubs with Hank Leiber and Gus Mancuso for Bill Jurges, Frank Demaree, and Ken O'Dea.

The Cubs were disappointed with Dick, and he with them. He liked Billy Herman, the best second baseman he'd played with so far, and he had affection and respect for his roommate Dizzy Dean. "A marvelous guy. Hard competitor. Poor loser. You hated him as an opponent, but when you were on his side he'd give you the shirt off his back. I always felt Frank Frisch used him up at St. Louis. With careful handling, Diz could have won 30 a year forever!"

He didn't get along so well with manager Gabby Hartnett. In training camp at Catalina Island he "pulled a groin," never got into proper shape, and played hurt for much of the year. It showed. In 105 games he hit a thin .238 and fielded .943, the bottom for regular NL shortstops. In December he was traded to Detroit for Billy Rogell.

The Tigers got much the better of the deal, and Bartell liked his new team. "We were older fellows. I was 32, Gehringer 37, Buck Newsom and Tommy Bridges 33, Pinky Higgins 31. Even Hank Greenberg, my road roomie, was 29. We were old pros and we had a good feeling." Gehringer? "He was the best. It was a great pleasure to play with him. Our rhythm, our continuity were smooth and easy.

"Del Baker, the manager, told me, 'You take charge of the infield.' I said, 'Hey, I'm a National Leaguer. I'm not coming over here and tell your guys what to do.' "

Nonetheless, he did. He set up the Giants' relay system and he ragged Newsom for being out of shape. "If you'd get some of that fat off," I told him, "you'd win 30 games." Well, almost. He shed some pounds and went 21–5, the best performance of his long and tangled career. Dick says he and Bobo developed a pickoff play that nabbed 13 runners at second. There was no signal, no count. In the stretch, Bobo watched Dick jockey and feint, "and anytime he saw me between the runner and second, he knew I'd keep going for the base."

He hit .233, his lowest average ever, although he doesn't think American League pitchers were any tougher than the National's, or the strike zone markedly different. "No excuses. I just didn't have a good year. That happens sometimes. I got my usual bunch of doubles [24] and seven home runs. I had a lot of walks [76, his career high] and 53 runs batted in, which was pretty good for me.

"Fortunately, we had Greenberg, Barney McCosky, Rudy York, and Gehringer all over .300 and belting the ball, so my defense was more of a contribution than my bat." He fielded .953, as well as Luke Appling, though less well than Lou Boudreau. The old Tigers edged into first place a game ahead of Cleveland and two over New York.

The Series was against Bill McKechnie's Cincinnati Reds, a not terribly memorable team, yet one that won 100 games and finished 12 ahead of the Dodgers. Its defensive strength was formidable. Frank McCormick, Billy Werber, and Harry Craft had the league's highest fielding averages at their positions. Billy Myers and Lonny Frey turned a fine double play. And their two aces, Bucky Walters and Paul Derringer, were stingy with runs. As a team the Reds allowed nearly 100 fewer runs than the next-best club.

It was a seesaw Series, with heavy pressure on the pitchers, for the seven games were played in a week, with no breaks for travel between cities. Overall, Bartell did well: .269 plus 26 chances and one no-harm error. He drove in two with a bases-loaded single in Game 1, scored in Two, singled in Three, had two hits, one a run-scoring double, in Five, and two hits and two fielding gems in Six.

The seventh game, at Cincinnati, saw Newsom and Derringer each pitching for the third time. The Tigers scored early and Newsom made one run stand up for six innings. In the Cincinnati seventh, two doubles, a sacrifice, and a long fly earned two runs, and by that margin the Reds became world champions.

By some accounts Dick Bartell was the "goat." Back to the seventh inning:

Frank McCormick doubles off the left-field wall. Jimmy Ripple follows with a drive off the right-field screen. McCormick, thinking the ball might be caught, is slow leaving second. Bruce Campbell fields the ball, heaves it to Bartell as McCormick rounds third. There is, however, no play at the plate and heavy-footed Frank lumbers in with the tying run. Ripple is sacrificed to third, and Myers' fly to deep center brings him home.

Why didn't Bartell throw? Explanations vary. One says Campbell's throw was meant for the plate, but Bartell cut it off. Another says that because Bartell had his back to the plate while taking the throw, he a) didn't know McCormick was going all the way, or b) couldn't hear his mates hollering "Home! Home!" over the crowd's roar.

What does Dick say?

> Ripple's hit went down the right-field foul line. Gehringer goes out for the relay and I head for second in case we can nail Ripple there. The throw goes over Charlie's head. It wasn't meant for [Billy] Sullivan. Bruce just overthrew Charlie. I go after the ball, taking a quick look at third. McCormick has slowed down, but made the turn. I retrieve the ball; now my back is to the plate. McCormick keeps going. Slow as he is, I decide there is no play, no assurance that even a perfect throw will catch him. Incidentally, nobody was yelling "Home!" Even if they were: For God's sake, I'd been playing major league shortstop for 14 years. I didn't need to be told where the play was. Remember, there were no outs and McCormick was only the *tying* run. Perhaps I should have made the throw, but it seemed safer not to.
>
> Del Baker and Pinky Higgins evidently squawked, though not to my face, and I think the press likes to single out a "goat." But I've watched movies of that game, and that play, over and over again, and I don't feel as though I lost the Series.

While he'd rather not have to argue the point, he discusses it calmly now. "In a seven-game Series, you know, someone has to lose four times. Schoolboy Rowe, our big stopper after Newsom and Bridges, was knocked out twice, once in a third of an inning. Did he lose the Series? Rudy York was unproductive. Charlie Gehringer hit .214 and banged into three double plays. Did they lose the Series? I don't think so. Detroit lost the Series."

At Lakeland, Florida, the following spring, Dick had painful twinges in his knees that Denny Carroll, the Tiger trainer, thought might be arthritic. Still, he covered the ground and was told the shortstop job was his: "You have nothing to worry about." In May, six weeks into the season, having played five games, he was released outright. Frank Croucher, a utility infielder, took over. Four days later Bartell was back with the Giants. He appeared in 104 games and hit .303. Jurges had a lock on short, so Dick spent most of his time at third, as he also did in 1942–43. He filled in at his old position occasionally, however, which made Mickey Witek, the principal second baseman of those last years, his twenty-first keystone partner.

In 1944–45 he served at the 12th Naval District headquarters at Treasure Island, in San Francisco Bay. In 1946 five games with the Giants ended his playing career.

V

The Missions were Koenig's last connection with baseball. He left them before the end of the 1936 season and went to work for a local brewery. There was a time, later on, when he felt the separation keenly enough to write the Giants for a coaching job. They had one, but nothing came of it. He bought a gas station in a good location—on the Peninsula, south of San Francisco—and operated it for 10 years or so. Baseball gave him a lifetime pass, but no pension. The most he ever made was $12,000. He got along.

Bartell's bigger career led to immediate opportunities in baseball. He became manager of the Sacramento Solons (PCL) in 1947, the Kansas City Blues (Double A), a Yankee farm, in 1948.

> After the season George Weiss asked me to manage their Class A Eastern League club at Binghamton, New York. "We're going to make changes in our farm system," he told me, "but we'd like to keep you in the organization." I should have listened to him. The Eastern was a lesser league, though, and it seemed like a step down. So when Red Rolfe, who'd just become manager at Detroit, asked me to be his third-base coach, I accepted.

In mid-season 1952, with the Tigers in the cellar, Rolfe was fired and Coach Bartell soon followed. He was out of baseball in 1953, then coached two years for his old teammate Birdie Tebbetts at Cincinnati, and managed Montgomery, Alabama, of the Sally League for one year. When the club was moved to . Knoxville, Tennessee, he left baseball for good.

For seven years he was a wholesale representative for an East Bay dairy products company, then ran a liquor store in nearby San Leandro for 10. In 1972 he retired.

Today, at 82, he has lost some of the pounds and inches of his playing days, but still has the bright, alert air of the take-charge shortstop and the quickstep stride of a man in spikes leaving the dugout for the stadium grass. He is pleased with his accomplishments, although, until they were compiled for him several years ago, he did not realize how impressive they are. In the long history of baseball only 125 men have played more games, only 117 have had more hits, only a dozen or so shortstops have made more putouts or averaged more chances per game. "I played 110 percent on the field," he says simply. Still does. When he was asked by the Giants to throw out the first ball at Candlestick a season or two ago, he geared up for the task. "Don't look feeble," he told himself. "Get up on your toes, throw overhand, and point for accuracy." He threw a strike.

He shoots excellent golf, with an occasional round in fewer strokes than his age! He has toured the country to plug his recent autobiography, *Rowdy Richard,* to appear at baseball card shows and on radio and TV.[11] He has been active in the Association of Professional Baseball Players of America, which is based in Los Angeles and helps old-timers with health problems. He lunches frequently at the Grotto, a waterfront restaurant in Oakland's Jack London Square. The welcome is warm and the company, which may include old buddies such as Augie Galan, is congenial.

Mark Koenig is rather more slowed down by age. He has a cottage on the family's 30-acre farm which produces oranges, olives, pecans, and almonds. He lives simply. He regrets, but accepts, his isolation which is now more a factor of time than of distance. He sees no distinction in being the last of the 1927 Yankees. In his mind he still is with them. Five or six years ago, as he was wheeled into the operating room to undergo serious surgery, he said, "Tell me, Doc. Am I going to join Babe and Lou?"

"Baseball made me," Dick says happily. "I loved the game and I have wonderful friends all around the country. It was a business," Mark acknowledges. "When you're through, you're through." But: "It was wonderful fun. I was born under a lucky star!"

NOTES

Direct quotations of Mark Koenig and Dick Bartell derive from intermittent interviews and conversations between 1983 and 1989.

1. Donald Honig, *October Heroes.* New York: Simon & Schuster, 1979, p. 98.
2. John Mosedale, *The Greatest of All: The 1927 Yankees.* New York: Warner, 1975, p. 56.
3. *Babe Ruth's Own Book of Baseball* (Christy Walsh). New York: A.L. Burt, 1928, p. 101.
4. *New York Times,* April 7, 1927, p. 17.
5. Mosedale, p. 80.
6. Honig, p. 126.
7. Telephone interview, August 1983.
8. July 6, 1932. With Jurges disabled by bullet wounds to right upper body and left little finger, the Cubs moved English back to shortstop and called on rookie Stan Hack for some of the first games of his long career at third.
9. Charlie Grimm, with Ed Prell, *Jolly Cholly's Story: Baseball, I Love You.* Chicago: Henry Regnery, 1968, p. 80.
10. Bartell says he learned of this from Terry after he joined the Giants.
11. Dick Bartell, with Norman L. Macht. Berkeley, CA: North Atlantic Books, 1987.

Happy Jack's Wild Pitch

BILL FELBER

The rivalry between Boston and New York has produced several chapters in the American League's book of classic pennant races. Even relatively young fans, for instance, recall Bucky Dent's home run to win the 1978 playoff game, the climax of a soul-stirring, weeks-long battle. Fans of a heartier vintage remember the perennial Boston-New York scraps of the late 40s and early 50s. Perhaps the most storied of those, on the final two days of the 1949 season, saw the Yankees twice beat the Red Sox at Yankee Stadium to overtake them for the pennant. On nine different occasions in American League history, the Yanks and Sox have finished one-two in either their league or division. Many trace the origin of the rivalry to the winter day way back in 1920 when the Red Sox sold their star player, Babe Ruth, to New York, essentially setting up the first great Yankee dynasty.

The truth is that both the rivalry and the tradition of Yankee-Red Sox late-season pennant theatrics predate Ruth's sale by two decades, hearkening well beyond the reach of the memory of the most veteran present-day fan. It dates from an upstart New York team's first challenge to the supremacy of a Boston dynasty in the obscure summer of 1904, a summer when the fabled "Royal Rooters" cheered Boston's Pilgrims, and a pitcher with the carefree sobriquet of "Happy Jack" lived one of the most melancholy moments in all of the game's lore.

To appreciate the full irony of that seminal event in the New York-Boston rivalry, this much must first be understood: In 1904, Jack Chesbro was a remarkable pitcher. A luminary with the National League Pittsburgh Pirates, for whom he had won a total of 49 games in 1901 and 1902 pennant seasons, Chesbro jumped to the rival American League's New York team, then called the Highlanders, in 1903 at the height of the interleague "war" for players. His acquisition was perhaps the centerpiece of a series of steps taken by club owner Frank Farrell, a saloon keeper, in direct concert with league president Ban Johnson, to improve the makeup of the Highlanders, who had moved from Baltimore at the start of the 1903 season. When they came to town, what baseball excitement did grip Manhattan could be traced directly to their hated rivals, the Giants of John McGraw and Christy Mathewson. New York's elite—those involved in entertainment, politics, and business—would be seen daily in the prominent boxes of the Giants' home, the spacious Polo Grounds.

Johnson knew the importance to his league of having a competitive team in the nation's largest city. That's why he lobbied for the transfer of the franchise; that's also why he talked the financially well-heeled Farrell into purchasing the team.[1] And that's why both men wanted Chesbro, indisputably the game's eminent pitcher, in New York American League livery.[2] He provided the Highlanders and the league with a recognizable personality, and in so doing fashioned them into a marketable commodity. "Happy Jack's" naturally smiling, relaxed demeanor, combined with his obvious talent, constituted an intangible quality that in later years would variously be labeled as charisma, credibility or stature. In 1904, of course, neither Johnson, Farrell nor anyone else thought to suggest that Chesbro might attract fans to Highlander Park in upper Manhattan because of charisma, or that his presence would give the toddler league credibility. But if they or anyone had thought to suggest it, they would have been right, because that is what Jack Chesbro did.

But Chesbro's acquisition was only part of the makeover process. With Johnson's assistance, Farrell undertook one of the boldest and most successful player raids ever conducted prior to the 1903 season, also stealing pitcher Jess Tannehill, third baseman Wid Conroy, outfielder Lefty Davis and catcher Jack O'Connor from the National League champion Pirates.[3] In a complicated deal, Johnson arranged for the outright transfer of Detroit shortstop Kid Elberfield to the New York roster.[4] The Johnson-Farrell team won another major bidding war when Farrell signed famed outfielder Willie Keeler, late of Brooklyn's National League entry, to play with the Highlanders, and Johnson arranged for the interleague dispute over Keeler's services to be settled in New York's favor.[5]

Those moves lifted the Highlanders—who, in Baltimore, had finished last with 50 victories—to fourth and 72 wins in 1903. But Farrell was not yet through. Prior to the 1904 season, Tannehill was sent to Boston and veteran pitcher Jack Powell obtained from St. Louis. In early May, pitcher Al Orth came over from Washington. Farrell's final deal solidified the outfield, sending utility player Bob Unglaub to the Red Sox for outfielder Patsy Dougherty. The trade stunned Boston fans, for Dougherty had hit .342 and .331 the past two seasons, and as an Irishman he was especially popular among Boston's "Royal Rooters," that band of 300 or so largely ethnic ultra-rabid partisans who rarely missed a home game, and who often followed the team on the road. Contract disputes had soured Dougherty's relationship with Boston management, and when he batted only .272 over the first 50 games of the 1904 season he became expendable.[6]

Even with the Dougherty problem, the Pilgrims quickly moved into first place as they had been expected to do. This was a superb Boston team, winner of the previous season's pennant by 16 games and surprise champions of the first "World's Series," defeating the Pirates five games to three. The heart of the Pilgrims lay in their imposing "one-two" moundsmen, Cy Young and Bill Dinneen. Together they had won 49 games in 1903. (They would equal that total in 1904.) Outfielder Buck Freeman had driven in a league-high 104 runs the previous season. And baseball experts agreed that the game had never seen a finer third baseman than Jimmy Collins, who held the position for Boston and doubled as manager. Their record as of June 1 was 25–10, and they seemed comfortable at the standing's apex.

Nobody expected the Highlanders, under pitcher-manager Clark Griffith, to do anything, and they started slowly, finishing April in fifth place. But, thanks in large measure to Chesbro, they climbed to fourth by June 1, then to second by the first of July. With a month of play remaining, the Highlanders had closed to within one game of the champions. Chesbro was pitching every second or third day, amassing prodigious totals that kept him at or near the league's top all summer in victories, winning percentage, strikeouts, complete games, innings pitched and fewest hits per nine innings.

For the challengers, the grueling climb toward the top neared a late-season climax filled with dual perils. The first was a three-week long odyssey through seven of the eight league cities, involving 24 games, a murderous 23 of them on the road. And if the Highlanders remained in contention after that, they faced a last-ditch, final weekend showdown with the Pilgrims themselves to decide the title.

The sojourn, a test to which it is inconceivable that any club would be subjected on a modern schedule, began with a series in Boston Sept. 14–16. Because of darkness-prompted ties, the clubs wound up playing three consecutive double headers, each team winning two games in addition to the two deadlocks. Chesbro accounted for both New York victories. The final double header attracted 22,983, a record crowd for Boston. Griffith's club returned following that series for its only home game of the stretch, defeating Washington. Then the Highlanders entrained westward, and this is how they did:

In Washington, three victories––two by Chesbro—and one defeat.

In Cleveland, two losses—Chesbro suffered one—one tie.

In Detroit, two victories—one by Chesbro—one defeat.

In Chicago, two victories—one by Chesbro—two defeats.

In St. Louis, three victories—one by Chesbro.

The Highlanders had undertaken a 24-game, seven-city tour under intense pennant pressure, and had emerged with 13 victories and only eight defeats. Three of the victories had been shutouts; in seven others, New York pitchers allowed a single run, Chesbro's personal register showed seven victories against five different teams, and only one defeat.

But at the same time the Boston juggernaut completed an only slightly less exhausting trip with a virtually identical record, so as the contenders returned east Oct. 6 for their showdown series, the margin separating them was a paltry percentage point. Boston led at .617, New York was second at .616.

The receptions accorded the two clubs along their return routes from the west illustrated the prevailing public mindset that the Pilgrims were the champions, the Highlanders pretenders. Throngs heralded the Bostonians at virtually every depot. When the Red Sox special stopped at Buffalo, friends, neighbors and townsfolk joined the family of player-manager Collins in greeting him. A few miles farther along the route, in Elkhart, fans saluted catcher Lou Criger, formerly of that area. Dinneen was similarly hailed in his home town, Syracuse.[7]

Jack Chesbro. (Photo courtesy of the National Baseball Library, Cooperstown, N.Y.)

No cheering fans waited to greet the Highlanders at any of their stops. In fact, they had to scramble to make the series' first game on time, arriving in New York only hours before the scheduled first pitch. Lacking even the opportunity to exchange their soiled grey uniforms for fresh home whites, the players detrained and immediately boarded hacks for the ride to the park at 160th Street.[8]

Never in the history of either the American or National League had a pennant race devolved into a head-to-head meeting of contenders on the season's final weekend, so fan interest was at maximum intensity. And never before or since had such a vital series been played on so strange a schedule. Originally, four games had been scheduled for New York, one each on Friday and Saturday, then a concluding double header Monday. (Sunday baseball was illegal.) But there remained one of the September ties in Boston to be made up and Farrell—in a move he would have cause later to regret—agreed to move his Saturday home date in order to play a double header that afternoon in Boston. Thus, following the Friday game, the clubs both would board trains again for Boston, returning to New York for the final two games Monday.[9]

With the race in a virtual tie, the only thing clear was that whichever team won three of the five games would be the champion.

OCTOBER 7

Raw temperatures and blustery winds greeted the returning Highlanders and the 9,500 topcoated fans who tromped to the Upper West Side park. Most came to cheer the home club, but not all. Boston's legendary "Rooters" had not organized a formal party for the Friday engagement—although plans had been developed for a large excursion Monday—yet numerous Pilgrim backers vociferously claimed seats behind the visitors' wooden third base bench. Griffith selected Chesbro to make his 53rd appearance and 49th start of the season—he had completed 45 of the previous 48—in search of his 41st victory. Collins turned from both of his veterans, Young and Dinneen, and chose instead Norwood Gibson, a 17-game victor in 1904, which was his best season in a four-year career.

Gibson matched Chesbro through the early innings, and Fred Parent's two-out, third inning single scoring Kip Selbach gave the Bostonians a chance to cheer a brief lead. But New York quickly offset that run. With one out in the bottom of the inning, Elberfield allowed a pitch to brush his pant leg, and was awarded first base. He stole second, and with two outs scored when John Anderson looped a ball just inside fair territory for a double.

A defensive foul-up gave the Highlanders the lead in the fifth inning. Dougherty, down two strikes to Gibson, fouled off several pitches and then flied to shallow left. Either shortstop Parent or left-fielder Selbach could have made the catch, but the screeching of the home crowd prevented the two from hearing each other, and the ball fell safely. With Dougherty secure at second, Keeler advanced him with a bunt and Elberfield drove a fly ball deep enough to score the run.

Chesbro's spitter checked Boston on only two hits through the seventh, and New York added to its lead in the bottom of that frame when Dougherty bunted safely, stole second, and scored on Button Williams' base hit. Boston's best opportunity of the afternoon glimmered in the eighth in the dust of a collision and a diving stop. Selbach walked leading off, and Parent followed with a slow roller toward second base. The ball, second baseman Williams and base runner Selbach arrived almost simultaneously, the fielder and runner collided, the ball skittered away and umpire Tommy Connolly signaled Selbach out for interference. Connolly's call proved costly after Stahl followed with a line single to left that might have scored Selbach. Then with two out, Buck Freeman drove a

The 1903 World Series at the Old Huntington Avenue Grounds, Boston, where the Red Sox defeated the Pittsburgh Pirates. (Photo courtesy of the National Baseball Library, Cooperstown, N.Y.)

smash toward short that Elberfield knocked down with a lunge. He could not throw the batter out, nor keep Parent from scoring, but he did hold Stahl at third with the game-tying run. Twice reprieved, Chesbro retired Candy LaChance to end the inning, and made quick work of Boston in the ninth to complete the 3–2 victory that edged the New Yorkers into first place.[10]

Highlander fans carried Chesbro from the field, and Griffith merrily shook hands with dozens among the crowd. But for most of the players on both teams, there was little time for either celebrating or second-guessing. They were due in Boston the next morning. Accompanied by Farrell, the Highlanders—who had not seen their homes in three weeks—left the ball park to catch the evening train. The Pilgrims followed on the midnight special.

OCTOBER 8

The excitement at Boston's Huntington Avenue Grounds was reminiscent of the atmosphere a year earlier, when the park had hosted the first World Series. Official attendance for Saturday's double header was placed at 28,040, easily breaking the park record the same two teams had set on Sept. 16. But nobody suggested that official attendance reflected the actual number of fans who found a way to witness the day's games. Some watched from rooftops of adjacent buildings; others perched atop fences to peer into the grounds. Enterprising young daredevils scaled telegraph poles and held on through the afternoon.

Well-meaning but larcenous enthusiasts used ladders to surmount the grounds' walls, while others literally tunneled underneath them. The best estimates as to the actual count of onlookers approached a staggering 35,000—far in excess of any audience for any previous game of baseball ever played anywhere. By way of comparison, the other three American League sites that same day drew a total attendance of about 4,000.

Boston fans, renowned as the nation's most rabid, strained at the bounds of emotional control at the thought of their great club facing elimination from the pennant race, which would occur with a double defeat. But they as quickly took heart from the realization that both of manager Collins' rested aces, Young and Dinneen, were prepared for the occasion. Dinneen would start the first game. All morning and the previous night, Griffith had refused to reveal his own pitching plans—he probably was truly undecided—fueling rampant speculation. Most of the grandstand talk focused on Powell, a 23-game winner, and perhaps even Griffith himself. At age 34, the pitcher-manager known as "The Old Fox" was past his prime, but that prime had seen him win 20 or more games in seven different seasons, and amass 238 victories for his career. But for the first game, Griffith went with neither Powell nor himself. Instead, he sent the imposing figure of Chesbro out to warm up again.

Only a pitcher of epic stature could have proposed to silence the world champions in such climactic contests twice within the span of a single sunset. But through the early innings, the marvelous spit baller seemed carved from that epic mold. He fanned two Boston batters in the first inning, and completed three having allowed no hits and just one walk. The Highlanders further dampened the mood of the Boston partisans when Dougherty, who had opened the game with a single and advanced on Keeler's bunt base hit, scored on sacrifices by Elberfield and Williams.

Indeed, through the first part of the game the only cause for Boston celebration was a contrived one. As Collins strode to the plate in the second he was called aside and the game briefly interrupted so that local fans might present their hero with a 26-inch high silver cup. Collins accepted the gift and the plaudits of the crowd, then flied to Keeler.

But Chesbro proved a flawed colossus in the fourth. Parent opened with the club's first hit, Stahl sacrificed, and Collins singled sharply to right, scoring the tying run. Freeman also singled, and when Dougherty misplayed the ball Boston runners reached second and third with but a single out. Williams fielded La-Chance's grounder and attempted to head off Collins at the plate, but his throw was late. Three more hits and a walk followed, the tally of runs mounting to six in a burst so delightful to the home crowd that they took to counting each score as it crossed home plate the way students at a high school football game might do today. "One, two, three, four, five, six!" they chanted in unison, yelling the final number with considerable emphasis. Griffith replaced Chesbro with young Walter Clarkson, a lad best known in Boston as the brother of John Clarkson, famed pitcher of an earlier generation. Walter had joined the Highlanders only weeks before upon his graduation from Harvard—for whom he had played most of the year—and had compiled a 2–2 record.

Young Clarkson proved no more effective in the fifth than Chesbro had been in the fourth. He hit Collins, walked Freeman, and one out later served up a pitch to Hobe Ferris that the veteran infielder drove far over Anderson's head in center for what under normal circumstances would have been an inside-the-park home run. It wasn't on this day, but only because the crowd had overflowed onto the field, and when the ball rolled into the ranks of fans it was declared a ground-rule double. Only Collins and Freeman were allowed to score.

The Highlanders posted one more run against Dinneen in their half of the sixth, but by that time the run-counting Boston fans were counting well-toward their team's final tally of 13. Dinneen finished with a four-hitter, his 22nd success of the season.

With the race virtually even again, Griffith and Collins chose Powell and Young, the latter already a lifetime 400-game winner, to meet in the second game. For five innings Powell was very much the match of the legendary fastballer, each escaping their only crisis in the fifth. In the Yankee half, Keeler slipped a hit past Parent into left, Elberfield again was struck by a pitch, and Keeler reached third on Williams' force-out grounder. The Highlanders, with runners at first and third, gambled on a double steal. But Parent took Criger's throw and—all the while watching Keeler at third—trapped Williams between first and second, finally running him down to end the inning. In the Boston half, Selbach's walk and Stahl's double placed two runners in scoring position with a single out. Either Collins or Freeman could have broken open the game, but Powell fanned them both, much to the crowd's dismay.

By the bottom of the fifth, darkness already was settling over the park, and the prospect of a shortened scoreless tie loomed. In the gathering twilight of the Boston sixth, Ferris' bad-hop grounder eluded Williams. Playing the sacrifice game so typical of the era, Criger laid down a bunt that advanced the runner into scoring position for Young. Never ranked among the more notable pitchers with the bat, Young lofted a fly ball deep enough to Anderson in center that Ferris elected to tag and try for third. The gamble paid off with a dividend when Anderson's throw bounced away from Conroy and skipped into the crowd on the field, enabling the runner to continue to home plate.

New York went down in order before Young in the seventh as well, and after Boston failed to score in the bottom of the inning the umpires ruled it too dark to continue. Young had fashioned a six-hitter for the 1–0 victory, his 26th of the season. Powell had lost despite giving up only four hits. And Boston's lead was a game. But a New York sweep on Monday could still swing the tightest pennant race in the history of the major leagues to that date. "I am still confident," Griffith said afterward. "Chesbro will go again Monday. We are all cheerful."

OCTOBER 10

The core of the Boston citizenry spent their "day of rest" finalizing plans for the trip to New York. So assiduously did the Royal Rooters' leaders, Charley Lavin, Johnny Keenan and "Nuf Said' McGreevey, organize that nearly 400 Pilgrims' partisans signed up for the train ride.

And what a train ride it was! All New England rode with the Pilgrims, and fans lucky enough to live along the route formed a virtual cordon to New York for them. At the New London, Ct. station, lunch counters were swept clean of sandwiches and fruits, and in the hubbub not all of the commodities were paid for. To make amends, the Rooters treated station personnel to a chorus of one of their best-known cheers:

Hobble, Gobble,
Hobble, Gobble,
Ziss, boom, bah!
Boston, Boston, Rah, Rah, Rah![11]

The same thing happened in New Haven, except that this time the serenade featured the Rooters' unique version of "In the Good Old Summer Time:"

In the good old summertime,
    Our Boston baseball nine
Beat the teams east and west,
    Now they're first in line.
The New Yorks are after us,
    Oh me! Oh my! Oh my!
We'll do them as we did the rest
    In the good old summertime![12]

On their arrival in New York, the Rooters were easily recognizable. They proudly wore bold red badges on their coats, each emblazoned with the words "world's champions." At the hotel Sunday evening and Monday morning, Pilgrim backers openly speculated that Griffith would not dare return Chesbro to the mound following the drubbing he had received Saturday, and that accordingly the pennant was virtually theirs by forfeit.[13] They staged a rollicking informal parade up 165th Street to the park Monday morning, led by Dockstader's band, a Boston troupe they had hired and brought with them for the occasion. A Boston police sergeant in the party procured a mascot, a 79-year-old black man who gave his name as Gabriel and whom the Rooters outfitted in a blue great coat with brass buttons. Gabriel's grey beard glistened in the mid-day sun as he marched at the head of the assembly, carrying aloft an immense bean pot, the traditional symbol of the city's baseball fortunes.[14] The parade rocked with chorus after chorus of the Rooters' trademark song, "Tessie," and the Rooters reprised the tune dozens of times once they took their seats directly behind the Boston bench at the park, including between every inning:

Tessie, you make me feel so badly;
    Why don't you turn around.
Tessie, you know I love you madly;
    Babe, my heart weighs about a pound.
Don't blame me if i ever doubt you.
    You know I can't live without you.
Tessie, you are my only, only, on-ly.[15]

The Highlanders had no similar theme song, but on this day they had their own home crowd of 28,000. And despite the Rooters' expectations, they also had Chesbro. Griffith, knowing he needed both victories, sent him to the mound in the hope that the full day's rest had invigorated him. Collins, who had planned to start Gibson, switched to Dinneen when the latter warmed up and reported no lingering soreness from his Saturday start.

William Dinneen. (Photo courtesy of the National Baseball Library, Cooperstown, N.Y.)

For four innings, neither team scored, although the champions escaped some tight jams. Dougherty walked and reached second base in the first; then, with one out in the third, Chesbro tripled along the right-field foul line. The hit came after Highlander fans, mimicking the presentation to Collins two days earlier, halted the game to bestow gifts including a sealskin coat, cap and gloves on their star moundsman. The New Yorkers hoped fervently for a hit, but Dinneen struck out both Dougherty and Keeler to end the threat.

Dinneen held the home team scoreless until Red Kleinow singled after two were retired in the sixth. Chesbro also singled, his shot caroming off Dinneen's glove, and the rattled pitcher surrendered a third straight hit to Dougherty that tallied Kleinow with the game's first run. That wasn't all. Dinneen walked both Keeler and Elberfield, forcing across a second score.

Through six innings Chesbro's spitter held Boston scoreless. But only nine outs from a victory that would have sent the race to a final and deciding game, he was betrayed by sloppy fielding. LaChance opened the seventh with a base hit, then Ferris drove a ball right between Williams' legs at second. It was scored an error. Criger laid down the anticipated sacrifice, bringing Dinneen to bat. He rolled an easy grounder to Williams, who fielded it and fired wildly toward Kleinow at home as LaChance scored easily and Ferris followed him around. That quickly, the game was tied at 2–2.

"Tessie" fairly echoed through the wooden park.

Still tied, the game moved through the eighth inning and into the ninth as 28,000 fidgeted under their autumn hats. Criger, leading off, scratched out an infield hit, his team's seventh. Dinneen bunted him to second. There was true tension throughout the ball park as leadoff hitter Selbach approached the plate. Chesbro himself grimaced, but he induced Selbach to ground a spit ball to Conroy for the second out as Criger took third. The next batter was Parent. He threw him a spitter; it was called a strike. Two more followed, both balls. Then a fourth, this time a fatal one. The pitch slipped from Chesbro's grasp, sailed over Kleinow's mitt and thudded dully against the park's back wall. Criger frantically lumbered across the plate with the run that gave Boston a 3–2 lead, touching off riotous glad-handing behind the visitors' bench, and sending the rest of the grandstand into a depression.

As if it could remove some of the onus from the most fated wild pitch in the game's history, Parent drove Chesbro's next delivery sharply up the middle of the diamond for a base hit.

Highlander fans rose a clatter as John Ganzel approached the plate to open the ninth in the hope that the din might rattle Dinneen. It did no such thing; Ganzel fanned. Dinneen thought he'd fanned Conroy as well on a 3–2 pitch. He complained shrilly when the batter instead was waved to first base on ball four. Kleinow flied to Stahl in center, and Griffith called on 41-year-old reserve Jim McGuire as his club's last hope. McGuire delivered, after a fashion, by drawing a second base on balls. That brought up the same Dougherty who had been dealt from Boston to New York earlier in the season. A .283 batter since his acquisition by the Highlanders, Dougherty took a curve for a strike, then a fast ball high and inside. Another curve broke low, Dougherty swinging and missing for strike two. The fourth pitch sailed judiciously high and wide.

On the mound, Dinneen raised two fingers of each hand, confirming the count of two balls and two strikes. Then he stepped back astride the rubber. The big pitcher rotated his arm in the winding motion that was common to pitchers of that day, then brought ball and arm forward. The pitch bore in close to Dougherty, who swung, and whoosh of air signalling strike three crowned Boston as champion for the second successive year. The Boston fans cheered and followed their band through "Tessie." Gabriel led an impromptu parade around the field, carrying a sign that drew attention to the avowed refusal of John T. Brush, owner of the National League champion New York Giants, to permit his team to play a World Series against the representative of a "minor league." The sign said:

> Mr. Brush, we're on plush,
>   Where are you?
> Don't be vain; give us a game.
>   One or two.[16]

One observer described the New York backers as "silent as grass."[17]

As if to heighten the aura of "what might have been," the Highlanders proceeded to win the meaningless second game 1–0 in 10 innings.

AFTERMATH

Because of the Giants' refusal to play, the Pilgrims had only the memories of their triumph in the most dramatic pennant race to that date to carry them through the winter. The Royal Rooters loyally cheered their heroes through hard times until the pennant was returned in 1912. By that time, Young, Freeman and Collins were gone, replaced by Smoky Joe Wood, Tris Speaker and Harry Hooper. The Huntington Street Grounds itself had given way to the vast and impressive new brick and steel ballpark built on the city's Fenway.

Chesbro was good for 19 more victories in 1905 and an additional 24 in 1906. He died in 1931, five years before the creation of the Hall of Fame, to which he was elected in 1946. Griffith was inducted with him; Young, Keeler and Collins already were there.

Highlander fortunes never again approached the doorstep of the destiny that they nearly achieved in 1904. The team took a new nickname in 1906—the Yankees. Ironically, it would be the sale of a Boston player, Ruth, to New York after the 1919 season that would alter the Yankees' fortunes for the better. But between 1904 and that sale, Johnson, Farrell and others pining for the arrival of a contender in New York must have wondered whether their dream had been left forever dashed in the bitterly ironic dust of Happy Jack's wild pitch.

NOTES

1. Eugene Murdock, *Ban Johnson, Czar of Baseball* (Westport, CT: Greenwood Press, 1982), p. 58, 63.

2. Ibid., 60.

3. Ibid.

4. Harold Seymour, *Baseball: The Golden Age*. New York: Oxford University Press, 1971, 12.

5. Murdock. Page 62.

6. Joe Reichler, *Baseball Trade Register* (New York: Macmillan, 1984).

7. *Boston Globe*. Oct. 7, 1904. Page 4, col. 4.

8. *New York Times*. Oct. 8, 1904. Page 7, col. 1.

9. *Boston Globe*. Oct. 7, 1904. Page 1, col. 8.

10. Details of the play-by-play and atmosphere were widely recorded in several newspapers the following morning. The best sources are the *New York Times, The New York World,* and the *Boston Globe*. Information concerning the play on the field for this article was drawn from all of them.

11. *Boston Globe*. Oct. 10, 1904. Page 8, col. 3.

12. Ibid.

13. *New York Times.* Oct. 10, 1904. Page 6, col. 5.

14. *New York World.* Oct. 11, 1904. Page 6, col. 6.

15. Frequent repetition of "Tessie," the long-time theme song of the Royal Rooters, was reported in several newspapers that covered the game.

16. *New York World.* Oct. 11, 1904. Page 6, col. 5.

17. Ibid.

Playing for John McGraw

NORMAN L. MACHT

Transcending time and space and mortality, we brought together seven men who played for John McGraw to talk about the man even his critics have called the greatest manager of them all.

A rowdy, boisterous, no-holds-barred, umpire-baiting third baseman on Ned Hanlon's three-time pennant winners, the Baltimore Orioles of the 1890s, McGraw headed the Baltimore franchise in the new American League in 1901, but jumped to the Giants in July of 1902, where he won 10 pennants and three World Series before he retired in June 1932.

Of the seven you will hear from, four played their entire careers with the Giants and for McGraw. One was Bill Terry, the great first baseman who never got along with McGraw, didn't speak to him for two years and succeeded him as manager although he was not McGraw's choice. Shortstop Travis Jackson was there for 15 years and four World Series. McGraw's last year at the Polo Grounds was the first regular season for Joe Moore and pitcher Hal Schumacher.

George Kelly had the dubious honor of following Hal Chase at first base for the Giants in 1920. A long-ball hitter and RBI man, he was shifted to second to make room for Terry in 1925, and was traded to the Reds in 1927.

Outfielder Ethan Allen was with the Giants 1930–1932 between stints with five other teams in his 13-year, .300 BA career.

Pitcher Carmen Hill came up from Indianapolis briefly in 1922, and got the benefit of some direct tutoring from McGraw. When he won 22 for the 1927 NL champion Pirates, Hill's batterymate was Earl Smith, a burr under McGraw's saddle when Smith was with the Giants in the early 1920s.

Terry, Jackson and Kelly are in the Hall of Fame.

While these men did not meet for the following conversation, all of their comments are based on interviews by the author between 1982 and 1985, and are their own words.

***

The seven: Bill Terry, Travis Jackson, George Kelly, Carmen Hill, Joe Moore, Hal Schumacher, Ethan Allen.

Moore: What I remember is that big sign he had in his office. It was right in front of you above that mirror when you walked in. It said: THINK in big letters. But you didn't think with him. Don't ever say I thought so about something to him; that was the wrong thing to say. You wanted to know for sure. He did all the thinking.

Kelly: He relied on discipline and smart baseball, but you were expected to be watching, thinking and learning all the time, on your own. He used to change the signs every three innings. You had to look at the card posted in the dugout to see what they were. Nobody told you when they were changed. You had to look for yourself. If you missed a sign it cost you. Rookies and veterans alike. He treated them all the same.

Jackson: That's true. He didn't teach you anything on the bench. I had to sit and watch and learn and see things for myself to try to improve myself.

Allen: That's why I liked McGraw. He treated everybody alike. Sure he got on the young players, and some writers jumped on him for that. But he got on the veterans too. Sometimes a manager will show favoritism toward an older player but will eat out a rookie. But the older player deserves it more when he makes a mistake. He didn't motivate anybody. He scared some of them, but he didn't motivate. You were supposed to supply that yourself.

Kelly: You're right. He called everybody you big stiff. His idea of motivating somebody was, he'd say to Christy Mathewson, "You big stiff, let's see you get somebody out." This was after the guy had won over 350 games for him. One day he said to me, "You big stiff, why don't you make a play at first base?" So I thought, what can I do out there? Maybe if I get some dumb baserunners, I'll get a chance to trap an infield fly and fool somebody. Sure enough, one day there were two on and one out and the batter hit an infield fly. Automatic out. So I trapped it. The runners went. I threw to second for a double play. I came into the bench feeling pretty good. I don't see McGraw on the bench. "Where's the old man?" I asked. "He went out to Belmont when we took the field," somebody said. He used to do that sometimes late in the game. It was the only time I made a play like that, and he didn't see it.

Allen: Even if he did see it, he probably would have taken credit for it. He would take credit for everything that happened. If he told you to hit to right and you did, he would take credit for it sitting on the bench.

Kelly: He took all the credit, all right. In 1921 late in August we were 7½ games back of the Pirates. They came into New York for a five-game series. They say McGraw gave us a big pep talk before the first game. Maybe so, but I don't remember him ever giving us any kind of pep talk. The first game, Babe Adams is pitching for Pittsburgh. We get three men on and I'm up. The count goes to 3-and-0. I look down at Hughie Jennings coaching at third and he's giving me the hit sign. I don't believe it. With McGraw, the 3-and-0 was always an automatic take. I step out of the batter's box and look again. Again he flashes the hit sign. If the Pirates had been watching me I'd have tipped them off for sure. But Adams grooved the next pitch and I hit a home run. Won the game. Afterwards,

McGraw comes by my locker and says to me, "If my brains hold out, we'll win this thing yet." That's all. Not a word about the homer I hit.

Terry: It's not true that he never had a word of praise for anybody. But there weren't many. While I was playing for him Pep Youngs—Ross Youngs—was his boy. He always had a good word for Pep.

Schumacher: He had that reputation for not praising anybody when I came up, but he did one good thing for me. During spring training I pitched against the White Sox coming north. We came into the Polo Grounds for the last exhibition game. It was a cold day. I worked the last two innings and struck out five of the six batters I faced. I walked into the clubhouse and was bent over the water cooler. Somebody patted me on the shoulder. I looked up and it was McGraw. He looked at me and said, "Schumacher, I want to congratulate you on the impression you made on the Polo Grounds fans in your first appearance here." And he just walked away. You were there, Travis.

Jackson: I remember, when the old man got out of range, I said to you, "Geez, the old man's gone soft." Maybe he was rough to play for, but I have to say he never cussed me out, even when I made a mistake. And he was fair. When I was the captain it was my responsibility to position the fielders. One day at the Polo Grounds we had a rookie, Jimmy Welsh, in the outfield. Somebody hit a line drive out there and Welsh was in the wrong place and it went for a triple. When we went into the dugout McGraw was just frothing at the mouth and cussing Jimmy out. Jimmy said to him, "Mr. McGraw, Jackson moved me." McGraw asked me, "Did you move him?" I said, "Yep." Mac said, "Forget about it, Welsh." That's all there was to it. I may have made a mistake, but as long as I was thinking and trying and hustling, he didn't get on me.

Moore: Yeah, he'd get on you, but if somebody else did, he was quick to defend you, too. In my rookie year I was playing left field one day against St. Louis. Bill Walker was pitching for us, The Cards had the bases loaded and a ball was hit to left. I charged it and booted it a little bit and two runs scored. We got back in the dugout and Walker starts chewing me out. He says, "Why did you charge that ball, there wasn't any play," and McGraw right away says, "No play—with the bases loaded there's bound to be a play somewhere."

Kelly: He could get on you, but he backed his men against everybody else. When he let Hal Chase go and put me on first base in 1920, that was a tough act to follow. I got off to a slow start, wasn't hitting much. The writers were getting on me. One of them wrote: I'm getting ready to retire, I saw Kelly get a hit. Another one wrote a poem, When Kelly Gets a Hit. Stuff like that. The fans picked up on it and they got on me pretty good, too. McGraw told me, "Don't read the newspapers. You're working for me. I do the hiring and firing." The club paid the writers' expenses on the road. If he didn't like what somebody wrote, he left them home.

Jackson: He didn't get on you for making mistakes if you were trying. It was the mental lapses, the missed signs, the disobeying orders that drove him crazy.

Hill: I can vouch for that. He didn't get on you if you remembered his instructions, but just couldn't execute them. I reported to the Giants for the last month of the 1922 season. We're playing Brooklyn a double header. McGraw called me over and sat me down beside him. As each player came up to bat he

John McGraw. (Photo courtesy of the National Baseball Library, Cooperstown, N.Y.)

said, "This is so-and-so and here's the way I want you to pitch to him." The next day he starts me. Late in the game the score was 1 to 1. They had a man on second with two out, and Andy High came up to bat. He was really the only one I remembered McGraw's instructions on; he'd told me to pitch low to High. I got a pitch up a little and he hit it into right center for a triple. When I came in McGraw says to me, "Where'd I tell you to pitch to High?" I says, "Low." "You didn't do it, did you," he says. I said, "No." He said, "Okay." That was it. But if you didn't follow orders, watch out. One day Irish Meusel comes up to bat with a man on base and the score tied. McGraw says to him, Irish, take a strike. He said that a lot, wanted you to take a good pitch before you swung. Well, Irish goes up there and hits the first pitch into the seats for a home run. He circles the bases, comes down with both feet on home plate and runs back to the bench, feeling mighty good. McGraw says, "What did I tell you to do?" Meusel says, "You told me to take one and I took it right out of the ball park." McGraw says, "It'll cost you 200." Irish says, "Make it 400." A madder Irishman I never saw. McGraw says, "It's 400." And it stuck.

Terry: One of his orders was calling all the pitches in a game. He drove poor Pancho Snyder crazy doing that. Snyder was a fine catcher. But he'd have to look over to McGraw to get every pitch. And then when we'd get in a spot where we were in bad shape, a couple men on and the pitcher behind the hitter, then he'd give Snyder a sign that said: you're on your own and you'd better get him out.

Hill: Earl Smith was another catcher who didn't like that. First time I pitched for McGraw, Smitty came out to me and said, "Hill, I don't know you and you don't know me. If I call for something you don't want to throw, just shake me off. But don't look in there at that potbellied sonofabitch on the bench or he'll try to pitch your ball game for you." I said, "Oh no he won't." "Well, just don't look at him," Smitty says, "and neither will I." McGraw was waving his arms and pacing around that whole game but we just ignored him.

Jackson: You're right, Carmen. If a pitcher didn't like him calling all the pitches, you'd be in Indianapolis the next day, as you found out. I saw him call 18–19 straight curve balls when Rosy Ryan was pitching one day. Every time Rosy threw a fast ball somebody hit it good. Mac had enough. He started calling curve ball, curve ball. Everybody knew he was doing it for meanness.

Schumacher: I can tell you, if you shook him off, there was hell to pay. Not even Hubbell got away with ignoring his calling the pitches. One day Carl was pitching against Brooklyn. Rube Bressler, a right-handed crouch hitter, was up. He bent way over the plate. McGraw signalled for the screw ball. Bressler hit it hard but foul. McGraw called for the same pitch and Bressler hit it hard but foul again. Hub thought in his own mind it would be a good idea to at least straighten the hitter up. So he shook off the sign and threw one up and in. Well, Bressler had been looking for a screwball down low and when it came in high he just threw the bat up and backed away, The bat hit the ball over the shortstop's head and the winning run scored. McGraw came into the clubhouse and he walked directly over to Hubbell and he really lambasted him, called him some names— none endearing—and said, "That's going to cost you 50 bucks." Well, 50 bucks in those days, 1931, was a lot of money.

Jackson: Talk about pitchers, I remember one time he was really stumped for an answer. He had a young pitcher making his first start. We were playing the Phillies. Gavvy Cravath had been hitting a lot of home runs over that short right-field fence at Baker Bowl. Before the game McGraw said to the boy, "When Cravath comes up, keep the ball low and inside. He can't hit that pitch over the fence." So what happened, when Cravath came up, the youngster pitched him high and outside and Cravath smacked the ball over the fence. When the inning was over, McGraw said to the pitcher, "Didn't you hear what I told you about Cravath?" and the boy answered, "Yes, but how did I know that was Cravath?"

Kelly: One time on the bench he was arguing with a pitcher. I don't recall what it was about. But we all knew the pitcher was right. The argument went on, and finally McGraw said, "Even if you are right, you're wrong with me." He could be stubborn, all right. And he didn't have much of a sense of humor. He was all business. After a loss, you sat in front of your locker until he was through talking. He had his way of doing things and his rules, and as long as you stuck to them, he'd back you up. I used to tell young players, don't ever lie to him because he knows everything you're doing. He had detectives follow some players who were drinkers and carousers. Sure, we had a curfew. The trainer came around checking the rooms at 11:30. If you were late coming in, he knew it, and if you lied about it, it cost you double.

Terry: That's the first thing I did when I replaced McGraw as manager, fire the trainer. He was McGraw's stool pigeon. McGraw and I never got along, but that's no secret. From the first day I met him we didn't get along. I didn't take anything off him. The last two years he was managing we didn't even speak.

Jackson: He knew the ones he could get tough with and who he couldn't.

Terry: He fined me once. We were in Chicago and somebody had a few tickets to a show. So we went and after the show we went backstage to say goodbye to one of the actors we knew. We looked at the clock and saw it was almost curfew time. We ran all the way back to the hotel and came in two minutes late. McGraw was sitting in the lobby and saw us. The next morning the club secretary, Jim Tierney, handed me a note. It said you are hereby fined $50. I handed it back to him and said, "Here, take this and tell him to make it 100 and I'll go home." I never heard any more about it. We went into St. Louis and I'm sitting on the bench. Late in the game McGraw says to me, get a bat. I got up and stopped in front of him and knelt down and tied my shoelaces, then picked up a bat. Alexander was pitching. He came down the middle with one and I hit it out of the park. That night in the hotel I said to Freddie Lindstrom and Travis Jackson, come on up to my room, I've got some free beer. I charged it to the old man, and I ordered a tub of ice to cool it down and charged that to him, too.

Kelly: Well, I always said the people who didn't like him were the ones who didn't like to follow rules.

Jackson: George, you had to take the brunt of it sometimes for the rest of us. You were pretty hardheaded, and wouldn't hold anything back. We knew that, so we let you be our spokesman.

Kelly: He had a temper, but he never carried anything off the field, and the next day it was all over and forgotten. Even with the umpires. He was not an umpire baiter or a showboat. When he had a beef coming, he let them know it and that was that. In those days the chief ump would pull a watch on you. After a few minutes of jawing you were through. One day the ump pulled his Ingersoll on the old man. McGraw was so mad he knocked the watch out of the ump's hand and stomped on it. Little springs were flying all over the place. . . . Of course he was thrown out of the game. The next day, after handing over the lineup card at home plate, he pulled out a new gold watch and gave it to the ump.

Jackson: I've seen him get mad at players on other teams. He'd say to them, "I'll trade for you and get you on my club and then I'll send you down to Timbuktu."

Hill: I didn't like McGraw, but Smitty really hated him. One year it cost Earl $2,500 in fines for not being in his room at curfew times. In '27 Smitty was my catcher at Pittsburgh. First time we played the Giants McGraw ordered Fitzsimmons to walk Earl by throwing at him four times. Four times Smitty went down. I went out there and decked their first three hitters. That ended it.

Jackson: Smith and McGraw didn't like each other, that's true. They'd go at it, shouting back and forth, in the clubhouse. Smith would needle him, call him Muggsy, and that would start it. We all had to double over or crawl into a locker to hide our laughing. It was quite a scene.

Kelly: Calling him Muggsy would really do that to him. He sure hated that name. One time, before a World Series against the Yankees, I'm sitting on the bench with him during batting practice. I look up and there's a young fellow peering down into the dugout. He calls out, "Muggsy?" McGraw bellows like a bull, "Who sent you down here?" Turns out he was a newspaperman from Iowa or someplace. He wants to know who's the starting pitcher for the next day. McGraw never gave out that information to anybody. He invites the fellow to sit down. "Those guys up in the press box put you up to this?" he asks. The writer nods. "They know I don't give out my pitchers," he says. "But I'll tell you what I'll do. I'll tell you who's going to pitch and you can scoop them all in your paper. Just don't tell them I told you."

Allen: Some players didn't like McGraw, but I liked him the best of all the managers I played for.

Kelly: Maybe, like some writers and players said, he was arrogant. Maybe he overdid the strategy business. Some players didn't like his style. But I, for one, liked him, as a man and a manager. He was tops.

Playing a Man's Game: Women and Baseball in the United States, 1866–1954

DEBRA SHATTUCK

Baseball has long been considered a man's sport. Books and articles on baseball history abound, but few give serious consideration to women's involvement with the national pastime. Articles that do mention women generally focus on their role as spectators or on the social derision they faced for daring to play a man's game. But women were playing baseball as early as 1866 and their defiance of social mores dictating separate roles for men and women raises some interesting questions to challenge baseball and social historians: What kind of women played baseball? Were they women's rights activists trying to make a social statement? Were they playing simply for the money such a novelty might net? Were they from the upper or lower classes, white collar or working class, married or single? Did their participation alter certain cultural attitudes toward female athletes?

This brief overview of the history of female baseball players cannot possibly permit in-depth analysis of the motivations and aspirations of female players, but a few generalizations will be offered. The women in this study came from all classes of society and walks of life. Some were married, some were single and most were white. But while all of them shared the distinction of challenging social mores by playing a "man's game," there is little indication that the female players in this study, from the pioneers at Vassar to the professionals of the All-American Girls Professional Baseball League, were specifically trying to change social mores. In fact most of the women went out of their way to demonstrate that they could still conform to social definitions of femininity even while playing baseball.

It appears that female baseball players were motivated by the same reasons that women took up activities like cycling, basketball and tennis before those were socially accepted pursuits for women—they simply enjoyed the game and found ways to play it. There is little evidence female baseball players saw themselves as anything particularly phenomenal. Sophia Foster Richardson and Minnie Stephens attributed the origins of baseball at Vassar and Smith colleges to the desire of students for some "vigorous exercise." When female players from Philadelphia were asked in 1883 why they played baseball, they remarked that it was "partly for the fun of it and to see the country." These are hardly the statements of women out to change the status quo.

Whatever their motivations, it is still significant that women were playing baseball at all in the nineteenth and early twentieth centuries when social custom dictated that a woman's place was in the home and that her greatest aspiration should be to bear and raise children. This article will introduce these women whose involvement with the national pastime may not have always been readily accepted but who, because of their actions, have enriched baseball's colorful history.

**

Women who wanted to participate in sports or games in early nineteenth-century America faced a host of social and cultural obstacles. Throughout this period, women were told that their ideal strengths were "moral and emotional and nonphysical."[1] Physicians warned women that failure to severely curtail physical activity after puberty, and especially during menstruation, would result in severe consequences including disease, miscarriage and possible sterility.[2]

Women who chose to participate in physical sport despite the warnings of well-meaning physicians often faced social ostracism. One article, published in 1834 in *New York Sporting Magazine,* summed up the attitude of many men toward women involved in sporting activities: "[W]e have a peculiar antipathy to ladies in gigs; . . . we nauseate all skating in the feminine gender; and . . . we have an extraordinary aversion to ladies riding to hounds." The article concluded with a threat which many self-respecting nineteenth-century women must have found hard to ignore: "We would not marry a downright, thorough-going, hurdle jumping, racing pace, fox hunting lady, if she had the planet, Jupiter, for her portion."[3]

Despite the threat of spinsterhood or debilitating physical maladies, scores of women participated in physical exercises in the first half of the nineteenth century ranging from horseback riding to dancing to ice-skating. Croquet was an especially popular sport for women in the mid-nineteenth century. In 1866 *Harper's Weekly* called croquet the "greatest outdoor game for women yet invented."[4]

If croquet was the greatest outdoor game for women, baseball was the greatest outdoor game for men—at least as far as Charles Peverelly, author of *The Book of American Pastimes,* was concerned. "The game of Base Ball," he asserted, "has now become beyond question the leading feature of the out-door sports of the United States."[5] Also "beyond question" was the fact that baseball was not a game for women. "There is no nobler or manlier game than base-ball. . . ," *Harper's Weekly* proclaimed.[6] *Cassell's Complete Book of Sports and Pastimes* went so far as to say that baseball, "when played up to the highest mark," was

Dorothy "Mickey" Maguire of the Muskegon Lassies. (Photo courtesy of the National Baseball Library, Cooperstown, N.Y.)

not even suited for boys, due to the "fatigue involved, and the injuries frequently sustained."[7]

Surprisingly, in this era of cumbersome hoop skirts, tightly laced corsets and high button shoes, there were women who were determined to play baseball. The archives of the nation's earliest women's colleges have preserved the history of what may well have been the country's first female baseball players.

In June 1866, *The Vassariana*, Vassar College's student newspaper, reported the existence of the Laurel and Abenakis Base Ball Clubs.[8] Thirty years later, in a speech to the Association of Collegiate Alumnae, Vassar alumna Sophia Foster Richardson (class of 1879) provided valuable insight into the game of baseball as played at Vassar in the 1870s. Richardson related that when she was a freshman at Vassar, "seven or eight baseball clubs suddenly came into being." She added: "The public, so far as it knew of our playing, was shocked, but in our retired grounds, and protected from observation even in these grounds by sheltering trees, we continued to play in spite of a censorious public."[9]

Pressure from the "censorious public" and "disapproving mothers" prevailed and baseball did not flourish for long at Vassar although, according to Richardson, "those of us who had learned the value of vigorous play succeeded in keeping alive enough interest in the game to support two clubs until our senior year."[10]

Vassar was not the only college where women had learned the value of vigorous play. An interesting account of baseball's first appearance at Smith College is provided by Minnie Stephens (class of 1883) in a letter to her former schoolmates: "Way back in Seventy Nine [1879], I was more or less active and full of fun.—It seemed to me that we ought to have some lively games in the way of wholesome exercise so I got a few friends together and we organized a base ball club."[11] The Smith girls formed another team soon after and, in Stephens' words, they "had a wonderful match game, never equalled in the history of athletics for 'intelligent gentlewomen.'"[12] The restrictive clothing styles of the day must have made the game especially challenging but, as Stephens related, fashion had its good points too: "One vicious batter drove a ball directly into the belt line of her opponent and had it not been for the rigid steel corset clasp worn in those days, she would have been knocked out completely."[13]

Baseball players at Smith College fared little better than their contemporaries at Vassar. "We were told . . . that the game was too violent," Stephens recalled, "and also there was great danger in breaking windows in the Hubbard House, so we were politely ordered to give it all up." She added that a tennis club was soon begun but "the fire of the base ball club still smouldered and we did want a safe place to play."[14]

As it turned out, the women at Smith College had to wait until 1891 before the college president approved baseball as an official club sport. The "safe place to play" was assured in 1899 when Stephen's husband, Frank Gates Allen, donated an Athletic field to the college on behalf of his wife and daughter.

While female college students had the advantage of trespassing on the male sphere of baseball in the relative seclusion of all-girl campuses, other women challenged social dictates off-campus. An illustration from an unidentified source in the files of the National Baseball Hall of Fame Library shows women playing baseball in front of a large crowd of well-dressed male spectators. The caption reads: "The Last [Latest?] Illustration of Women's Rights.—A Femele [sic] Base-Ball Club at Peterboro, N.Y." The drawing is dated Saturday, July 3, 1869. The caption also mentions an article about the game, but until the source of the illustration can be determined, little else can be learned about the team.

It is impossible to tell whether the Peterboro women played baseball by official rules but, consistent with the times, none was wearing baseball gloves. Also, while the caption attributes the game to an "illustration of women's rights," there is no way to substantiate that. The women wore bloomer style pants which many "proper" ladies shunned, but all the players were wearing typical high button shoes and many wore earrings—a feminine touch to what might otherwise have been construed a rather masculine style uniform.[15] It is very possible the reference to "women's rights" was made by a disgruntled male observer and was not an accurate reflection of the players' motives. If the women at Smith and Vassar are any indication, women played baseball because they enjoyed it; they weren't necessarily trying to use baseball to challenge cultural definitions of male and female spheres.

While women on-campus and off played baseball for enjoyment, it didn't take long for a few enterprising men to see the financial possibilities of promoting women's baseball as a spectator sport. Consequently, sometime in 1875, three men organized two women's baseball clubs in Illinois for the sole purpose of making money. The "Blondes" and "Brunettes" played their first game on September 11, 1875 in Springfield, Illinois. One newspaper called it the "first game of baseball ever played in public for gate money between feminine ball-tossers," a claim which may or may not be true.[16] The women used modified rules and equipment. Baselines were only 50 feet instead of the regulation 90 feet, and a lighter ball and smaller bats were employed. There is no indication whether the pitching was overhand or underhand. A box score of the game makes it evident that the women were not experienced ball players. Though the final score in the 2 hour and 45 minute game was 42 to 33 in favor of the Blondes, only three of their runs were earned. The Brunettes managed only one earned run. Errors abounded: the Blondes reached first base 13 times on blunders; the Brunettes nine times.

Poor ball playing probably did not concern the clubs' organizers much since financial success did not depend on their clubs' win-loss record. As one news-writer put it: "The troupe contains some pretty fair players, but as a general thing the attraction is the novelty of seeing eighteen girls prettily attired in gymnastic dress playing in a game of baseball."[17]

Apart from their names, listed in newspaper accounts of their games, nothing else is known about the women who made up the "Blondes" and "Brunettes." It is significant, however, that one article refers to them as "a selected troupe of girls of reputable character."[18] Projecting a clean-cut image of their players was critical to the clubs' owners. The novelty of the game was women acting like women playing a man's game, not women acting like men playing a man's game. Spectators would have been especially critical of the latter and gate receipts would have dwindled.

Fortunately for women, after 1880 social mores did grant women far more freedom to pursue vigorous physical exercises like cycling, field hockey, golf and track. As historian Lois Banner states, "The ancient belief that a woman was controlled by her reproductive organs was on the way out."[19] Author Henry Hall reflected the view of an increasing majority when he wrote in 1887: "Exercise . . . adds materially to woman's charms and greatly to her effectiveness and the ease and safety with which she performs the great functions of her life."[20] This view still emphasized women's traditional roles as housewife and mother, but acknowledged that exercise could actually benefit women in those endeavors.

Society's more lenient attitude toward female exercise did not extend to women who wanted to play baseball, however. "The female has no place in base ball, except to the degradation of the game," proclaimed an editorial in *The St. Louis Globe-Democrat* in 1885.[21] Five years later, a disgusted gentleman lamented: "Probably the most disgraceful feature in base ball is the female base ball crowd now travelling over the country giving a burlesque of the sport."[22] And indeed, it did seem there was a "crowd" of women who had decided that, socially approved or not, they were going to play baseball.

The campuses of women's colleges continued to offer a relatively safe haven where girls could pursue their love of baseball. The women at Mount Holyoke organized their first formal team in 1891 although photographs in the school archives indicate students played baseball there in the mid-1880s. At Wellesley College, beginning in 1897, women could play baseball on club teams, and in 1911 the physical education department began offering formal instruction in the sport. The records of the Radcliffe College Athletic Association first mention baseball in 1915 and the student handbook issued in 1920 for the Women's College at Brown University noted: "Last year was the very first year that baseball at the Women's College was a definite sport."[23]

Unless specifically stated in contemporary sources, it is difficult to determine which form of baseball rules were used on college campuses. There were many from which to choose. In addition to regulation men's baseball or softball (the first women's softball teams appeared in the mid-1890s), schools could adopt any number of variations of indoor baseball rules available. Indoor baseball had been invented in the late 1880s by a group of men determined to play baseball despite inclement weather. The game was soon modified for all sorts of conditions and players. In 1920, in *Basketball and Indoor Baseball for Women*, Helen Frost and Charles Digby Wardlaw described indoor baseball games using 12″ balls with 35′ baselines, 14″ balls with 27′ baselines and 16″ balls with 18′ baselines.[24]

Since there were no official standardized rules for women's baseball until the Sub-Committee on Baseball of the National Committee on Women's Athletics of the American Physical Education Association adopted rules devised by physical educator Gladys E. Palmer in 1926, schools played one or more modified versions of baseball. (Even the official rules, once approved, allowed for four different-sized diamonds, four different-sized balls and either overhand or underhand pitching depending on the size of the diamond or the ball. The Sub-Committee specifically rejected the official men's 90-foot diamond on the grounds that it was not suited to the "abilities and needs of the average girl.")[25]

There were a few women's colleges which played baseball by official men's rules. Frost and Wardlaw observed in 1920: "Certain women's colleges have been playing baseball for years, and some under outdoor rules with a regulation ball, gloves, masks, etc."[26] One of these schools was Barnard. When baseball was officially added to the list of approved sports at Barnard in 1910, an article in the *Cincinnati Enquirer* noted: "The Barnard girls will play on a diamond of regulation size, with bags, mitts, bats and other accouterments from a regulation sporting goods house. They will play genuine baseball, with all its complications and regulations."[27]

Despite more lenient attitudes toward women playing sports, women playing baseball on college campuses couldn't entirely escape criticism. A scathing commentary in *The Reach Official American League Guide for 1911* viewed the addition of baseball as an official sport for women's colleges as "One more indictment against the modern unsexing system of female education and training."[28] The anonymous writers continued: "We hold, and we know, that base ball is not a game for any woman, not even the most masculine of that sex." They concluded bluntly: "So far as such essentially masculine games as base ball and foot ball are concerned women's only relation thereto should be as spectator."

While female college athletes continued playing baseball despite occasional

The Young Ladies Baseball Club in 1891. (Photo courtesy of the National Baseball Library, Cooperstown, N.Y.)

criticism, a growing number of women outside of the colleges took up the sport. Some played on organized teams; others, like a group of women in Gilmore, Pennsylvania, played, what might be termed today, "pick-up" games. An article in the *New York Clipper* on October 2, 1886 reported that a "novel" game of baseball had been played the week before in Gilmore between two women's teams, the "Marrieds" and the "Singles." "A woman umpired the game, which was witnessed by a large crowd, and terminated at the end of seven innings in a victory for the married women by a score of 25 to 17. The women all wore long dresses and gave a good exhibition."[29]

A few women had the opportunity to play baseball on organized teams. In August 1883 the "Young Ladies Baseball Club" was founded in Philadelphia. Like the women's team at Springfield in the 1870s, the Young Ladies Baseball Club was organized by men eager to capitalize on the financial potential of women's baseball. The owners billed their club's games as entertainment spectacles, not serious competition and, like the Springfield managers, stressed the femininity and moral respectability of their players.

A newspaper account of one of the club's first games relayed the management's claim that players were "selected with tender solicitude from 200 applicants, variety actresses and ballet girls being positively barred."[30] The article further stated: "Only three of the lot had ever been on the stage, and they were in the strictly legitimate business. . . . Most of the others were graduates of Sunday-schools and normal colleges. . . ."[31]

63

While the players' social pedigrees may have been impeccable (according to their managers) their playing abilities were questionable to say the least. When the Young Ladies Baseball Club played its first game on August 18, 1883 at Pastime Park in Philadelphia, 500 spectators laughed themselves silly as the girls attempted to play baseball on a regulation diamond. As one writer observed: "A ball thrown from pitcher to second base almost invariably fell short, and was stopped on the roll. The throw from first to third base was an utter impossibility."[32]

When the Club played again at the Manhattan Athletic Club on September 23, 1883 the players were still woefully lacking in playing skills. While one writer did concede that "four of the girls had become expert—for girls," the remainder of his lengthy article described the comical antics of their teammates.[33] The score was 16 to 3 after only one inning and by the fifth inning the players were exhausted. Many "doggedly refused to run from one base to another, until it became morally certain that the other side was hopelessly tangled up with the ball."[34]

Evidently "novelty" as opposed to quality continued to be enough to draw fans to contests between female baseball teams. The Young Ladies Baseball Club endured under various managers for at least two years and possibly longer. Newspaper articles attest to their appearance in cities like Chicago and New Orleans. In the winter of 1884, a group of the players made an extensive trip throughout the south. During this trip the women were pitted against men's teams instead of against each other. Despite the new tactic of using competition between male and female teams to draw fans to the games, the managers continued to promote games the same way. Advertisements stressed novelty and entertainment as selling points. In New Orleans, the players "paraded the streets in full uniform, and created an impression that base ball, played by shapely, activs [active] girls, must be attractive."[35]

By the late nineteenth and early twentieth century, scores of "Bloomer Girls" baseball teams were traversing the country demonstrating their baseball prowess—or lack thereof. As one writer noted, Bloomer Girls was "a name without copyright" adopted by a variety of barnstorming baseball teams "trying to scratch a buck out of the sandlots of early 20th century America."[36] There were Bloomer Girls teams organized in Texas, Chicago, New York, Kansas City, Boston and anywhere enough interest could be generated. Bloomer Girls was actually a bit of a misnomer since it did not refer to teams composed entirely of women. Many of the teams contained one or more "toppers," baby-faced boys or men dressed in women's wigs. Despite the abundance of Bloomer Girls teams, they did not play each other and no formal league was established. Instead, they journeyed from town to town challenging men's amateur and semi-professional teams.

Unlike the women's teams of the past little, if any, emphasis was put on promoting the femininity of Bloomer Girls players. In fact, at least one manager stressed just the opposite. This gentleman, mentor of the Tennessee Bloomer Girls, claimed his girls "were equally talented at playing baseball and chewing tobacco."[37]

64

It is hard to say why managers would no longer wish to promote the femininity of their players. One reason may be that since Bloomer Girls teams often contained a number of male players, managers realized the futility of trying to claim respectability for women who blatantly disregarded social mores against women playing on the same teams as men.

If managers could not promote the fine morals of their female players, at least they could promote their playing skills. One female player who received a great deal of praise in newspapers for her playing ability was pitcher Maude Nelson (sometimes spelled Neilson) who began her career with the Chicago Bloomer Girls as early as April 1899 and was still playing six years later with a group called the Chicago Stars. Her excellent pitching was frequently cited as the main attraction at her team's games.[38] Nelson's teammate, "Miss" Day (first name unknown), also received acclaim. One sportswriter contended: "She is without doubt the greatest lady ball player in the business, and deserves all the nice things that have been said by the press throughout the country about her."[39]

Despite the occasional praise of a kind-hearted sports-writer, life for a Bloomer Girl was difficult. Teams played grueling schedules (the Boston Bloomer girls once played 28 games in 26 days without a loss[40]) and there were no luxury airliners or air conditioned tour buses to take them from place to place.

The Bloomer Girls teams were not the only option available to baseball-playing females. There were numerous women's teams and co-ed teams throughout the country. On August 31, 1903 an article in the *Boston Herald* announced an upcoming game at Forest Hills between the "Hickey and Clover clubs," both composed of five women and four men. The article noted that the Hickey team had already played a number of similarly organized teams with great success due in large part to the excellent play of pitcher, Elizabeth Conry, and catcher, Mary Howe.[41] One year later in Flat Rock, Indiana, a group of women organized two baseball clubs, one consisting of only married players, the other only single players. The *Cincinnati Enquirer* commented that a game played between the two teams "would make the bloomer girls sick with envy."[42]

It is difficult to determine the social class of most female ball players. While the majority of female players in colleges were from the middle and upper classes, the majority of "Bloomer Girls" were probably from the lower classes. It is unlikely that upper class women made up the contingent of tobacco chewing players about which the Tennessee Bloomer Girls coach boasted. Another questionable group of "ladies" was the New York Bloomer Girls team which, according to one account, "ended a tour of North Carolina [in 1913] by wrecking a hotel in Raleigh." When a police officer arrived on the scene, they pelted him with "shoes, bats, masks and baseball weapons."[43]

There is evidence that upper class women did play baseball outside of a college setting, however. For example, two of the women who played in Flat Rock, Indiana were wives of prominent members of that community.[44] In addition, in April 1908, Roy Somerville penned an article called "Feminine Baseball De Luxe" for *The Baseball Magazine*. Somerville introduced the "charming daughters of Mr. Howard Wood, multi-millionaire iron manufacturer," who had organized two baseball teams of "society buds."[45] Somerville contrasted these players with the "collection of 'pie-faced' females, in spotted uniforms who travel through the bush countries as 'professional ball-players.'"

Somerville attributed "society's invasion of the plebeian baseball field" to the girls' love of outdoor sports, but added: "Secure in their social position, they could afford to show the natural American love for the game of baseball."[46] His statement indicates that women baseball players were not highly respected. The Wood sisters could "afford" to play because their social position was secure. Few would dare speak ill of them. Such was not the case for lower-class female baseball players who were frequently denounced by the public as whores and freaks.[47]

Considering public disapproval for women baseball players and the social taboo regarding women competing "against men in the more rugged masculine sports,"[48] it is surprising to find evidence of a number of women who played on otherwise all-male teams. One of the most successful of these women was Ohioan Alta Weiss.

Born in Ragersville, Ohio on February 9, 1890, Weiss was the daughter of a prominent physician, Dr. George Weiss. Perhaps because he had three daughters and no sons, Weiss enthusiastically nurtured the athletic talent Alta demonstrated from an early age. When she was 14 she played baseball with a local boy's team. According to a history of Ragersville her father, acting in his capacity as president of the Ragersville Board of Education, even established a two-year high school "so Alta could play with a high school team."[49] He later had a private gymnasium built near his home so Alta could keep her pitching arm in shape during the winter months.[50]

Alta's rise to fame as a baseball player began in the summer of 1907 when her family made a trip to Vermilion, a popular resort town about 20 miles west of Cleveland on the shores of Lake Erie. During the visit Vermilion's mayor, purportedly "elected five straight terms on nothing less than a 'baseball' ticket,"[51] spotted Weiss playing catch with some local youth and convinced the manager of the semi-professional Vermilion Independents to give her a try. Fortunately for Weiss, the team had just lost one of its best pitchers and needed help in that area.

More than 1,200 fans showed up for Weiss's pitching debut on September 2, 1907 in Vermilion. She pitched five innings giving up only four hits and one run. By the time Weiss made her second appearance on September 8th, she was already being heralded as the "Girl Wonder" in the press.[52] The *Vermilion News* reported that so many fans were expected for Weiss's next game that "an effort is being made to have either the L.S. & M.S. or the Nickel Plate run a special train from Cleveland so as to give the Cleveland people a chance to see this girl wonder."[53]

Weiss attracted more than 13,000 fans to the eight games she pitched for the Independents in 1907. The following year her father bought a half-interest in a men's semi-professional team in Cleveland which became known as the Weiss All-Stars. Weiss played in more than 30 games for the All-Stars in 1908 as the team travelled throughout Ohio and surrounding states. She generally pitched five innings and then played first base for the remainder of the game.[54]

Weiss was very popular with Cleveland sportswriters. They even began a half-serious campaign to get her signed with Cleveland's professional team, the Naps. A headline in the *Cleveland Press* on March 22, 1908 questioned: "If the Nap Pitchers Can't Win Regularly, Why Not Sign Alta Weiss to Help?" Larry Lajoie, the Nap's manager, was not about to sign a female player although, after seeing her pitch a game with the Independents, he had conceded: "I was surprised to find that she could pitch so well."[55]

After the 1908 season Weiss dropped out of the limelight to enroll in college. She attended the University of Wooster and later studied at the Starling Ohio Medical College where she became the only female graduate in the Class of 1914. She served in the medical profession for more than three decades.

After entering college, Weiss did not completely give up baseball. In 1910 a newspaper reported that she had signed to pitch with an all-male team in Ragersville and would "twirl in all the big games."[56] An article in the *Vermilion News* dated October 5, 1922 noted that Weiss "again appeared in action and is still a marvel among women baseball players."[57]

Weiss's enduring popularity among northern Ohio baseball fans went beyond her feminine gender. She was not just a female ball player, she was a good female ball player. One sportswriter commented that though there were many "would-be women ball players" in the country, "Miss Weiss can easily lay claim to being the only one who can handle the ball from the pitchers box in such style that some of the best semi-pros are made to fan the atmosphere."[58] His remarks are typical of the numerous accolades Weiss received from the press.

Thanks to the abundant source material available on Weiss it is possible to address her motives for playing baseball. The newspaper articles about her playing days make it clear that she loved the game and was thrilled to have the opportunity to play it. She was not a women's rights activist. Her reluctance to wear bloomers is one indication of this. A few years after becoming a baseball sensation Weiss told a newswriter how she had finally been forced to give up skirts in favor of bloomers: "I found that you can't play ball in skirts. I tried. I wore a skirt over my bloomers—and nearly broke my neck. Finally I was forced to discard it, and now I always wear bloomers—but made so wide that the fullness gives a skirtlike effect."[59] Weiss also had ample opportunity in the press to speak out on behalf of women's rights but never did so. At one point she even stated: "No, I don't believe that there ever will be any distinguished women base ball players. Women haven't the nerve. . . . They may get up some wishy-washy girl's nines, but they'll never have any real players."[60] (Weiss was obviously a better ball player than a seer, however, as the later section of this article on the outstanding athletes of the All-American Girls Professional Baseball League will attest.)

Though Weiss was far and away the most well known female baseball player in northern Ohio at the time, she was not the only one. When she returned to Cleveland in 1908 to begin her second season she was already facing competition from other female pitchers. Her scrapbook contains numerous clippings about her female rivals like 14-year-old Carita Masteller, Irma Gribble, Anna Singleton, Verds Bailagh, "Miss" O'Brien and sisters, Irene and Ruth Basford.

None of these girls received near the acclaim Weiss enjoyed. Part of Weiss's success was, no doubt, related to her social standing. Her father was a respected physician and community leader. He had the financial means to build her a gymnasium for winter workouts and to assure her a place on the Weiss All-Stars by purchasing a half-interest in the team. These financial advantages were not available to Elizabeth Murphy who, from about 1915 to 1935, was known as the "Queen of Baseball" throughout New England and eastern Canada.

Born Mary Elizabeth Murphy in Warren, Rhode Island on April 13, 1894, "Lizzie," as she liked to be called, was the daughter of a mill hand. At the age of 12 she joined her father in one of Warren's woolen mills. But, according to Murphy, she spent much of her time in front of the looms "dreaming of the outdoors and baseball."[61] She recalled that even when she was too small to play: "I used to beg the boys to let me carry the bats."[62]

It was not long before Murphy impressed her playmates with her baseball savvy. By the time she was 15 she had earned a spot on a number of men's amateur teams in Warren.[63] Not long after, she was being paid to play. The 1913–1914 edition of *The Bristol, Warren & Barrington Rhode Island Directory* listed the occupation of "Mary E. Murphy," boarder at a home on Arlington Avenue, as "ball player."[64] Few women could make such a claim in 1913.

Murphy was indeed a ball player—and a good one at that. Like Alta Weiss, she did not depend on her gender alone to draw fans; she was an expert player. She played first base and, as one of her managers put it: "She swells the attendance, but most important, she produces the goods."[65] After earning $5 per week plus a share of the gate receipts playing for local Warren teams, Murphy signed with the semi-professional Providence Independents in 1918. A few years later she signed with Ed Carr's All-Stars of Boston and spent a number of seasons touring with them through New England and Canada.[66]

Murphy played baseball until 1935 when she returned to Warren and settled down. She married in 1937 but her husband died a few years later. Unlike Weiss, Murphy had not been as frugal with her earnings and was forced to work in the woolen mills and on oyster boats to support herself. During this period her love for baseball diminished considerably. Toward the end of her life she rarely reminisced about her baseball glory days and once remarked, "It's hard to explain why I liked baseball so much. And the more I think about it the less I understand the reason."[67] Murphy died on July 27, 1964.

It is difficult to ascertain exactly how much money female ball players like Weiss and Murphy were paid. One article in Weiss's scrapbook stated that she was to receive $100 for her debut at Cleveland's League Park.[68] It is highly unlikely she earned anything close to that sum for every game. Another article did note, however, that during at least one game in which Weiss appeared, the fans threw money on the field whenever she struck out a batter or reached first base.[69]

A look at Murphy's earnings indicates that female players were sometimes exploited by managers. After her initial appearance on a semi-professional team in Warren, Murphy failed to receive a penny of the $85 gate receipts. She subsequently refused to play until the manager guaranteed her $5 per game and an equal share of the gate.[70] When she played for Carr's All-Stars she earned somewhat more though the exact figure is unknown. Another ploy Murphy used to bolster her small salary was to sell autographed pictures of herself in the stands between innings. At one game in Dorchester, Massachusetts she reaped almost $50 in this manner.[71]

While Elizabeth Murphy was impressing New Englanders with her baseball expertise, 14-year-old Margaret Gisolo was helping her Blanford, Indiana American Legion men's baseball team win county, district, sectional and state championships in 1928. In seven tournament games, Gisolo had nine hits in 21 at-bats for a .429 batting average. She scored 10 put-outs and 28 assists in the field with no errors charged against her.[72] A protest filed by opposing teams against her participation in the games went all the way to the American Legion's National Americanism Commission who referred it to Major League Baseball Commissioner, Kenesaw Mountain (Judge) Landis. Landis determined that American Legion rules did not specifically ban the participation of women and the protest was disallowed.

Little did Landis know, but just three years after he approved Gisolo's participation in the American Legion tournament he would have to address a similiar situation in minor league baseball when the "Barnum of Baseball," Chattanooga Lookouts manager Joe Engel, signed 17-year-old Jackie Mitchell to a contract with his Class AA team.[73] Engel knew that the novelty of seeing the first female ever signed to a professional contract in organized baseball would draw fans to his ball park, but he also knew that Mitchell was a superb pitcher. She had been taught to pitch by major leaguer Dazzy Vance and had once struck out nine men in a row in an amateur game. Engel wasted no time putting Mitchell's abilities to a true test—he immediately scheduled her to pitch against the visting New York Yankees in an exhibition game on April 2, 1931.

That date has forever gone down in baseball history as the day that a woman struck out Babe Ruth and Lou Gehrig back-to-back. Speculation continues as to whether Ruth and Gehrig were merely putting on a show or really trying to hit Mitchell's pitches. Mitchell contended that it was not a setup, and that the only instructions given to the Yankee hitters was to try not to hit the ball straight through the pitcher's box. A number of Yankee players later commented they were not aware of any special agreement to take it easy on Mitchell.[74] Other witnesses pointed out that Mitchell was a left-handed pitcher pitching to two left-handed batters, and that she had an excellent sinker pitch—sufficient advantage for many pitchers to accomplish the same feat.

Unfortunately, Mitchell never had an opportunity to repeat her performance as a professional ball player. A few days after her debut, Landis informed Engel that he had disallowed Mitchell's contract on the grounds that life in baseball was too strenuous for a woman.[75] Mitchell spent the next six years barnstorming the country with a number of men's teams and then settled down to live out a quiet life in Chattanooga.

While Murphy and Gisolo and Mitchell dazzled fans with their baseball savvy, the social debate over the propriety of strenuous athletic competition for women continued. Despite the political gains made by women's rights activists during the early 1920s, and the symbolic defiance of thousands of young "flappers" challenging the mores of Victorian culture, many physical educators were determined to keep men's and women's athletics in two separate spheres. In

Athletics in Education, published in 1930, physical educators Jesse Feiring Williams and William Leonard Hughes wrote: "The error in athletics for women is not in allowing them to play games but in permitting them to imitate both the activities of men and the manner of conducting men's competitions."[76]

One key organization of physical educators which worked to keep women from merely copying men's athletic endeavors was the Women's Division of the National Amateur Athletic Federation (WD/NAAF). In 1926 the WD/NAAF resolved to "promote the study of existing rules of all sports to the end of adapting them, wherever indicated to the special needs of girls and women."[77] Throughout the 1930s and into the 1940s, the WD/NAAF represented a bastion against women's involvement in serious competition. By the 1930s, the Women's Division had succeeded in eliminating gate receipts for women's competitions at almost all schools and colleges.[78]

While the WD/NAAF could exert considerable influence over collegiate sporting activities for women, it had little influence over the female athletes, both amateur and professional, who competed outside the collegiate arena in national and international competitions. In addition, as more women entered the nation's work force, especially during World War II, the WD/NAAF found itself unable to counter a trend toward female participation on industrial league teams coached by men and under men's rules.[79]

In 1942 32 amateur women's softball teams from the Midwest banded together and created the International Girls' Major League (IGML),[80] and by 1943 there were 40,000 women's semi-professional teams scattered across the country. One contemporary noted that "every city of any consequence" had a women's softball league made up of teams sponsored by various businesses and industries.[81] Another observed: "It has been no secret to sports fans in the Midwest that girls' softball in Chicago has been outdrawing the major-league baseball clubs."[82]

Major league baseball struggled throughout the war and many minor league teams were forced to shut down completely due to lack of players. In 1943, to conserve fuel and money, 16 major league clubs broke a long-standing tradition and agreed to conduct spring training in or near their home cities.[83] This measure, coupled with a shortened season, was still not enough to guarantee baseball could survive the war. Although President Roosevelt believed "it would be best for the country to keep baseball going," he emphasized to Baseball Commissioner Landis that "individual players who are of active military or naval age should go, without question, into the services."[84] Roosevelt refused to exempt players from the draft, pointing out that baseball would retain its popularity even if older or less skilled players were used.

Faced with the bleak possibility that major league baseball might have to suspend operations, Chicago Cubs owner Philip K. Wrigley decided to capitalize on the popularity of women's softball to provide entertainment for war-weary industrial workers. In 1943 he created the All-American Girls Professional Softball League with the intent that the teams would play their games in the major league baseball stadiums for the duration of the war.[85] As it turned out, few league games were played in major league stadiums and, within a year, the league modified its rules and became the first women's professional baseball league.

Wrigley was not content to merely create another IGML. He knew that female softball players were often referred to as "Amazons" in the press and that many tried to mimic the mannerisms of male big league players. Wrigley was adamant that his girls would be ladies first and ball players second. According to one writer, Wrigley's challenge was to convert "somewhat uncouth Amazonian spectacle into something nearer to the Wellesley, Vassar, Smith, and Stephens standard of competition."[86] The challenge was one Wrigley had every intention of meeting. As had been the case with promoters of women's baseball in the past, Wrigley was determined that his league would gain "respectability" in the eyes of the general public.

The official contract of the All-American Girls Professional Baseball League (AAGPBL), as it came to be called, stated that the league's purpose was to oversee baseball in such a manner that it would "secure approval of the American public."[87] One of the most visible manifestations of Wrigley's emphasis on the femininity of league players was the dress code. On the field the players wore skirts; off the field, they were admonished to "always appear in feminine attire when not actively engaged in practice of playing ball."[88] In 1951 this general guidance was clarified: "Masculine hair styling, shoes, coats, shirts, socks, T-shirts, are barred at all times."[89] Players were forbidden to appear in public wearing slacks or shorts. Proof that the league placed high priority on proper dress is that while players were fined $10 for being ejected from a game for arguing, they could be fined $50 for appearing in public with an unkempt appearance.[90]

Wrigley was not content with having his players just look like ladies, he wanted them to act like ladies too. For awhile he even insisted that every member of his league attend charm school.[91] To ensure that league rules were upheld and to convince wary mothers that their daughters were involved in a respectable enterprise, Wrigley stipulated that every league team have its own chaperone. The chaperones were combination policewomen, nurses, business managers, surrogate mothers and best friends for the more than 500 girls and women who played in the AAGPBL during its 12-year existence.

The AAGPBL made its debut in 1943 when four teams, the Rockford [Illinois] Peaches, the South Bend [Indiana] Blue Sox, the Racine [Wisconsin] Belles and the Kenosha [Wisconsin] Comets, squared off during the league's 108-game schedule.[92] Attendance that year was 176,000 which, according to one source, meant the league was "drawing a higher percentage of the population [in league cities] than major-league baseball ever did in its greatest attendance years."[93] (AAGPBL teams were located in communities with populations ranging from 50,000 to 150,000.[94]) In 1944 the Milwaukee Chicks and Minneapolis Millerettes joined the league (neither team lasted more than one season) and attendance soared to 259,000 for a 152-game schedule.[95]

Wrigley's idea to provide wartime entertainment to the American public was a resounding success and the AAGPBL continued to flourish after the war. Attendance figures climbed year after year, reaching a peak in 1948 when the

The Kenosha Comets with Connie Mack. (Photo courtesy of the National Baseball Library, Cooperstown, N.Y.)

league's 10 teams drew almost 1,000,000 fans.[96] League cities fell in love with their teams and their players. Sportswriters in these communities devoted as much attention to AAGPBL teams as was given to major league teams in other cities. At least one city, Racine, introduced live, play-by-play coverage of its team's games on the radio.[97]

The success of the AAGPBL goes beyond its emphasis on the femininity of its players. While a few prospective players were turned away for being "too uncouth, too hard-boiled or too masculine,"[98] league scouts signed some of the premier female athletes in the country. Every player in the AAGPBL was a top-notch athlete. Many were veterans of championship school, community or industry softball teams and some, like Wilma Briggs, Glenna Sue Kidd, Mary Lou Studnicka and Sarah Jane Ferguson, had even played on boys' or men's baseball teams.[99]

It is impossible in this article to give an adequate recounting of the tremendous skills of the AAGPBL players. Just as men's baseball had its Babe Ruths and Ty Cobbs, women's baseball had its standouts as well; women like Jean Faut who pitched her way to three pitching championships, hurling two perfect games in the process, and Joanne Weaver who won three consecutive batting titles from 1952–1954, amassing a .429 average in 1954.[100]

Contemporary articles about the league are filled with comments about the superb playing abilities of the players. Sophie Kurys was dubbed "Tina Cobb" by one sportswriter for her ability to steal bases like the great Ty Cobb.[101] (Kurys averaged over 100 stolen bases per season and swiped a phenomenal 201 bases in 1946. She was thrown out only twice in 203 attempts that year.[102])

The baseball expertise of AAGPBL players can be attributed, in part, to the men who taught them the finer points of the game. Many of the AAGPBL managers were experienced professional ball players; some, like Bill Wambsganss (the only player to achieve an unassisted triple play in a World Series), Max Carey, Jimmy Foxx, and Dave Bancroft, were legends.

Despite enjoying great support from fans and the press for many years, the AAGPBL eventually folded in 1954. League historians and former players have offered a number of explanations for the league's demise, ranging from the resurgence of men's Major League baseball after the war, to a change in the AAGPBL management system which saw the individual team owners taking over the league and drastically cutting publicity and recruiting budgets. The most significant factor in the league's final collapse was probably the advent of television. League teams had always been sponsored on a non-profit basis by local communities (any profits made were used in the communities for special projects and charity work[103]), but once television arrived on the American scene, it became harder for communities to maintain fan interest and keep their teams out of debt. Many men's minor league teams failed during this same period as television began broadcasting Major League games to a wider audience.

Some effort was made to sustain interest in women's professional baseball after 1954. When the league folded Bill Allington, a team manager, took a selected group of players on a cross-country barnstorming tour. The women played 90 games in 107 days against a host of men's teams. The venture enjoyed some success and was repeated in 1956 when the players travelled throughout the North and West playing 65 games in 88 days. By 1957, however, women's professional baseball was breathing its last gasps. Jean (Geissinger) Harding and Fran Janssen related the tribulations of the travelling team: "endless hours on the road, cheap motels, living out of a suitcase; eating, sleeping and laundry done when time allowed."[104] The glory days of women's baseball, when one million fans turned out to watch league games and when players earned good salaries and slept in fine hotels, were over.

***

Had the All-American Girls Professional Baseball League continued to flourish until today, this article would merely have been a chronological survey of the transformation of baseball from a male-dominated sport, to a non-gender-specific sport as occurred with games like tennis, golf and basketball. But the AAGPBL did not endure—and baseball continues to be dominated unofficially and officially by men.

Baseball has been able to maintain its status as a "man's" sport despite the number of women who have been serious baseball players. While no specific quantitative figures can be offered concerning the number of women who played baseball during the period studied, enough examples have been given to demonstrate that more women played baseball than previous literature on baseball has admitted.

One possible reason baseball is still regarded as a man's sport is that it has been identified as such far longer than sports like basketball and tennis. These sports were introduced in the United States in the late nineteenth century at a time when women were gradually being allowed more freedom to participate in athletic activities. But baseball had been dominated by men for decades prior to that and, as such, it was easier for them to maintain dominance over the game.

For years social disapproval of women competing against men was sufficient to keep most women from playing baseball, but when these social restrictions weakened, and women like Alta Weiss, Lizzie Murphy and Jackie Mitchell began competing against men, baseball's upper hierarchy resorted to written legislation to ban women from men's major and minor league professional baseball teams. This legislation was officially passed on June 21, 1952 after the Class B minor league Harrisburg Senators attempted to sign Eleanor Engle to a contract as a publicity stunt.[105] Minor League President George Trautman and Baseball Commissioner Ford Frick moved quickly to block the attempt and succeeded in barring all women, capable or not, from organized baseball. It is impossible to predict how long the ban against women in professional baseball will stand in the face of determined efforts by women to change it.

In 1974, in the wake of a series of lawsuits, the courts ordered Little League Baseball to admit female players. In 1984 a women's baseball team attempted to join the Class A Florida State League—unsuccessfully for the time being.[106] In June 1987 the first issue of *Base Woman: Darlene Mehrer's Newsletter of Women in Baseball* was published. One of Mehrer's goals is to unify efforts to challenge male domination of baseball. She abhors softball, the baseball surrogate for women, and lumps its invention in with such infamous events as the Chicago Fire, the St. Valentine's Day Massacre and the Black Sox scandal (all originated in Chicago).[107] Mehrer's attitude is shared by many women determined to extend equal rights to the baseball diamond.

As more and more young girls play baseball on Little League teams, and as more women's teams attempt to gain access to minor league circuits, baseball may well become, as basketball, tennis and golf before it, a game for either sex. It may take legal battles to break Organized Baseball's ban against women, but it seems quite possible that an exceptionally talented female baseball player (most likely a pitcher) will someday get the chance to prove her abilities on a men's major league team and open the door for baseball to become an accepted sport for women.

NOTES

1. Stephanie L. Twin (ed.), *Out of the Bleachers Writings on Women and Sport*, (Old Westbury, NY: The Feminist Press, 1979) xviii.

2. Carroll Smith-Rosenberg, "Puberty to Menopause: The Cycle of Femininity in Nineteenth Century America," *Clio's Consciousness Raised: New Perspectives on the History of Women,* eds. Mary S. Hartman and Lois Banner (New York: Harper & Row, 1974) 26.

3. Sylvanus Swanquill, "Feminine Fox Hunter," *New York Sporting Magazine* (Jan. 1834) 505–506; Reprinted in: Jeannie Holliman, *American Sports (1784–1835)* (Durham, NC: The Seeman Press, 1931) 163.

4. Herbert Manchester, *Four Centuries of Sport in America* (New York: Derrydale Press, 1931) 160.

5. Charles A. Peverelly, *The Book of American Pastimes, Containing a History of the*

Principal Base Ball, Cricket, Rowing, and Yachting Clubs in the United States (New York: Chas. Peverelly, 1866) 337.

6. Harvey Green, *Fit For America: Health, Fitness, Sport and American Society* (New York: Pantheon Books, 1986) 210.

7. [?] Cassell, *Cassell's Complete Book of Sports and Pastimes Being a Compendium of Out-Door and In-Door Amusements* (London: Cassell and Co., Ltd., 1896) 129.

8. See: Dorothy A. Plum and George B. Dowell, *The Great Experiment: A Chronicle of Vassar* (Poughkeepsie, NY: Vassar College, 1961) 10.

9. Sophia Foster Richardson, "Tendencies In Athletics For Women in Colleges and Universities," *Appleton's Popular Science Monthly* (Feb. 1897) 1–2.

10. Ibid.

11. Letter from Minnie Stephens Allen (Class of 1883, Smith College) to her former classmates, [c. 1903?] Smith College Archives.

12. Ibid.

13. Ibid.

14. Ibid.

15. Bloomers, a type of baggy culottes, were adopted in the mid-1800s by feminist pioneers like Amelia Bloomer, Elizabeth Cady Stanton, Lucy Stone and Susan B. Anthony. From that point on, people often equated bloomers with feminism and so many women hesitated to wear them even though they offered more freedom of movement than long, bulky skirts. See: Eleanor Flexner, *Century of Struggle: The Woman's Rights Movement in the United States* (Cambridge, Mass.: Belknap Press, 1975) 83–84 .

16. Details on the Blondes and Brunettes are from two unidentified newspaper articles in the National Baseball Hall of Fame Library's (NBHFL hereafter) "Women in Baseball" file. The articles are probably from the *New York Clipper* and *Sporting News* and were published circa Sept. 1875.

17. Ibid.

18. Ibid.

19. Lois Banner, *Women in Modern America: A Brief History* (New York: Harcourt, 1974) 14.

20. Henry Hall, *The Tribune Book of Open-Air Sports* (New York: The Tribune Assoc., 1887) 234.

21. David Quentin Voigt, *American Baseball,* Vol. 1 (Norman: U of Oklahoma P, 1966) 211.

22. Unidentified clipping, NBHFL "Women in Baseball" file. Reprinted from the *New York Tribune* [c. Aug 20 1890].

23. *Student's Hand Book of the Women's College in Brown University* ([?]: YWCA of Brown U, [c.1920]) 20.

24. Helen Frost and Charles Digby Wardlaw, *Basketball and Indoor Baseball for Women* (New York: Chas. Scribner's Sons, 1920) 91.

25. *Official Handbook of the National Section on Women's Athletics of the American Physical Education Association Containing Official Rules for Aquatics, Track and Field Athletic Games, Baseball and General Policies of the Committee 1928–1929* (New York: American Sports Publ. Co., 1928) 177.

26. Frost and Wardlaw 91.

27. Even the "genuine baseball" of the Barnard women was slightly modified as the title of this article suggests: "Base Stealing Will Not Be Allowed in Barnard College Girls' Games," *Cincinnati Enquirer* 23 March 1910.

28. "Base Ball Not for Women," *The Reach Official American League Guide for 1911* ed. Francis Richter (Philadelphia: A.J. Reach Co., 1911) 169.

29. *New York Clipper* (Oct. 2, 1886) 457, col. 1.

30. "A Base-Ball Burlesque," *New York Times* 23 Sept 1883.

31. Ibid.

32. "Girls at Base-Ball: A Ridiculous Exhibition at Philadelphia Park," *New York Times* 19 Aug. 1883.

33. "A Base-Ball Burlesque."

34. Ibid.

35. "The Female Nine in Town," *The New Orleans Daily Picayune* 26 Dec. 1884.

36. Larry Keith, "Not Every Bloomer Held a Girl," *Sport Illustrated* (Jan. 4, 1971) E3.

37. Ibid.

38. The *Cincinnati Enquirer* carried regular coverage of the Chicago Bloomer Girls games. A few of the articles which mention Nelson appeared on Aug. 23, 24, 25, 26, 1900 and Aug. 23, 1903.

39. "Bloomer Girls May Play Abroad," *Cincinnati Enquirer* 7 Oct. 1905.

40. Keith, "Not Every Bloomer," E3.

41. "Teams Made Up Mostly of Girls To Play Baseball at Forest Hills," *Boston Herald* 31 Aug. 1903.

42. "Bloomer Girls Outdone by Ladies of Shelbyville, Ind.—Great Game," *Cincinnati Enquirer* 19 Aug. 1904.

43. Keith, "Not Every Bloomer," E3.

44. "Bloomer Girls Outdone."

45. Roy Somerville, "Feminine Baseball De Luxe," *The Baseball Magazine* (May 1908): 18, 19.

46. Ibid.

47. [David Q.] Voigt, "Sex in Baseball: Reflections of Changing Taboos," *Journal of Popular Culture* 12 (Winter, 1978) 393.

48. "Man's Athletic Crown in Danger," *The Literary Digest* (July 28, 1923) 56.

49. Untitled section from local history of Ragersville, Ohio. 190. (NBHFL "Women in Baseball" file).

50. Ibid; See also: "Girl Pitcher Will Go on the Road," [?] 9 March 1908. (Weiss Scrapbook.)

51. "Base Ball Notes: Girl Pitcher," *The Vermilion News* 19 Sept. 1907: 6.

52. "Girl Wonder to Pitch Tomorrow: Will Hold Down Box for Vermilion Against Norwalk at Crystal Beach," *The Lorain Times-Herald* 7 Sept. 1907: 6; "Vermilion vs. Norwalk, Miss Weiss, the Girl Wonder to Pitch for Vermilion," *The Vermilion News* 5 Sept. 1907: 8.

53. "Base Ball Notes," *The Vermilion News* 12 Sept. 1907.

54. Details of games appear in the *Cleveland Leader, Cleveland Press* and *Cleveland Plain Dealer* as well as numerous other newspapers throughout Northern Ohio.

55. "Lajoie Surprised at the Work of Alta Weiss, the Girl Pitcher," [?] c. late Oct 1907, (Weiss Scrapbook).

56. "Alta Weiss to Play with Ragersville," [?] c. 1910; (Weiss Scrapbook).

57. "Joppa Down Pirates," *The Vermilion News* 5 Oct 1922.

58. "Ladies Want to See Miss Weiss Pitch," *The Lorain Times-Herald* 18 Sept. 1907: 6.

59. Sara Moore, "The Women You Meet: The Ball Player," [?] c. 1909 (Weiss Scrapbook).

60. Ibid.

61. John Hanlon, "Queen Lizzie Plays First Base," *Sports Illustrated,* NBHFL "Lizzie Murphy" file.

62. Ibid.

63. Ibid.

64. *The Bristol, Warren & Barrington Rhode Island Directory 1913–1914* (Boston: Union Publ. Co., 1913) 31.

65. Ed Carr. Reprinted in: "Lizzie Murphy Larivee, 70, One Time Ballplayer Dies," *The Providence Journal* 29 July 1964.

66. Hanlon, "Queen Lizzie."

67. See also: "The Queen of Baseball," *Yankee* [1985?] 15–16. (NBHFL Lizzie Murphy file.)

68. *[?] Daily Reporter* 28 Sept [1907] (Weiss Scrapbook).

69. Unidentified Clipping. (Weiss Scrapbook.)

70. Hanlon, "Queen Lizzie."

71. Ibid.

72. Ralph Burris, "The Story of Gisolo, Unique Legion Star," [?] 19 July 1975 (NBHFL "Women in Baseball" file.)

73. Cy Yoakam, "She Struck out Babe Ruth," *Sports Heritage* (March/April 1987): 23.

74. Ibid., 89.

75. Ibid.

76. Jesse Feiring Williams and William Leonard Hughes, *Athletics in Education* (Philadelphia: W.B. Saunders Co., 1930) 114–115.

77. Alice Allene Sefton, *The Women's Division National Amateur Athletic Federation: Sixteen Years of Progress in Athletics for Girls and Women 1923–1939.* (Stanford: Stanford UP, 1941) 11.

78. Williams and Hughes 114.

79. Sefton 60.

80. Robert M. Yoder, "Miss Casey at the Bat," *Saturday Evening Post* (Aug. 22, 1942) 16.

81. Morris Markey, "Hey Ma, You're Out," *McCall's* (Sept. 1950) 68.

82. Herb Graffis, "Belles of the Ball Games," *Liberty; a Weekly Periodical for Everybody* (Oct. 16, 1943) 26.

83. "Pitch Camps in North for First Time in Generation," *The Sporting News* 14 Jan. 1943.

84. Letter from President Franklin D. Roosevelt to Kenesaw M. Landis, January 16, 1942. Reprinted in its entirety in: Sue Macy, "War, Women, and Pro Baseball," *Scholastic Search* (April 30, 1982): 10.

85. For an extensive study of the AAGPBL see: Merrie A. Fidler, "The Development and Decline of the All-American Girls Baseball League, 1943–1954," thesis, 1976, 293.

86. Graffis 26.

87. Official AAGPBL contract supplied by Lois A. Barker.

88. Reprinted from: Fidler 286.

89. Ibid.

90. Eric Zorn, "The Girls of Summer," *Chicago Tribune* 12 July 1982.

91. "Baseball, Maestro, Please," *Time* (July 31, 1944) 40.

92. Ibid.

93. Graffis 26.

94. Max Carey, *All American Girls Baseball League* [AAGPBL publication] (1947) n.p.

95. Carey [1946 publication] 139; see also: James Gordon, "Beauty at the Bat," *The American Magazine* (June 1945) 24.

96. Max Carey, *All American Girls Baseball League* [AAGPBL publication] (1949) 6.

97. Carey, [1947 publication] n.p.

98. "Ladies of Little Diamond," 73.

99. Interview with Wilma Briggs, June 1987. Also, survey of former AAGPBL players by Debra A. Shattuck, August 1987.

100. Statistics supplied by former player, Faye K. Dancer.

101. "Baseball: Babette Ruths," *Newsweek* (July 29, 1946).

102. Sharon L. Roepke, *Diamond Gals—The Story of the All-American Girls Professional Baseball League* (N.P.: AAGBL Cards, 1986) 14.

103. See *Peoria Redwings* [a yearbook] (1948) n.p.

104. Jean (Geissinger) Harding and Fran Janssen, "Touring Team 1954–1957," Fort Wayne Reunion Souvenir Program, 1986.

105. Miscellanous news releases and photos in "Engle, Mrs. Eleanor" photo file at the NBHFL.

106. "A Diamond These Girls' Best Friend," *[?] Daily Star* 18 Sept 1984; "Women Get Their Shot in Baseball," *[?] Times/Union* 18 Sept 1984. (NBHFL "Women in Baseball" file).

107. Darlene Mehrer, "Happy Birthday Softball, Wish You'd Never Been Born," *BaseWoman: Darlene Mehrer's Newsletter of Women in Baseball* 1.1 (June 1987) 1.

The Man Who "Owned" Babe Ruth and Other Tales of Success Against the Babe

WAYNE STEWART

The career of America's most colorful, popular, and legendary sports figure, Babe Ruth, touched many other players. Interestingly, in numerous cases those who are now important historical footnotes in Ruthian lore were actually obscure players. Sure, there were stories of Ruth vs. Cobb, but more noteworthy in many ways are the tales of Ruth vs. Pruett or Ruth vs. Bush (Guy, not George). For those anecdotes let's explore a man who actually dominated the Babe, and then glance at some pitchers who faced the Bambino in his final days.

In baseball jargon, a pitcher who dominates a particular batter is said to "own" that hitter. When you marvel at the incredible numbers Babe Ruth carved into the record books, you get the impression that *he* "owned" the entire pitching staffs of the American League during his illustrious career. Ruth not only hit for power (714 HR), he also slashed the ball at a lofty .342 clip.

Keeping that in mind, imagine this scenario: The year is 1922. You're standing on the mound facing the New York Yankees. You glance around the Polo Grounds (the Yanks wouldn't play in the "House that Ruth Built" until the next season). First you notice the unique Roman Colosseum facade frescoes. Then your gaze falls upon the looming figure of Babe Ruth in the batter's box, a mere 60 feet, six inches from you; and only 256¼ feet away from the inviting target of the right-field fence. Does your heart palpitate? Are you intimidated? You shouldn't be if your name is Hub "Shucks" Pruett. Hard to conceive, but this obscure St. Louis Browns pitcher managed something few men could do— Pruett totally befuddled the Babe.

Partly due to Pruett's mastery over the Bambino, the 1922 season was labeled an off-year for the consummate slugger. Ruth hit "only" .315 (almost 30 points below his par); had 99 RBI (he was usually good for nearly 130 ribbies); and he propelled 35 homers (but he averaged over 40 for each full season).

The first time Pruett faced the "Sultan of Swat" was on April 22, 1922. "It didn't bother me, facing Ruth for the first time," said Pruett. "All I knew was that he batted left-handed and I didn't have much trouble with left-handers. When I went out to the mound, I didn't know who he was. I struck him out on three pitches."

It was no fluke, the 21 year-old rookie southpaw continued to baffle the Babe. During Ruth's first unlucky 13 plate appearances versus Pruett, the usually omnipotent Ruth tapped out pitcher-to-first, drew two walks, and fanned a staggering 10 times! Overall, in 1922, Ruth batted 21 times against Pruett and whiffed 13 times, an amazing 62 percent K ratio. Incidentally, Pruett recorded 70 strikeouts for the entire campaign with nearly 20 percent of those strikeouts at the expense of one man—Ruth.

Pruett spent three seasons in the American League and came in contact with Ruth 30 times. The "Colossus of Clout" managed only four hits in 21 official at bats, which translates to a microscopic .190 average. Ruth grounded out twice, hit one sacrifice fly, coaxed eight walks, hit one homer, and whiffed 15 times, exactly half the times they battled. Pruett's reaction? "Seeing the Babe strike out was almost as exciting as seeing him hit a home run."

Ruth's lone home run versus Pruett came at Sportsman's Park in St. Louis in the second game of a key three-game series between the two contending clubs. The blast came in a 5–1 New York loss to Pruett's Browns. The Yanks won the next game, however, and eventually went on to win the flag by one game over St. Louis. Nevertheless, that home run is worth recalling for its historical significance.

Pruett wanted to throw his favorite pitch to Ruth, but he let his catcher, Hank Severeid, use his power of veto, "He shook me off," said Pruett, "and called for the curve. I hung it and Ruth hit a line drive over the low right-field wall. There was no screen then, as there is in Busch Stadium today. Today Ruth's homer would be a double."

And just what was Pruett's favorite pitch? Reporters of the time called it "the pitch that Bamboozled Babe," "the pitch that mesmerized Ruth," and, simply, "The Pitch." Pruett labeled it a fadeaway. "It was a rather uncommon pitch in those days. Modern terminology has changed it to a screw ball. It's just a reverse curve," Pruett said. In fact, he explained, the pitch required a twist of the wrist in a motion that was the opposite of that used for his curve.

"When I was a small boy, my baseball idol was Christy Mathewson. Matty's most famous pitch was the fadeaway. When he threw it, the ball would break in on a right-handed hitter and away from a lefty. I got to thinking if a righty pitcher like Matty could throw it, why couldn't a lefty like myself do it?" Men such as Warren Spahn, Tug McGraw, Fernando Valenzuela might owe a great deal to pioneer Pruett, father(?) of the modern screw ball.

The evolution of the "scroogie" continued: "By the time I got to college I had a good one. I could make the ball break sharp and wide. I threw it three ways. Thrown overhand, it acted somewhat like a slider—it moved out. Underhand, the ball nose-dived—this was my big strikeout pitch. I also threw it with a three-quarter motion. I could break it down from head to foot (at times)." Little wonder Ruth associated Pruett's hypnotic pitch with sheer futility. According to Pruett, "I don't think he ever hit my fadeaway."

The 5'10", 135-pound Pruett began his pro career in the old Western League.

In August of 1921 while hurling for Tulsa, he tossed a no-hitter against St. Joseph. Not only did he possess his fadeaway but, according to the *St. Louis Post-Dispatch,* he also had an "excellent curve." Armed with these weapons, he moved up to the "big show" in 1922 with the Browns. By the way, despite his mastery over Ruth that year, and despite a sparkling 2.33 E.R.A., he was only a .500 pitcher then at 7–7.

Ironically, Pruett had almost signed with the St. Louis Cardinals; if he had, he never would have opposed Ruth. Originally, Pruett had been spotted by Cards scout Charley Barrett, but when he reported to the ball park and walked into the Cardinals office, the Redbirds were on the road. No executive was there to meet him. Instead, as Pruett recounted, "Bob Quinn, general manager of the Browns, asked if it would make any difference which team I signed with, and I told him no." Call it destiny.

Pruett was sent to the minors in 1925. Although he couldn't know it then, he was finished with his wars with Ruth. He wasn't, however, completely through as he won 23 for Oakland of the Pacific Coast League. His success prompted the Phillies to draft him in 1927. After an uneventful year-and-a-half stint there, he was shipped to the Newark Bears. By the end of the 1928 season, Pruett decided to retire to devote full time to his medical studies. Instead, he came to an agreement which allowed him to quit pitching in September to return to college. Under this setup, he won 15 for the Bears in 1929.

This time his ability and resiliency led to a signing with the New York Giants in 1930. That proved to be his only winning year in the Bigs (5–4). He impressed Giants skipper John McGraw who promised Pruett a pay hike for 1931. Pruett agreed, but told McGraw he would have to skip spring training as the aspiring doctor-to-be had to intern. The feisty McGraw snapped, "I'm running a baseball team, not a Mayo Clinic." Except for a brief stay with the Boston Braves in 1932, that succinct McGraw quote ended Pruett's big-league career.

His lifetime slate was 29–48 over seven scattered seasons. His E.R.A. stood at 4.63. "Actually," said Pruett, "I was a mediocre pitcher after 1923." However, the man *Sports Illustrated* called, "one of the original firemen" wasn't all that bad considering he was a sore-armed hurler from late 1922 on. Due to his injury, which some accounts say occurred when he "made a strikeout pitch, a screwball, to Ruth," Pruett no longer enjoyed the game. "It became a drudgery, but I needed the money to pay for my medical studies."

Pruett contended his injury was due to overwork, not his fadeaway, "The curve was harder on my arm," he said. "I pitched in six or seven straight games (in 1922). After I hurt my arm it hurt so much I'd have to tie a pillow to it in order to get some sleep."

Finally, by late 1932, he no longer needed the pain or the game. He got his M.D. at St. Louis University, the sixth university he attended (while also pitching in various ports of call) over eight years, twice the normal time it then took to earn the degree.

***

Born in Higginsville, Kentucky, on September 1, 1900, Pruett moved to Dexter, Missouri as a youth. He was given the nickname "Shucks" because that was the strongest expression he used. Pruett fit the stereotypical mold of the country boy. A writer once recalled Pruett's early days with the Browns, "Shucks was laid up in our hotel in Detroit with the flu. The manager and coach walked past his room saying, 'Too bad we'll have to send the kid (Pruett) back to St. Louis.'

"Shucks overheard them, as expected, and he was down in the lobby in five minutes." It was clear the country boy, never having been east of the Mississippi, wasn't going to pass up New York, Washington and Boston, according to the St. Louis reporter.

Later, as a doctor, he was a bit more sophisticated, but friends agreed the doctor of 41 years' experience was still a down-to-earth kind of guy.

***

Pruett spoke to Ruth only once in his life. As players they passed each other without speaking. "But every once in awhile Ruth did something that gave me a kick, he would wink at me," recalled Pruett. Much later, about two months before Ruth's death in 1948, they met at a baseball dinner at the Chase Hotel in St. Louis. "I went up and introduced myself and said, 'Thanks, Babe, for putting me through medical school. If it hadn't been for you, nobody would ever have heard of me.' The Babe remembered me. 'That's all right, kid, but,' he rasped, stricken with throat cancer, 'I'm glad there weren't many more like you or no one would have heard of me.'"

Pruett realized, of course, that were it not for his success against Ruth, called one of "the most notable jinxes in baseball" by a St. Louis writer, he would forever be just an obscure name in *The Baseball Encyclopedia*. "What got me a reputation in baseball *and* kept me in baseball were those dramatic strikeouts of Ruth." What a remarkable way to be remembered . . . the man who "owned" Babe Ruth.

Ironically Pruett, like Ruth, was a heavy smoker and also died of cancer. Although he was not a big name or winner on the field, he endured over Ruth once again, far out-living Ruth. Pruett died on January 28, 1982, at the age of 81. For the record, Ruth was 53 years old when he died on August 16, 1948.

***

It would be wonderful to inform you that Babe Ruth, in his final at bat, dueled the legendary Walter "The Big Train" Johnson. It would be marvelous to tell you that Ruth, at the age of 40, conjured up his magical prowess one last time and launched a Johnson fast ball over the fence, then trotted slowly, yet majestically, in his Ruthian waddle around the bases. It would be splendid to relate that Ruth, always a showman, beamed at the crowd, tipped his cap as he crossed home plate, then disappeared into the dugout for the final time. Yes, it *would* be grand, but it simply would not be true. In reality, Johnson had already retired and, more to the point, Ruth's last at bats—in the American League as a Yankee, and his very last at bat which was in the National League—were rather uneventful.

The pitcher who did oppose the "Bambino" in his last trip to the plate in the American League was an obscure 26-year-old southpaw (who was also a switch hitter—.152 lifetime). It was ironic that these two met in 1934 as their battle represented Ruth's last appearance in the A.L., and the climax to Cohen's first

Sidney H. Cohen. (Photo courtesy of the National Baseball Library, Cooperstown, N.Y.)

year in the majors. It was the classic aging superstar in the batter's box versus the young gunfighter on the hill. Even more ironic and coincidental is the fact that both were born in Baltimore. Destiny seemingly brought them together that autumn afternoon when they faced each other. For the record, Cohen won the dispute; he fanned Ruth.

Just who was Sid Cohen? Well, his whiff of the Babe was actually his only claim to fame. His '34 pitching slate was 1–1 with an E.R.A. of 7.50 in three games, two as a starter. He pitched only 18 innings and K'ed six men in all. His career (all of his three seasons were spent with the Washington Senators) was hardly sterling, either—55 games, 109 innings, three victories, seven defeats and a 4.54 E.R.A. Often working in relief, he managed five lifetime saves in an era when aging, fading pitchers and other such misfits often inhabited the bull pen.

Cohen died recently (on April 9, 1988) at the age of 81, but his name lives on in the Trivia Hall of Fame. His legacy: he was the last man to face Ruth as a Yankee.

But back to Babe, now. Even as early as May of '34 everyone felt this would be the last season for the "Colossus of Clout." Ruth slumped, suffered a serious wrist injury when hit by a pitch, feuded with the Yankee brass (sound familiar??), and complained that he should be the Yanks' manager. Thus it was not surprising when he announced in late August, after he had hit his 700th round tripper, "I'm definitely through as a regular player after this season." Therefore, as he made his last trips into various A.L. cities, he was believed to be making his farewell tour. So, when Ruth faced Cohen it was a significant event (especially now in retrospect to baseball historians).

There was a fine crowd on hand that last day but the Yankee organization, perhaps because it was disenchanted with the Babe, didn't exactly make a major production out of Ruth's adieu, as would certainly happen now (if only to draw an even bigger throng).

At any rate, less than one-half year later, on February 26, 1935, the Yankees released Ruth. After some negotiations, Ruth ended up with the Boston Braves for the next season. He agreed to become an assistant manager (with no real authority or function) and player. From the start the 40-year-old, now up to 245 pounds, struggled.* He would play in only 28 games that final season, never once playing the entire contest. He wound up hitting a paltry .181 with six homers, 12 RBI, and 24 strikeouts in a mere 72 at bats.

As was the case with the Yankees, the disgruntled Ruth argued with the front office, and suffered minor ailments as well. On May 12th Ruth told the Braves owner he was done as a player. However, Babe was persuaded to stick it out at least until he had paid a final visit to the "western cities." Those cities, he was told, already had a large advance sale of tickets for "Babe Ruth Days." He stuck it out, but did poorly for the next 12 days.

Ruth did enjoy one last binge of leviathan glory and power, though. On May 25th in a game against the Pirates, Ruth faced Red Lucas and propelled a first-inning homer, a two-run belt. Two innings later he went up against reliever Guy Bush. The last time these two had squared off, Bush plunked Ruth in the arm with a fast ball. This time Ruth took him deep for another two-run shot. Next time up Ruth slapped an RBI single before culminating his grand day with yet another home run (solo) against Bush. The ball soared over the double-deck right field stands in Forbes Field, clearing the towering roof there. No one had ever done this before (and few have since). They say, at about 600 feet from the plate, it was the longest blast ever hit in Pittsburgh.

---

*Although on Opening Day in Boston, Ruth displayed his electrifying, crowd-pleasing ways. In a 4–2 win over Carl Hubbell, Ruth drove in all four runs including two on a homer.

What a hitting spree! Ruth had gone 4-for-4 with six ribbies and three homers. His longest poke was his grand finale, the last Babe Ruth hit of all (he owned 2,873 lifetime hits).

With that dramatic game under his belt, Ruth was now urged to quit right then, on top of the baseball world one last time. He refused, keeping his promise to finish the current road trip.

That set the stage for his very last at bat of his 22-year career. On May 30, 1935, in a game against the Philadelphia Phillies, Ruth stood at the plate for the final time. It must have felt strange; having stood there for 8,399 official at bats (plus 2,056 times when he drew walks), this was it.

Ruth's adversary that day was Jim Bivin, a 25-year-old who, like Ruth, was also in his swansong season. However, for Bivin 1935 actually was his first, last, and *only* year in the Bigs. His slate that season showed a 2–9 won-loss mark with a sky high 5.79 E.R.A. in 47 games (14 as a starter).

What happened against Bivin? Sorry, no dramatics this time, a routine infield ground out. That's all folks. Ruth had started the first game of the Memorial Day double header that day in left field. After his one at bat, he got hurt in the outfield going after a fly ball and was replaced by Hal Lee (trivia lovers, put that one in your data bank). Ruth never played again.

If Ruth were playing today, every at bat would be on videotape for posterity. In those days, however, little was preserved of his last at bat. In fact, to be fair, who was to know for sure that that particular trip to the plate would be the end of the line for the great slugger?

When Ruth didn't play in the next afternoon's twin-bill, little mention was made by the media. The June 1st edition of the *New York Times* simply stated, "Babe Ruth didn't get into either game (versus the New York Giants). He fears he has a touch of water on the knee and, likewise, that he will be unable to get into the series."

In truth, his knee did bother him, but he also was bickering with Braves president Emil Fuchs once again. And, one day later on June 2nd, Ruth made it official. He was retiring. No real fanfare, but Ruth's playing days were indeed over.

***

Interestingly, instead of some classic matchup as mentioned in our "Walter Johnson vs. Babe Ruth" marquee scenario to end his career (as was sometimes arranged in those days), it was two obscure men who faced Ruth in his last at bats. Instead of hoopla it was a quiet hush which marked the end of his long stay in the majors. Yet, when it was all over, fans and the media could have borrowed a phrase from Shakespeare's *Julius Caesar* to describe the departure of the great Bambino, "Here was a Caesar! When comes such another?"

SOURCES

Official American League Pitchers' Records (1922–24) from the Hall of Fame archives.
Sports Illustrated article/interview from their "Yesterday" column—interview conducted by Gerald Holland, 1963.

Other clippings from various newspapers obtained from the Hall of Fame Library—includes obituaries (e.g., March 6, 1982, *The Sporting News*); numerous papers circa 1922–24 (most often the *St. Louis Post-Dispatch*); a July 18, 1961, *Post-Dispatch* by W.J. McGoogan; a *New York Times* article by Arthur Daley (9–17–61); and Bob Broeg's piece in *Post-Dispatch* of April 7, 1981.

Most of the material on Pruett appeared in the May/June 1987 edition (Vol. 1, No. 3, pp. 54–57) of *Sports Heritage*.

Two No-Hitters in Five Days

WALTER LANGFORD

It was June 1938. FDR was in the middle of his second term, the Depression had not fully run its course, war clouds were gathering as Hitler's madness pushed inexorably toward global conflict. And in baseball Joe McCarthy's New York Yankees were World Champions, already heading for their third such title in a string of four.

Meanwhile, in the National League, last year's doormats, the Cincinnati Reds, under the astute handling of Bill McKechnie, were emerging in a revival that would bring them pennants in both of the next two seasons. In fact, Deacon Bill in '39 would become baseball's first manager to lead teams from three different cities into the World Series (only Dick Williams in later times has equalled that accomplishment).

One of the reasons for the resurgence of the '38 Reds was a 23-year-old southpaw named Johnny Vander Meer who, in his first full season in the majors, was to compile a 15–10 record.

"I could have had a lot better year than 15–10," recalls John today, "had I not been lying in the hospital for a month. I had seven boils in one ear and six in the other. I lost about 15 pounds. They didn't know much about inside boils at that time, and all I could do was put heat lamps on them. Today they have anti-biotics."

Anyway, Vander Meer's season record stood at 5 wins and 2 losses on the morning of June 11, 1938. That afternoon he was to pitch against the Boston Bees (both previously and later known as the Braves) in Cincinnati's Crosley Field. Blessed with a potent fast ball, Johnny also possessed a very good curve ball. Up to this point the main obstacle to his advancement had been control, or rather his lack of same.

When he first came up with the Reds in '37, Vandy handed out 69 free passes to first in 84 innings, an unacceptable ratio. McKechnie, always a deft handler of pitchers, worked with him to reduce his wildness, with some success. Even so, through his career in the big leagues, Vander Meer issued an average of about

86

5½ walks per nine innings. In contrast, Bill Hallahan, a solid left-hander with the Cardinals for a decade starting in 1925, who for his wildness was nicknamed "Wild Bill," averaged only 4½ walks per game.

Johnny's opponent on the afternoon of June 11 was Danny MacFayden, a journeyman hurler who was nearing the end of a 17-season career with half a dozen teams in both leagues. The total attendance at the game was reported at 10,311, though only 5,814 were paying customers.

The game was scoreless through the first three innings, during which Vandy set down nine straight batters. He walked Gene Moore leading off the fourth, but Johnny Cooney popped up to catcher Ernie Lombardi on a hit-and-run play, and Ernie gunned down Moore before he could return to first.

The no-hitter almost evaporated in that same inning when Vince DiMaggio smashed a liner off Johnny's glove. Fortunately, the ball was deflected to Lew Riggs at third, who retired Vince on a bang-bang play at first which provoked a strong protest by Bees' manager Casey Stengel. This was more than a decade before Casey began his long and sensational run as manager of the Yankees.

Vander Meer walked Tony Cuccinello in the fifth, but Lombardi again came to the rescue by picking him off. This was one of Lombardi's main strengths, according to Vandy. "Lom," he says, "would pick about five to seven guys a year off of first base, throwing sidearm behind left-handed hitters. Great thrower." Later in the same inning Johnny gave up his third and final walk to Gil English. English was stranded and was the only man the Bees left on base.

The Reds got the winning run in the fourth, when Wally Berger was given a triple on a ball which caromed off the third baseman and eluded the left-fielder. Ival Goodman brought Berger home with a long fly ball. Berger also walked in the sixth and scored ahead of Lombardi when Ernie propelled a pitch over the left-field wall.

Stengel called on three straight pinch hitters in the ninth, but none could produce against Vander Meer, and the historic game was over. It had been reeled off in one hour and 48 minutes, a time not too uncommon in those years.

Since two of the three hitters who walked were retired on the bases, Johnny faced only 28 hitters, one over the minimum. "I think there were only about five fly balls in the ball game," he says.

I had a pretty good sinker that day. I wasn't real quick, didn't have my real good stuff, but it was one of the few days I had control, especially of my curve in the last four innings. They were hitting the ball into the ground a lot.

I didn't go for a no-hitter until the ninth inning. In that way I didn't put pressure on myself. And I had a bit of philosophy about the ninth inning. I liked to finish anything I started, and I'd get to the ninth inning and I'd always say to myself, "You've got 20 good pitches left." I'd start counting with 20, then 19, and so on. Waite Hoyt used to do this, and that's how I picked it up. So that gave me a bit of incentive in the last inning that I pushed myself with.

Any no-hitter is big news in the baseball world, even though about 200 of them have been recorded (including 20 of less than nine innings and 5 in the Federal League in 1914–15). So, Vander Meer's feat on June 11, 1938 brought him lots of deserved attention and recognition. But, after all, it wasn't a perfect game (of

John Vander Meer. (Photo courtesy of the National Baseball Library, Cooperstown, N.Y.)

which there had been only four up to that time in the twentieth century). Even so, baseball added his name to the 74 others who had achieved no-hit fame in the majors (10 of whom had even thrown a second no-hit game at one time or other).

Vander Meer's next start came on June 15 in Ebbets Field, home of the Brooklyn Dodgers. This time the circumstances were different.

Naturally, there was more than usual interest in the game because Vandy was just coming off his no-hitter of the 11th. More than that, there was immense excitement over the fact that it was to be the first night game in Ebbets Field.

Larry MacPhail, known as "the roaring redhead," had recently taken over as executive vice president of the Dodgers, and his farsightedness told him night ball was the key to financial stability for the major league teams. While previously vice president and general manager of the Reds, MacPhail had gained hard-earned approval of the National League owners to introduce night baseball with a limit of seven games per season.

Under his guidance the first night game in the majors was played in Cincinnati's Crosley Field on May 24, 1935. Now Larry had installed lights and engaged in lots of promotional activities for the first game under the lights in Ebbets on the date of June 15, 1938.

The response of the rabid Dodger fans was more than enthusiastic. The game was a sellout, and then some. Fans were arriving hours before starting time. Finally, 38,748 of them were crammed into the cozy confines of Ebbets Field and the gates were closed almost an hour early. Estimates are that 15,000 aroused fans were turned away.

A band was on hand, as well as a fife and drum corps and Jesse Owens, who in '36 had put on the one-man show at the Olympics in Berlin. Jesse raced against some of the players and also demonstrated his broad-jumping skills. Babe Ruth was on hand, too, to salute the crowd and receive a tumultuous ovation. To top off the pregame show, there was a huge fireworks display.

The New York Times reported the event the next day in these words:

The game, before it was played, was partly incidental; the novelty of night baseball was the major attraction. But Johnny Vander Meer, tall, handsome 22-year-old Cincinnati southpaw pitcher, stole the entire show by hurling his second successive no-hit, no-run game, both coming within five days, and making baseball history that probably never will be duplicated.

The above lines put it all in a nutshell, yet it wasn't quite that easy. In contrast to his performance four days earlier, Vander Meer on this occasion was wild, walking a total of eight batters. But they were the only Dodgers to reach base and all were left languishing on the basepaths. He struck out seven of the Brooklyn hitters.

According to Johnny, there was just one moment when he was in danger of allowing a base hit. "The only close call was when Buddy Hassett (Dodger left-fielder who was batting third) hit a line drive back through the box that I knocked down. I really had to scurry to pick it up and throw him out on a close call at first. That was probably the closest thing to being a hit in either of the two ball games."

The game-winning blow for the Reds came in the third inning on Frank McCormick's three-run homer. They added another run in that same inning and picked up single runs in the seventh and eighth for the final score of 6–0.

Vander Meer's wildness in at least two innings had his teammates biting their nails and the crowd in a frenzy. In the seventh he retired the first batter before walking Cookie Lavagetto and Dolf Camilli. He survived this threat by whiffing Ernie Koy and getting Leo Durocher on a ground ball to second.

Again in the ninth wildness almost cost him at least the shutout, if not the no-hitter. Hassett opened the inning with a slow bouncer down the first base line. Johnny got over fast to grab it and tag the runner as he went by. Then Vandy walked Babe Phelps, Lavagetto, and Camilli in succession. Manager McKechnie and the whole Red infield gathered around Vander Meer on the mound, urging him to take his time and get the ball over the plate. This he did, and the next batter, Koy, sent a grounder to Lew Riggs at third. His throw to Lombardi forced the runner coming home from third. Durocher then chilled everybody in the place with a drive high into the right field stands. But it was just a foul ball, and then Leo hoisted a fly to Harry Craft in short center for the out which made baseball history. The game had lasted two hours and 22 minutes.

Understandably, the crowd went wild as it surged onto the field trying to reach the hero of the moment. Only quick work by all the Cincinnati players kept him from being mauled. They converged from all directions—the bullpen crew, the onfield players, and the rest of the team from the bench—to form a ring around him and escort him to the dugout and on to the clubhouse.

It is hard to imagine a situation more felicitous and emotionally exciting than the combination of the first night game in Ebbets Field, the first double no-hitter in baseball, and nearly 40,000 out-of-control Brooklyn fans. It was truly a great night for MacPhail, Vander Meer, and baseball.

And Johnny's reaction to it all? He told the mob scene of reporters and others in the dressing room: "I'm going fishing, and I'm not telling you where." It quite likely was some place near the family home in nearby Midland Park, N.J. Some 500 persons from that small town had attended the game. Most fitting of all, among them were Vander Meer's parents, brother, and girlfriend.

John Vander Meer was not the first—nor the last—to pitch two complete-game no-hitters in the majors. Seven others turned the trick before him, including such notables as Christy Mathewson, Cy Young, and Walter Johnson. Fifteen more have done it since 1938, among them Bob Feller, Warren Spahn, and Jim Bunning. Four besides Vandy have thrown two no-hitters in the same season—Allie Reynolds in '51, Virgil Trucks in '52, Jim Maloney in '65, and Nolan Ryan in '73. Maloney tacked on a third such gem later. Sandy Koufax racked up four no-hitters, one each season for four straight years (1962–65). And of course Ryan is the king of the no-hit pitchers, having accomplished the feat five different times thus far, the latest coming in 1981.

In 1954 Sam "Toothpick" Jones of the Chicago Cubs equalled the scary ninth inning that Vander Meer lived through in his second masterpiece. On June 12 of that year, Jones was leading the Pittsburgh Pirates, 4–0, going into the final frame. He promptly walked the first three batters; earlier he had walked four others. Manager Stan Hack hurriedly got two pitchers warming up and held a conference at the mound with Jones and the infielders to settle down the young hurler. It worked. Jones tossed three curves in a row past Dick Groat, then fanned Roberto Clemente on five pitches (two of which were fouled off), and polished it off in style by getting Frank Thomas on a called third strike to strike out the side and preserve his no-hitter.

The year 1988 marked the fiftieth anniversary of Vander Meer's double feat. Since no one had been able to match this deed before Johnny's time and no one has duplicated it for 50 years more, it seems safe to classify it among the handful of baseball's "unbreakable" records. Someone someday may do it again, but it hasn't happened yet in almost a century.

Actually, one pitcher came maddeningly close to two no-hitters in succession. In 1947 Vandy's teammate, Ewell Blackwell, pitched a no-hitter against the Boston Braves on June 18. On the 22nd he went against the Dodgers and proceeded to no-hit them until one man was out in the ninth inning, when a base hit wrecked his hopes of joining Vander Meer in double no-hit fame.

There is another point that bears mention. In 1904 the legendary Cy Young (511 wins) strung together 23 innings of no-hit pitching. He did this in four outings starting on April 25 and ending on May 11. Only one complete game was involved in the streak.

Vander Meer threatened Young's total of 23 innings without yielding a hit, but he fell just short. In his next game following his two record-setting performances, Johnny went 3⅔ innings before giving up a hit. Adding the final out in the game prior to his no-hitters, we come up with a total of 22 innings without a hit. And Vandy has a postscript to add to that.

> The game prior to my first no-hitter I had a 3-hitter. I gave up two hits in the first inning to the New York Giants but shut 'em out. There were no more hits until the ninth. With two out Hank Lieber came up to pinch hit. I threw one in on his fist and he managed to punch it just over Lonnie Frey at second base for a base hit. If it hadn't been for that sloppy hit of Hank's, I would have had 29⅔ innings without giving up a hit.

Despite the fame of his double no-hitters, Vander Meer feels they weren't his biggest thrill in baseball.

> I think my biggest thrill was having the right skills to get to be a big league ball player. When I finally got to Cincinnati after about five years, I got my own locker with my own name over the top of it, and my uniform, and I was in the big leagues. I realized a boy's dream. If I had to pick an individual thrill, that was it.
>
> And, you know, I participated in the longest scoreless game in the major leagues. That was right after the war. I think I pitched either 15 or 17 innings in Brooklyn in that 19-inning ball game. Harry Gumbert finished it. It ended 0–0 on account of darkness, because they weren't allowed to turn the lights on at that time to finish a game. I think that was probably the greatest game I ever pitched.

Maybe we'd better stop right here, before Johnny tries to tell us he can't even remember those two no-hit games he pitched in a row.

Out with the Crowds: Counting, Courting and Controlling Ball Park Fans

DAVID Q. VOIGT

As America's venerable "national pastime," major league baseball owes its enduring popularity to the buoyant support of its fandom. While this is obvious to any student of the game, what is less obvious is that so little is known of the more than one billion fans who have attended major league games since 1871 or of other species of fans who have evolved over the years.

In pondering the various forms of fans who have emerged over the years it is the ball park denizens who first leap to mind. And why not, for surely the ball park spectators are the oldest type. After them came newspaper fans who were followed by radio fans and more recently by burgeoning numbers of television fans. Indeed, so numerous are the latter that not only do they now outnumber other species but they also account for most of the revenues of the major league baseball industry. Of course, no insurmountable barriers exist between the varieties of fans. Interfertility is rife, and any individual fan likely fits all afore-mentioned categories with some forming sub-types (such as collectors, re-searchers, table game players, formally organized research and player appreciation groups, and a host of others). But the godsplenty of forms only adds to the complexity of the problem of understanding the game's fandom.[1]

Although we need to know of all forms of fans, it is the purpose of this essay to shed more light on the ball park fans. Once known as "kranks" and "bugs," ball park fans have been thronging major league parks for over a century. Their importance has been underscored by the hoary adage that "at the gate is baseball's fate." And to keep them coming is the once and future goal of baseball promoters who have always been challenged by the problems of counting, courting and controlling this vital segment of fandom.

COUNTING THE BALL PARK FANS

One of the mysteries wrapped in the enigma of baseball's fandom is the question of how many fans have attended major league games over the years. Curiously, general histories of the game only skirt this question. In accounting for this oversight, it is apparent that historians have been more concerned with other aspects of the game. Moreover, available data tend to be sketchy and often unreliable, especially for the nineteenth-century seasons. Buried mainly in newspapers, sporting journals and annual guides, irregular reports were often censored and at times inflated by competing major leagues.

Although nineteenth-century attendance figures are particularly clouded, recent studies have been shedding light on this neglected subject. Thus, George Kirsch's study of baseball crowds prior to the beginnings of major league play in 1871 reports peak crowds of 15,000 and 20,000 on hand to watch the Brooklyn Excelsiors battle the Brooklyn Atlantics in 1860 and the Atlantics versus the New York Mutuals in 1865.[2] And in 1869 the all-conquering Cincinnati Red Stockings attracted an estimated 200,000 spectators overall for an average of 3,000 a game. Among the larger crowds to watch the Reds were the 6,000 at Brooklyn's Union Grounds (one of the earliest fenced parks when it opened in 1862) who saw the Reds defeat the Mutuals; later the Reds attracted the largest crowd of their undefeated season when 15,000 watched them play in Philadelphia. That year the Reds played six games in the New York metropolitan area, attracting a total of 23,217 spectators. In 1870, when the Brooklyn Atlantics finally ended the Reds winning streak, 9,000 spectators at the Union Grounds saw the Atlantics score an 8–7 extra-inning victory.[3]

Even if such large crowds were rarities, the prospect of attracting big paying crowds prompted the new breed of professional players and their patrons to organize the first commercial major league in 1871. Dubbed the National Association of Professional Base Ball Players, the jerry-built league lasted only five seasons. During that time the league's innovations included the construction of larger wooden parks (some seating more than 6,000 fans), sales of season tickets, and a hefty $1,440 advertising outlay by the 1875 Boston team. But the league's unresolved problems, including a lack of a fixed playing schedule, annual dropouts by disenchanted teams, widespread profitlessness, the sullying influence of gamblers, and Boston's pennant monopoly, affected attendance. According to one historian attendance at National Association games rarely exceeded 5,000, although games pitting such rivals as Boston, Philadelphia and Chicago might lure crowds of 10,000 and more. In 1875, the last season of the National Association, the Boston Red Stockings attracted an estimated 70,000 at their home games as they romped to a crushing 71–8 win-lost gait over their outclassed rivals.[4]

In the wake of the National Association's demise major league baseball grew to sturdy adolescence under the succeeding National League (NL) and the later arriving American Association (AA). The enduring National League opened play in 1876 with the American Association following suit in 1882. Fixed playing schedules, relatively stable franchises located in sizable cities, professional umpires, and the curbing of player movements by reserve clauses in contracts were major innovations. Nevertheless Boston's 1875 attendance as a member of the National Association was unsurpassed by any National League club until the early 1880s. In 1879, for example, the NL's Providence champs attracted only 42,261 fans at their home games, and in 1883 the champion Boston team averaged 2,800 spectators at its home games.[5]

By the mid-1880s attendance at major league games was stimulated by the rivalry between two established major leagues. A combination of a cheap 25-cent basic admission price, optional Sunday games and liquor sales, and well-located franchises enabled the American Association to surpass the older National League's attendance during most seasons. Under the National Agreement of 1883 the AA was recognized as a major league and the dual major league system popularized World Series play between the two majors. In 1887 the 15-game World Series played between the AA champion St. Louis Browns and the NL champion Detroit Wolverines attracted 51,453 spectators.[6]

As seasonal attendance rose, clubs in both leagues increased the size of their parks; in 1883 the three largest parks included the NL's New York (12,000) and Chicago (10,000) and the AA's Philadelphia park (8,700). But these were dwarfed by the 1887 opening of the NL's Philadelphia "Palace Park" with its seating capacity of 20,000 and by the 1891 expansion of the NL New York Giant's Polo Grounds which increased its capacity to 16,000.[7] Moreover, mounting attendance and profits during the late 1880s prompted both leagues to increase their seasonal playing schedules. From a modest 60 games a season in 1877–78, the NL upped its playing schedule to 140 games by 1888; meanwhile the AA's seasonal schedule rose to 140 games in 1886.

During this golden era, attendance at major league games peaked in 1889 when the two major leagues attracted nearly 3 million spectators. That year the NL hosted 1,353,000, paced by the champion Giants who attracted 201,000 at its home games. In bettering the NL total that year, the AA was fronted by the champion Brooklyn Bridegrooms whose record 353,000 home attendance included the largest Sunday crowd (16,974) and weekday crowd (20,914) to date. But this was the high water mark of nineteenth-century attendance. The following year three embattled major leagues, including an interloping Players League, fell short of the 1889 mark. Although inflated attendance figures were used as a propaganda weapon by the warring leagues of 1890, contemporary observers agreed that attendance at Players League games led the NL by over 150,000 admissions with the hard-pressed AA lagging far behind.[8]

The collapse of the Players League in 1890 followed by that of the AA in 1891 enabled victorious NL owners to form a monopolistic, 12-club major league which lasted from 1892–1899. During the brief era of this "big league" monopoly, attendance annually fell short of the high water mark of 1889. During the big league's inaugural campaign of 1892, played under a split season format with each team playing a total of 154 games, first half attendance was estimated at 1,812,239. But the second half of the campaign attracted only 713,190 spectators.[9] Over the next five seasons, with the annual playing schedule reduced to 132 games, attendance rose to 1,849,000 by 1894 and peaked at 2,883,630 in 1897.[10] Emboldened by this illusory trend, the owners hiked the playing schedule to 154 games, but faltering attendance in 1898–99 contributed to growing disenchantment over the 12-club format.

Although external factors like the faltering national economy and the Spanish-American War affected attendance, divisive internal factors plagued the big league. With Boston, Baltimore and Brooklyn teams winning all eight of the campaigns, each season saw envious losers grousing over attendance imbalance. The issue provoked a serious factional problem as the league's "big five" teams of Boston, New York, Chicago, Philadelphia and Pittsburgh attracted the lion's share of attendance. In retaliation the "little seven" clubs banded together and forced the big five to accept an even division of gate receipts. But this concession failed to stem the tide of financial losses. Indeed, annual attendance was too small to support the unwieldy league. Over the years 1892–98 one of the big five teams, the Phillies, averaged 318,000 fans at its annual home games.[11] By comparison, the powerful Baltimore Orioles, while drawing well on the road, ranked with the little seven in home attendance. In hopes of improving their attendance four teams in 1899 formed two controversial, joint ownership "syndicates." But this misguided scheme of fielding two strong teams and two weakened teams not only failed to boost attendance, but fueled the mounting antipathy among club owners. In 1899 one syndicate weakling, the Cleveland team, after playing before home crowds averaging fewer than 200 through June, played the remainder of its scheduled games on the road with disastrous financial result. By posting a 20–134 won-lost log, the Cleveland "Wanderers" set an unmatched record for competitive futility. But other NL teams of 1899 were suffering, including Louisville which elected to play its last 14 games on the road.[12]

The end of the 12-team big league came in 1900 when NL owners voted to return to an eight-team circuit. The unremunerative Cleveland, Louisville, Washington and Baltimore franchises were dropped and their owners paid off. At the same time the playing schedule was reduced to 140 games. In the wake of this drastic surgery 1.9 million fans attended NL games in 1900, but the following year attendance fell to 1.6 million.[13] By then the American League (AL) was waging its successful war for major league recognition. When confirmed by the 1903 National Agreement, the AL and NL returned major league baseball to the popular dual-league format of the 1880s. With both leagues playing 154-game schedules (from 1904–60, except for the war years of 1917–18), with World Series play restored, and with no franchise shifts until the early 1950s, major league baseball enjoyed a half century of unprecedented stability.

TWENTIETH-CENTURY ATTENDANCE TRENDS

A fast growing and increasingly urbanized American population with increasing leisure time and discretionary dollars were potent external factors contributing to surging attendance at major league parks (see Figure 1). Equally important were forces closer to the game such as increasing newspaper coverage, sprightly pennant races, and fan identification with diamond heroes. Bolstered by such forces, annual attendance, fronted by the American League (see Figures 2 and 3), rose steadily in the first decade of this century and climbed above the 7

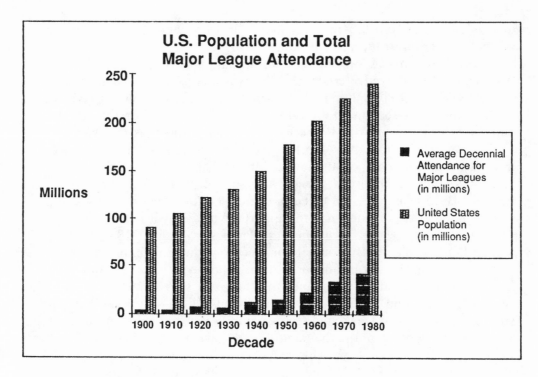

U.S. Population and Total Major League Attendance

Millions

250
200
150
100
50
0

1900 1910 1920 1930 1940 1950 1960 1970 1980

Decade

■ Average Decennial
Attendance for
Major Leagues
(in millions)

▦ United States
Population
(in millions)

Figure 1.

million mark in 1908 and 1909. But such figures are not wholly reliable, and as always attendance was unevenly distributed among teams. In these years home attendance for the Giants and Cubs far exceeded that of other NL clubs, and in the AL the Red Sox, White Sox and Athletics perennially led others in attendance. Indeed, over the years 1901–24 no team surpassed the lordly New York Giants in attendance strength; in those years the New Yorkers hosted more than 20 percent of NL fans. Nevertheless, the AL generally topped the NL in annual attendance (see Figure 4).

By 1910 the rising attendance trend and the pressure of stricter local building codes prompted major league owners to build bigger parks of durable concrete and steel construction. Over the years 1909–15 the boom continued with 11 new parks opening their gates. And with the addition of New York's Yankee Stadium (1923) and Cleveland's Municipal Stadium (1932) this phase of park construction ended. These parks housed major league fans until they were replaced by a post-World War II building boom. But some of these classic structures, including Fenway Park, Comiskey Park, and Cleveland Stadium, still endure. What's more, none of the parks constructed after World War II have matched the 80,000 plus spectators which on several occasions packed Yankee and Cleveland Stadiums.[14]

Ironically as the ball park building boom of the 'teens was under way, annual attendance slumped. After falling to 6.4 million in 1910 and hovering above the 6 million mark over the next three seasons, annual attendance fell below 5 million over the 1914–15 seasons. For this decline external factors such as a business recession and such diversions as movies and automobiles have been cited. But internal factors like the Federal League incursion and fan disenchantment with the low scoring style of play were equally important. In the aftermath of the Federal League collapse attendance rebounded to 6.5 million in 1916, but over the next two seasons attendance was affected by the nation's entry into World War I and by the deadly influenza epidemic of 1918. After falling to 5.2 million in 1917, annual attendance sank to its lowest point of this century when 3 million fans attended games during the shortened 1918 season. Under the circumstances, club owners expected little improvement for 1919, but the end of the war and the lessening of the flu epidemic contributed to a resurgence that saw 6.5 million attend games during that shortened and ill-starred season.

As the 1920 season began, newspaper exposés of the 1919 World Series scandal blemished the game and stirred fears of eroding attendance to come. But nothing of the sort happened. Instead attendance rose to a record 9.1 million, with the Yankees and their newly acquired hero Babe Ruth attracting 1,289,000 home fans. That year also saw the AL champion Cleveland Indians and the NL Giants top 900,000 in home attendance. Nor did the upward trend falter for over the years 1921–30 annual attendance averaged better than 9 million a season with a record 10.1 million attending games during 1930.

Fueling the attendance boom of the 1920s were such external forces as rising urban populations, national prosperity, and a growing public appetite for sports spectacles and sports heroes. And with the most popular sports hero of the decade wearing a Yankee uniform and playing in the biggest park, the Yankees averaged a million home fans each season. A slugging virtuoso, Babe Ruth personified the "big bang" offensive style of play which fans then and now seemed to prefer over low-scoring pitching-dominated games so characteristic of the early years of this century. Indeed, major league baseball's record atten-

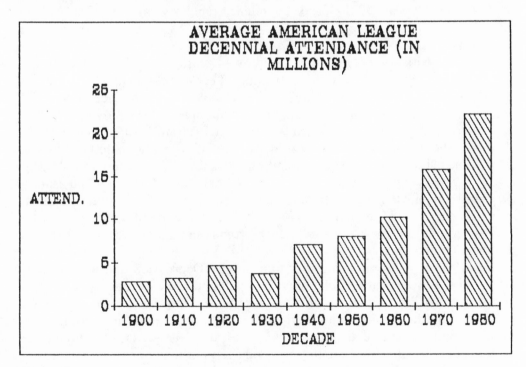

Figure 2.

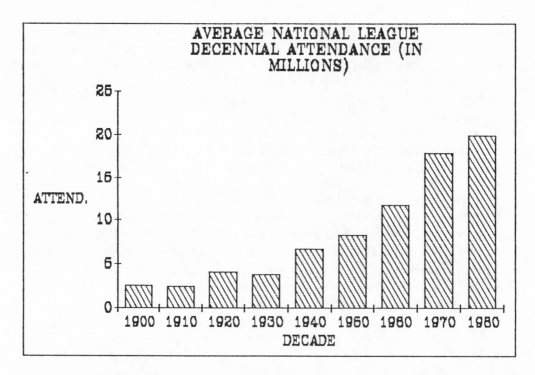

Figure 3.

dance mark of 1930 coincided with a batting spree that saw NL hitters average
.303 while smiting 892 homers. In topping AL hitters by a wide margin in both
categories that year, the NL attendance topped that of the AL by 800,000.
Indeed, over the years 1927–33 NL attendance regularly surpassed the AL's, a
turnabout blamed partly on the pennant monopoly by the AL's Yankees and
Athletics.

But these years of plenty were followed by 14 years of flagging attendance as
the game and the nation reeled under the impact of Depression and total war. As
the Depression gripped the nation during the 1930s, attendance fell to 8.4
million in 1931, to 7 million in 1932, and to 6 million in 1933. Recovering slowly
thereafter, total attendance reached 9 million in 1938 and topped that mark in
1940–41. The nation's entry into World War II dealt the game another blow as
attendance fell to 8.5 million in 1942 and sank to a low of 7.4 million in 1943. But
if club owners expected more of the same thereafter, they were pleasantly
surprised. Despite the ersatz brand of ball forced by the nation's total war effort,
attendance rose to 8.7 million in 1944 and posted a record 10.8 million in 1945.
That latter total set a new standard; henceforth annual attendance would always
top the 10 million mark.

During these years the austerities imposed by Depression and war affected
attendance. But innovations like night baseball and radio broadcasts of games
were attractive lures that popularized the game. Combined with peacetime
prosperity and racial integration of major league teams, these innovations contributed to the great attendance surges of the early postwar era. So did a brief
display of competitive balance that was reflected in the pennant races of 1946–
48. But thereafter the AL Yankees reasserted their domination with crushing

impact while the NL Dodgers waged a lesser tyranny in that circuit. Still while it lasted, the brief postwar attendance boom set lofty records—in 1946, 18.5 million; in 1947, 19.8 million; and in the years 1948–49 attendance twice topped 20 million. In these halcyon attendance years the AL twice topped 10 million and the NL bested that mark once. And if new home attendance marks were set by most clubs, the Yankees led all by topping the 2 million mark five times while the 2.6 million hosted by the 1948 champion Cleveland Indians of the AL set a record that lasted until 1962.

The vigorous postwar attendance boom deflated in 1950. Over the next dozen seasons total annual attendance never reached 20 million and only twice did a league's annual total exceed 10 million. On both these occasions it was the NL which turned the trick. Moreover, in seven of the 12 seasons after 1950, NL attendance surpassed its rival. This upturn in NL fortunes owed much to franchise shifts, especially the occupation of Los Angeles and San Francisco by the Dodgers and Giants. By comparison, AL franchise relocations to Baltimore and Kansas City produced modest gains in attendance strength. And as usual the Yankee pennant monopoly diverted the lion's share of AL attendance to that team's games.

In explaining the attendance reversal of the 1950s observers of the major league scene cited such factors as the lack of competitive balance, televised games, the length of games, and deteriorating parks. Among external causes cited were population shifts away from baseball's familiar urban haunts and competition from rival sports and new leisure activities. Certainly stagnating attendance was a matter of serious concern to promoters of the 1950s. Over the years 1951–53 annual attendance declined from 16.1 million to 14.3 million

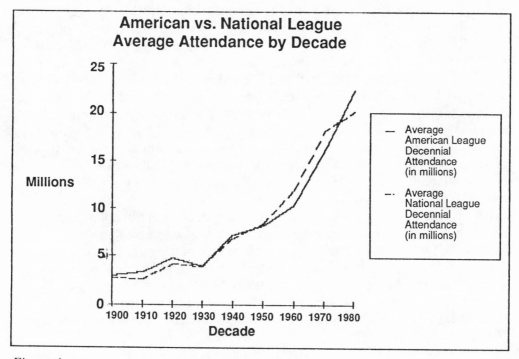

Figure 4.

before recovering under the stimulus of franchise relocations. From 1955–57 annual attendance topped 16 million and rose to 17.4 million in 1958 as the Dodgers and Giants commenced playing on the West Coast. The following year attendance totaled 19 million and in 1960, the last year of major league baseball's long standing 16-team format, attendance rose to 19.8 million.

As the decade of the 1960s began, forces were prodding tradition-bound owners to expand the game's horizons. No longer could club owners ignore the demographic realities of the nation's shifting population centers. Already enterprising pro football promoters were tapping newer population centers and a rival group of baseball promoters threatened to establish a competing major league in these sites. To undercut this Continental League threat, major league owners in 1961–62 expanded each league to 10 teams; the movement pre-empted four of the sites eyed by Continental promoters. But like the 12-club major league of the 1890s, this unwieldy 10-team format made for too many losers, although fans of the New York Mets turned out in large numbers to support this hapless team. Moreover, by the mid-1960s pitching domination sharply reduced offensive production, a situation remedied by rules makers in 1969 who decided to lower pitching mounds and to narrow strike zones in hopes of encouraging heftier hitting.

Such measures were in reaction to the flagging attendance which soured baseball's first expansion move. In 1962, the year the NL followed the AL in expanding to 10 teams and upping its playing schedule to 162 games, major league attendance rose to 21.3 million. Rising slowly thereafter, attendance reached 25 million in 1966, but sagged to 23 million in 1968, the year that impotent batting matched low points of this century. In these years the AL lagged far behind the NL in annual attendance; over the years 1962–68 NL attendance surpassed the AL's by 15 million. Worse still for AL fortunes, in three of those years its annual attendance failed to top 10 million.

For this alarming attendance imbalance, the AL's choices of Washington and Los Angeles as expansion sites were cited. At this time both franchises were liabilities: Washington, which had been abandoned when the original Senators moved to Minnesota, was reoccupied but was overshadowed by nearby Baltimore; and the Los Angeles Angels could not compete with the enormously popular NL Dodgers. For its part the NL occupied Houston and New York where both teams prospered. Furthermore NL teams benefited by the drawing power of new parks; of the eight new parks that opened in the years 1960–68, six housed NL teams. And in these years the NL, with more black stars in its ranks, topped the AL in most offensive categories.

Nevertheless both major leagues were concerned about attendance and were willing to take drastic new measures to increase the numbers of fans. To this end in 1969 the two leagues altered rules to encourage batting and, more important, voted to replace the unwieldy 10-team formats by another round of expansion. In imitation of pro football's successful divisional format, each major league added two new teams and subdivided into Eastern and Western divisions. By producing two divisional winners each season, the new format had the magical effect of redistributing the annual victory laurels. At the same time the current park building boom played its part; over the years 1969–82 10 new parks were opened. Of these five were in the AL, which also benefited from extensive renovations to such structures as Yankee Stadium.

Such tinkering produced intended results as attendance rose dramatically. From 27.1 million in 1969, annual attendance topped 30 million by 1973. Then, after receding slightly over two seasons, attendance exceeded 31 million in 1976 (the year officials calculated that one billion spectators had attended major league games since 1900). Thereafter attendance continued its upward spiral. From 38.7 million in 1977, annual attendance reached 40 million in 1978 and climbed above 43 million in 1979 and 1980.

During these bullish years the AL managed to gain and hold the lead in annual attendance. After falling behind the NL by 22 million admissions over the years 1969–76, AL owners used two strategems to turn the tide in their favor. In 1973 the AL unilaterally adopted the designated hitter rule which restored the league's offensive parity and boosted attendance. And by unilaterally expanding to 14 teams in 1977, the AL thenceforth held the annual edge both in attendance and home run production over its outnumbered rival.

In the decade of the 1980s, except for the crippling strike year of 1981 that shortened the playing season by some 50 games and dropped annual attendance to 26.5 million, attendance at major league games rose to new heights. Rebounding from the 1981 hiatus, attendance rose to 44 million in 1982 and by 1987 surpassed the 50 million mark. By this time the NL Dodgers led all rivals in home attendance; since the opening of Dodger Stadium in 1962, Dodger home attendance averaged 40,000 a game, and by 1988 the Dodgers boasted 27,000 season ticket holders. Thus, annual attendance at Dodger games regularly topped 2 million and on several occasions bettered 3 million. Indeed, by the 1980s major league baseball's present center of gravity showed a decided West Coast tilt with six major league franchises planted in the populous urban region from Seattle to San Diego. By then, like the fast growing nation that for so long embraced the game, major league owners were weighing the prospects of further expansion.

THE ENIGMA OF BALL PARK CROWD COMPOSITION

Although well over a billion spectators have already attended major league games and with future prospects bullish for sustaining the flow, it is surprising that so little has been learned of the makeup of ball park crowds. Indeed, as uncertainty surrounds the actual count of spectators in attendance over the years, we know even less of the composition of ball park crowds. But students of ball park crowds need not hang their heads in shame for little enough is known of the composition of most crowd forms.

A most difficult subject of inquiry, crowd composition and behavior has been studied for at least a century and has yielded little more than vague classifications of crowd forms with some murky explanations of crowd behavior. As temporary clusters of individuals, human crowds tend to be transitory, unstable and prone to emotionalized behavior—characteristics that defy sober probings into their composition. Not surprisingly, then, crowd studies have attracted few serious students. Even though crowd forms have long been discussed in social science textbooks under the heading of "collective behavior," as recently as

A Brooklyn Dodger fan. (Photo courtesy of the National Baseball Library, Cooperstown, N.Y.)

1974 only 17 percent of American colleges offered courses with scarcely a hundred scholars specializing in crowd studies. Such studies offer various classifications of crowd types, including such forms as audiences, spectators, demonstrations, queues, traffic jams, mobs, riots, panics and a host of others. But one must pity the poor student specializing in the study of some of these forms; one can imagine him sitting about waiting for such a crowd to take shape and hoping to arrive on the scene in time to commence his research! Nevertheless, in addition to such forms several theories of crowd behavior have been proposed. In the main such explanations focus on the disruptive aspects of crowd behavior while conceding the social usefulness of much crowd activity. But little light has thus far been shed on the composition of most crowd forms.

Thus cautioned, students of baseball history should be wary of studies purporting to explain the makeup of ball park crowds. This caveat applies to recent statements by some historians on the class, ethnic and gender composition of ball park crowds. In venturing conclusions on the class composition of ball park crowds three historians recently employed the dubious assumption that the American population has fitted neatly into an inclusive three-class system of upper, middle and lower rankings. And by using this simplistic model each arrived at different conclusions on the class composition of ball park crowds. Thus, Allen Guttman argued that "almost from its origin baseball has attracted lower class fans," while upper class urbanites "spurned the diamond." But Steven Riess, using the same model, concluded that ball park fans of the 1900–1920 era of major league history were predominately middle class. And to further confound the issue of class composition of ball park crowds, George Kirsch concluded that ball park fans of the 1855–1870 era were predominately upper or middle class with a sprinkling of lower class representatives.[15] Indeed, such disagreement over the class composition of baseball crowds should alert students to the pitfalls of using a simplistic social class model. To do so invokes the fallacy of misplaced concreteness; far better to assume that the class structure of American society is too complex a phenomenon to be said to speak for itself.

Moreover, the same warning applies to attempts at essaying an ethnic analysis of ball park crowds. In this endeavor the likelihood of simplistic explanations is compounded by the risk of reinforcing mythical ethnic stereotypes. Thus, on the basis of such gossamer evidence as the sale of the Irish-American star "King" Kelly to the Boston team in 1887, the popularity of the German-American star Honus Wagner of the early 1900s, and the presence of three dozen Italian-American players in 1941, Guttman airily concluded that "disproportionate" numbers of ball park fans of those eras were Irish-American, German-American and Italian-American. For his part, Riess wisely hedged his conclusion on the ethnic composition of fans of the 1900–1920 era, stating only that baseball owners tried to recruit ethnic players to please large ethnic segments in major league cities.[16]

Nor does the historical evidence admit firm conclusions of the gender makeup of crowds. That ball park crowds have been predominately male is well known, but little is known of the numbers of female fans amongst crowds of seasons past. By studying newspaper accounts of games played before 1871, Kirsch found females in attendance. But his claim that they were "middle and upper class women" is questionable. And far more suspect are Guttman's conclusions that as the popularity of baseball increased, female attendance lessened, or that middle class women "have always shown resistance" to baseball.[17]

Such unwarranted conclusions about the composition of ball park crowds of the past are likely to crop up as long as scholars fail to acknowledge the complexity of the problem. Truth to tell little is known of the makeup of past ball park crowds. Moreover, available evidence is spotty and limited mainly to newspaper accounts and written reports from eye witnesses. Thus, historical studies of past ball park crowd compositions are likely to yield only impressionistic glimpses. Some insights can be gleaned by monitoring newspapers as G. H. Fleming did in his day-by-day account of the frenzied 1908 National League pennant race. Although Fleming focused mainly on the campaign, his narrative is studded with interesting glimpses of crowd behavior. Likewise similar works of limited focus cast light on spectators.[18] But thus far no scholar has undertaken the formidable task of gathering and interpreting the spotty data on crowd behavior over the long span of major league baseball history.

Although gathering information on the composition of past baseball crowds poses an awesome problem, modern market research studies are enhancing knowledge of present-day crowds. This is because modern baseball promoters are bullish over the potential of such studies for attracting fans to ball parks. Thus, recent studies convincingly show that black spectators comprise less than 10 percent of ball park crowds of recent years. And a 1986 survey of Los

Angeles Dodger season ticket holders counted only 50 blacks among 27,000 purchasers.[19]

Since the 1970s an increasing number of market research studies have been undertaken. A pioneer in the movement is Matthew Levine whose staff study of 300,000 ball park fans, conducted over the years 1974–80, produced some iconoclastic findings about the makeup of recent ball park crowds. One of Levine's findings challenged a prevailing assumption that such crowds were mostly composed of young, affluent, "middle class," married people with children. Instead, Levine's findings showed crowds to be mostly composed of older, "working class" people whose limited income made them vulnerable to ticket price increases. Moreover, three-quarters of those surveyed attended at least five games a season. And another finding suggested that the most zealous of baseball fans preferred to watch games on home television sets rather than going to ball parks.[20]

Such studies offer promising insights into the composition of present and future ball park crowds. So do on-the-spot studies of fans like Lonnie Wheeler's recent study of bleacher seat spectators at Chicago's Wrigley Field. Wheeler spent the summer of 1987 watching Chicago Cub home games from the vantage point of the bleacher sections where he mingled with the spectators. By observing the antics of the bleacherites and listening to informants, Wheeler constructed an interesting description of a semi-permanent segment of an otherwise amorphous crowd scene. Among his findings, Wheeler learned that the much publicized "bleacher bum" subculture was a spontaneous phenomenon until the late 1960s when the media focused attention on fans occupying these dollar seats. At the time some self-styled "bleacher bums" wore yellow helmets, brandished heckling signs, quaffed much beer, and badgered both visiting and home players. According to an informant, the unwanted publicity led to the dispersal of that generation of bleacher bums; but by 1987 a new generation was thriving. The new breed tended to be younger, more affluent, and more female. More prone to drinking, flirting and betting than their forebears, these successors were scorned by old timers as intrusive dilettantes. Indeed, by 1987 bleacher seats had become prized status symbols; on weekends such seats sold out early and scalpers might fetch $15 for a $4 seat in the bleachers.[21]

Although Wheeler's account is often hyperbolic and unsystematic, the approach promises insights into ball park crowd composition by using a participant observation technique. Still, like the present-day market research techniques, participant observation is a tool for studying the composition of present-day crowds. Of the composition of past ball park crowds it is possible that we shall never be well informed, because the subject is a recent interest of baseball promoters and students of the game. In the past the subject of crowd composition was of little concern to either. For their part, promoters of the past were mainly interested in luring patrons to their parks. For more than a century promoters plied trial-and-error means to entice fans and if little was noted of crowd composition, much was learned of the courting and controlling of ball park crowds. Thus, we leave the enigmatic challenge of crowd composition to future scholars while turning to the topics of courting and controlling ball park crowds.

COURTING BALL PARK FANS

More Than Just a Game—Early Promotional Insights

In the formative years of American baseball, games played on open fields attracted crowds of spectators who paid nothing for the experience of watching diverse forms of the game. But after the New York Knickerbocker Club formalized the playing rules in the 1840s, the game became standardized. Thereafter clubs proliferated and competition among teams attracted partisan spectators, triggering a baseball mania in eastern towns and cities by the late 1850s. This baseball boom prompted some clubs to enclose their playing fields and charge admissions, ranging from a dime to fifty cents, for the privilege of watching colorfully uniformed teams vie with rivals for vaguely defined championship honors. And during this amateur era which lasted until 1871, American baseball was loosely regulated by the National Association of Base Ball Players. Organized in 1858, the Association codified playing rules, but failed to establish leagues or playing schedules, or to regulate recruiting practices of member teams. But if attendance was adversely affected by the muddled question of seasonal championship honors, it was stimulated by competitive recruiting of players. Thus, strong teams lured fans by recruiting good players often with cash payments or by offering sinecure jobs. From such practices professional players emerged, and promoters soon recognized the spectator appeal of such stars as pitcher Jim Creighton or infielders like Al Reach, George Wright, Dickey Pearce and Joe Start.

As promoters wooed spectators by fielding star players, they also benefited from free publicity provided by newspaper and magazine coverage of games. By 1860 such coverage included extended accounts of games along with primitive box scores. Thus, like the fabled marriage of the Jack Spratts, an enduring symbiotic relationship between baseball and the print medium was formed; the latter benefited from increased readership while the former gained converts and spectators. And grateful promoters accommodated reporters at parks, including the zealous Henry Chadwick whose contributions as an innovative reporter, statistician, editor of guides, and adviser to baseball officials earned him deserved acclaim as the "Father of the Game."

With paternal interest Chadwick watched baseball's lusty growth as a popular spectacle. As the Civil War ended, a second wave of popular interest in baseball boosted the number of organized clubs to over 300 by 1867. But this bullish growth also exacerbated problems like creeping commercialism and the chaotic championship issue. For his part Chadwick sided with the professional players in their struggle with the amateur proponents. That festering issue and the unresolved matter of annual championships undermined the authority of the weak National Association and contributed to the disorganized state of baseball.

In 1869 the controversy over professionalism came to a head when Cincinnati promoter Aaron B. Champion decided to field an all-salaried team against all comers. With Harry Wright as the team's playing manager the Cincinnati Red Stockings barnstormed the country as apostles of commercialized baseball. Undefeated in 58 games that year, the Reds attracted over 100,000 spectators in a convincing demonstration of the popularity of the professional cause. Inspired by the Reds' success, other teams followed suit, prompting a National Association decision to exclude professional players from its ranks. But the professional teams countered by forming a league of their own in 1871, a move that destroyed the National Association and thenceforth enabled professional interests to dominate organized baseball in America.

As the first professional major league, the National Association of Professional Base Ball Players lasted five seasons, time enough for pioneer promoters to learn some workable and unworkable techniques for attracting spectators. On the positive side, the concept of an organized league with member teams required to play each other five times went far to clarify the seasonal championship issue. Other innovations included a suggested 50 cent admission price, but ticket prices and accommodations varied among National Association clubs. Some clubs sold season tickets and pried more money from fans wishing to watch games from the comfort of their carriages. For his part, manager Henry Wright of the Boston Red Stockings urged clubs to adopt standardized practices. As the league's most successful manager, Wright argued that fifty cents was a fair price for seeing a good game. And Boston spectators, who were treated to the best brand of ball in the league, outnumbered all other clubs in attendance and made folk heroes of the team's starring "big four" of Al Spalding, Jim White, Ross Barnes, and Andy Leonard.

Had there been more innovative managers like Wright who wooed fans by scheduling games at appropriate dates, designing scorecards, overseeing the care of his grounds, outfitting his team in attractive uniforms and, above all, fielding a perennial winning team, the first major league might have survived. But serious problems such as the lack of a fixed playing schedule, a low entrance fee allowing teams to enter and drop out of contention with ridiculous ease, poor officiating by volunteer umpires, and a woeful lack of competitive balance doomed the league. For the latter problem Wright himself was to blame; over the years 1872–75 his team won four consecutive pennants over outclassed rivals. Indeed once raised, the problem of competitive balance plagued major league promoters until recent years. But the National Association's most vexing problem was a lack of control over players who often jumped contracts and deserted teams. Such actions and rumors of players conspiring with gamblers who frequented games were blamed for low attendance. But the popularity of betting at games also suggested that spectators wanted more than just a game, an insight that eluded promoters of this time.

In 1876 Chicago promoter William A. Hulbert staged a coup that replaced the National Association with a new league, the National League of Professional Base Ball Clubs (NL). Determined to correct the shortcomings of the discredited league, Hulbert imposed a fixed playing schedule of games, limited league membership to well-financed teams located in cities with populations of at least 75,000, and effectively bound players to teams by inserting reserve clauses in player contracts. In time the reserve clause became a divisive issue but, by stabilizing lineups, it fostered fan identification with players.

But such positive measures were offset by some fan alienating moves. For one, Hulbert banished the New York and Philadelphia clubs for failing to play their full complement of games in 1876, thereby depriving fans in these most populous sites of National League baseball until 1883. Moreover, Hulbert sanctimoniously banned betting, Sunday ball and the sale of alcoholic beverages from NL parks.

The weakness of this moralizing stance was convincingly demonstrated in 1882 by promoters of the rival American Association who struck a popular note by allowing optional Sunday games and booze sales along with a 25-cent basic admission price. By drawing well in its initial season, the American Association forced National League officials to grant major league status to the league and to reoccupy Philadelphia and New York. From 1883 to 1889 the game enjoyed a brief era of unprecedented popularity under this dual major league format.

Record setting attendance and profits characterized this golden age and these were fueled by bold promotional innovations. Of major importance was a spate of rule changes that transformed the game into a livelier, more exciting spectacle. These included overhand pitching over an increased distance, a single strike zone, and a reduction in the number of called balls. Such measures speeded the pace of games and heightened the dramatic duels between batters and pitchers.

The sprightly style of play produced a host of star players whose exploits enthralled fans who could also follow their deeds in the columns of two popular weekly baseball journals, *The Sporting News* and *Sporting Life*. Thus, folk heroes were made of pitchers like Charles Radbourn and John Clarkson, hitters like Pop Anson, Dan Brouthers, Roger Connor, Pete Browning and Tip O'Neill, and versatile performers like John Ward and King Kelly. By paying high salaries to stars and by selling stars for dazzling prices, promoters exploited the folk hero factor. By such transactions as the selling of star players King Kelly and John Clarkson for $10,000 apiece, promoters discovered a sure-fire tactic for revitalizing teams and boosting attendance. Indeed, partisan fans of this era joyously responded to victorious teams by staging victory parades and benefits in honor of their heroes. This era also saw the emergence of organized groups of cheering fans like General "Hi Hi" Dixon's coterie at Boston and the "Ladies Auxiliary" of the Philadelphia Athletics. Such groups were the forerunners of many others over the years; included were "Nuf Ced" McCreevy's Boston Royal Rooters of the early years of this century, the "Ice Wagon Boys" of St. Louis, Chicago's "Stockyard Boys," Pittsburgh's "Steel Puddlers" and, more recently, Chicago's "Bleacher Bums."[22]

Encouraged by rising attendance, promoters of both major leagues increased their seasonal playing schedules and built larger wooden parks. In 1887 the NL Phillies opened the largest of these. Dubbed the "Palace Park," its double-decked stands could seat 20,000, and its amenities included a bicycle track and a clubhouse swimming pool. But after a fire ravaged its stands in 1894 a limited reconstruction effort reduced its capacity to 16,000 seats with space for 4,000 standees. During the 1890s a rash of ball park fires foreshadowed the ending of the wooden parks.

Meanwhile inside such parks, fans of this era were often frustrated by decisions of newly credentialed professional umpires. Indeed, canny promoters encouraged umpire baiting by paying the fines of kicking players. Thus, the enduring ritual of booing and scapegoating of umpires played a part in luring

MAJOR LEAGUE BASEBALL PLAYING SCHEDULES, 1876–present

1876–1899

Years	NL	AA	UA	PL
1876	70			
1877–78	60			
1879–81	84			
1882	84	80		
1883	98	98		
1884	112	112	112	
1885	112	112		
1886	126	140		
1887	126	140		
1888–89	140	140		
1890	140	140		140
1891	140	140		
1892	154			
1893–97	132			
1898–99	154			

1900–present

Years	NL	AA	FL
1900	140		
1901–03	140	140	
1904–13	154	154	
1914–15	154	154	154
1916–17	154	154	
1918*	125	125	
1919	140	140	
1920–60	154	154	
1961	154	162	
1962–present**	162	162	

*Schedule curtailed as World War I measure.
**1981 schedule shortened by player strike.

UA = Union Association; PL = Players League; FL = Federal League.

Sources: Ron Liebman, "Playing Schedules Since 1876," *Baseball Research Journal*, 1973. The *Baseball Encyclopedia*, New York: Macmillan, 1969.

fans to games.[23] Moreover, teams of this era fed the emotions of fans by adopting a rowdy, deceptive, rule-stretching style of play; popularized by players like King Kelly, such tactics made a virtue of winning games at the expense of sportsmanlike canons.

While pandering to the emotions of fans, promoters also catered to their creature comforts. At this time four American Association promoters profited from that league's policy allowing for optional liquor sales and Sunday games. Among this quartet the rotund Chris Von der Ahe of St. Louis emerged as the most innovative promoter of the century. Even if his knowledge of the game was limited, Von der Ahe was a promotional genius who lured fans to Sportsman's Park by fielding a winning team and by plying fans with booze sales, Sunday ball, and such extra entertainments as a picnic area, band music, fireworks, boxing matches, horse racing, a merry go round, a shoot the chute, and an artificial lake.[24]

If Von der Ahe's ploys inspired few imitators and much ridicule, other promoters profited modestly from concession sales of lemonade, peanuts, pies and tobacco. The profit potential from feeding hungry spectators inspired Harry Stevens to introduce hungry Giant fans to the delights of hot dogs and soda pop. By the early 1900s the widespread popularity of these items had transformed Stevens from a hawker of nickel scorecards to a budding millionaire concessionaire. In the distant future revenues from food and drink sales and other concessions would approach that of ticket sales at ball parks, but this potential was dimly understood by promoters of this era who were heavily dependent on revenue from ticket sales.

Indeed, American Association promoters soon regretted their policy of fixing a basic quarter admission price. On the one hand, the cheap rate boosted AA attendance above that of the NL, but on the other, revenues from such sales lagged behind rising expenses. Thus, when AA promoters raised minimum ticket prices to 50 cents in 1888, lagging sales forced a return to the quarter rate. It was a damaging retreat which contributed to the demise of the AA by 1891.

Meanwhile the AA's policy of allowing Sunday games also stirred controversy. Although popular in some cities, in others the games drew rabid opposition from religious groups. With battle lines drawn, a 30-year struggle ensued before the opponents of Sunday games gave up the ghost. Not that the outcome was ever in doubt for fans welcomed Sunday games. When the struggle ended

St. Louis fans at Sportsman's Park in 1926. (Photo courtesy of the National Baseball Library, Cooperstown, N.Y.)

with a complete victory for proponents, religious moralizers realized that churchways could not override leisureways; present-day moralizers do not show much taste for renewing the battle either.

At this time a lesser controversy followed the practice of staging Ladies Day games at parks. Given the prevailing sexist standards of the times, this revival of an earlier experiment was a bold move. Of course, promoters only vaguely grasped the attendance potential of this vast segment of the population. In the main promoters of this era assumed that the presence of more female fans might have a salutary effect on the behavior of predominately male crowds. Hence, cautious promoters offered free admission only to escorted women on designated days and Von der Ahe primly advertised the availability of ladies toilets at his park. However, Ladies Days became popular events, so much so that the AA Brooklyn team in 1885 and again in 1889 made Ladies Days of all home games except Sunday and holiday games. And when the Cincinnati promoter observed female fans doting on handsome pitcher Tony Mullane, he made every Monday home game a Ladies Day with Mullane assigned the pitching duties. But disenchanted promoters soon regarded females as a divisive presence. Numerous complaints, including males blaming ladies for distracting their attention and from women complaining of abusive males, persuaded promoters to discontinue the practice.[25] By the early years of this century Ladies Days were abolished and were not revived until the 'teens.

Despite the fumbling approaches to Sunday and Ladies Day games, or their inability to see merit in night baseball experiments staged in these years, promoters of the 1880s left a legacy of successful innovations for later generations of promoters to exploit. However, their immediate successors merely followed well-trodden paths. Thus, promoters of the 1890s got several seasons of heavy hitting by extending the pitching distance to its present length. Although the passage of time showed fans preferring this slugging style of play, teams of the 'nineties settled on the pitching-dominated, low-scoring "scientific" style of play. If this was a promotional blunder, the establishment of a single monopolistic big league in this decade was even more short-sighted. After eight seasons of disappointing profits and attendance, in 1900 NL promoters cut back to an eight-team circuit. And by granting major league status to the rival American League three years later, baseball officials restored the dual major league format of the prosperous 1880s.

With the added safeguard of a strong National Commission for settling disputes between the two major leagues, the game entered an era of unprecedented stability. And by reviving annual World Series competition between the two leagues, a move that proved to be both profitable and popular (see Figure 5), the restoration was completed. Fan support was evidenced by rising attendance, prompting owners to build durable new parks with average seating capacities of 35,000 over the years 1909–32.[26] Safer and more comfortable than the wooden parks, these sturdy structures offered more ticket booths and wide ramps leading to the seats. Inside the parks improved crowd control was achieved by distancing seated fans from the playing fields and by deploying larger scoreboards and loudspeaker systems to better inform spectators. Located inside rapidly growing cities, the new parks were accessible by various forms of intra-

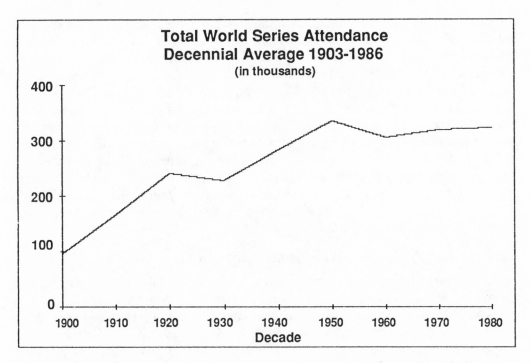

**Total World Series Attendance
Decennial Average 1903-1986**
(in thousands)

Figure 5. Sources: Richard Cohen, David Neft, Roland Johnson, The World Series, *New York, 1976.* World Almanac, *1977–87.*

urban transportation. However, the growing popularity of automobiles posed formidable parking problems which by the 1920s foretold the coming obsolescene of these structures.

But promoters of this era were more preoccupied with meeting mortgage and operating expenses of their privately owned parks and were mainly concerned with attracting a steady flow of spectators. Since more than 80 percent of club revenues came from ticket sales at ball park ticket booths, prudence dictated that ticket prices be affordable to fans. In these years sales of season tickets were meager, so that baseball's financial fate was truly at the gates of its parks. Thus, in the early years of this century ticket prices ranged from a quarter to $1.50 with the cheaper tickets accounting for a quarter of all sales as late as 1916. Moreover, frequently scheduled double headers allowed thrifty fans to watch two games for the price of one. Even World Series tickets at double the price of regular tickets were relatively cheap. In 1913 a fan after attending two World Series games in New York calculated that his total expenses, including lodging, came to $12.80.[27]

In other ways promoters relied on time-honored practices to attract spectators. Through the 1920s revenues from leased concession sales, fronted by the popular trinity of soft drink, hot dog and ice cream sales, accounted for only 5 percent of annual revenues. By then state and federal prohibition laws barred sales of alcoholic beverages. But if booze sales were curbed, legalized Sunday games in all states except Pennsylvania attracted large crowds. So did Ladies Day games, revived during the 'teens. In 1912 the St. Louis Browns admitted escorted ladies free of charge on designated days. Then when wily single women circumvented the escort rule by enticing single males to act as surrogate escorts, the club extended free admission to all ladies in 1917. By then other clubs did the same and Ladies Day games again became popular attractions.[28]

A departure from hidebound promotional practices came with the adoption of the "big bang" style of play in the 1920s, personified by Babe Ruth. This style of play attracted record numbers of fans. Ruth popularized the slugging game and reigned as the game's premier folk hero. The most photographed American of his day, Ruth was lionized by fans everywhere; lavish media coverage, including movies and radio, bolstered his image and that of major league baseball. Indeed, Ruth's greatest legacy was the perpetuation of the star system in baseball. Thus, canny promoters, recognizing the public's hunger for diamond heroes to worship, began subsidizing baseball writers and numbering player uniforms to facilitate fan recognition of stars.

Entertaining the Spectators—Recent Promotional Techniques

To be sure more than star players were needed to lure fans to ball parks during the austere years of Depression and World War II. As attendance slumped in the 1930s and again during the war years, promoters cautiously turned to radio broadcasts and night baseball to hype public interest. Admittedly neither ploy was new. As early as the 1880s the feasibility of night ball was demonstrated and in that decade telegraph augmented reconstruction of games displayed on illuminated boards in some major league cities heralded the coming of the electronic media era. And when radio sets became household appliances in the 1920s, broadcasts of World Series games and some seasonal games attracted millions of listeners. However, fears of such broadcasts affecting live attendance were rampant among promoters until the 1930s.

By then promoters were also alerted to the attendance-boosting potential of night baseball games that were being staged in 15 minor league cities in 1934. Brushing aside faltering opposition, Cincinnati general manager Larry MacPhail won permission to play seven night games in 1935. The games drew well, but no club followed suit until MacPhail moved to Brooklyn in 1938 and illuminated Ebbets Field. There the first night game played became an historic epic as 38,748 fans saw Cincinnati pitcher Johnny Vander Meer hurl a second consecutive no-hit game. Thereafter other promoters saw the light; by 1940 six NL and four AL parks staged night games. And during the war years, with President Roosevelt's blessing, night games became more numerous and popular. In the early postwar years all clubs except the Cubs (holdouts until 1988) scheduled night games. By the 1960s most championship games were night contests as were most World Series games a decade later.[29]

Meanwhile radio broadcasts of games made fans of millions while returning welcome revenues to promoters. By the mid-1950s more than a thousand radio stations broadcast play-by-play accounts of games over the land. It was a boon for major league baseball, but a bust for upstaged minor league promoters who also suffered the inroads of television broadcasts of big league games. Ravaged by falling attendance, the number of minor leagues dwindled, forcing major league clubs by the 1960s to subsidize surviving minor leagues. For not only were the minors important nurseries of future players, but they also served as proving grounds for promotional innovations like night ball, post season play-offs, rule changes and other crowd-pleasing ploys. Indeed, the most successful big league promoters had honed their skills in the minors.

One such apprentice, Bill Veeck Jr., went on to become the most innovative major league promoter since Von der Ahe. In 1942 this gifted son of a former big league general manager acquired control of the moribund Milwaukee Brewers of the American Association. Using limited funds to strengthen his team and refurbish his park, Veeck lured fans with a contending team and a variety of promotional gimmicks that excepted only free tickets. During that wartime season Veeck lured war workers with morning games and free breakfasts and night games with free coffee and doughnuts. Veeck also entertained fans with music, clowns, giveaways, and beer sales and regularly mingled with spectators to learn more of what was wanted to keep them coming. Of course, three consecutive championship teams provided the best lure, although military service kept Veeck from witnessing the last two victories. Returning in 1945 with a crippling injury, the convalescing Veeck sold the team for a $250,000 profit.

In 1946 Veeck organized a syndicate that acquired control of the lackluster major league Cleveland Indians. Moving swiftly, Veeck strengthened his team. In a bold and controversial move in 1947 he signed Larry Doby as the first black player in the AL and the following year he added the legendary black star Satchel Paige to his pitching staff. Joining the team in July, the venerable Paige made his debut before a record home crowd of 78,382 and pitched a shutout. Such moves attracted large numbers of black fans, but other ploys like staging Saturday Ladies Day games, giving free orchids and stockings to women, and opening a nursery for children lured thousands of female fans. On one Ladies Day an unexpected throng of 40,000 women showed. Nor did Veeck's telecasting of Cleveland home games toll on live attendance. On the contrary, while romping to a World Championship, the 1948 Indians hosted a record 2.6 million home spectators. It was a promotional triumph that won Veeck the recently established Executive of the Year Award.

Although financial problems forced Veeck to sell his interest soon afterwards, the demon promoter emerged in 1951 as a co-owner of the faltering AL St. Louis Browns. So desperate was this team's plight that not even Veeck's promotional acumen could keep it afloat. But Veeck lodged his family in the clubhouse and wooed fans with such ploys as playing a midget. Incensed by that caper, the AL president tried to expunge midget Eddie Gaedel's base-on balls from the record books, but 20,000 fans saw the game and objective statisticians kept the record straight. Other Veeck ploys like allowing placard-waving fans to vote on tactical decisions boosted attendance, but the Browns were too far gone to save. Forced to sell and harried from major league baseball by hostile owners in 1954, Veeck returned in 1959 as co-owner of the pennant-starved Chicago White Sox. That year the White Sox won the AL pennant and set a club attendance record. During this brief stint, Veeck refurbished the park, added a $300,000 scoreboard that exploded after each home team homer, and placed player names on the backs of uniforms. But the 1959 victory was Veeck's last. After selling his interest in 1961, he returned to the White Sox in 1975. Although winning another Executive of the Year Award in 1977, failing health and financial problems ended his career in 1980.

Although much scorned as a maverick, even the late Veeck's greatest detractors now concede his genius. His knowledge of the game and his ability to lure fans were unsurpassed and his two books detailing his promotional philosophy were widely read. Indeed, the designated hitter rule suggested early by Veeck boosted AL attendance when adopted in 1973.

In the main, Veeck's promotional philosophy stressed winning teams and entertaining diversions for luring fans to ball parks.[30] In his view the two were inseparable, but after World War II the entertainment dimension loomed larger. By then it was evident that Americans craved fun and entertainment with postwar prosperity supplying the means to those ends. With rival leisure activities offering tempting alternatives, baseball promoters responded by scheduling more night games. By 1950 half of all games were nocturnal, and by the 1960s day games and double headers were rare events. That fans preferred this scenario was evinced by the findings of two 1967 polls; one showed a strong preference for shorter single games played at night, and the other a preference for high-scoring games, colorful uniforms, and more comfortable and better policed parks.[31] In responding to the wish for higher scoring games a 1969 rule change penalizing pitchers ended a hitting famine in both leagues, and the AL's unilateral adoption of the designated hitter rule in 1973 boosted its offensive production above that of the NL thereafter. As for colorful uniforms, in the 1970s teams like the Oakland Athletics and Pittsburgh Pirates set new fashions with their gaudy, trim-fitting garb.

Meanwhile the latest park building boom produced 20 new parks over the years 1953–82 with average seating capacities of 50,000. Of these, all but Dodger Stadium were publicly financed and most were designed to accommodate other spectator sports. And because of major league expansion to 26 teams by 1977, many were located in new population centers. The new parks were commodius and comfortable and three were air-conditioned domed structures. Costly to build and to maintain, the new parks exacted higher ticket prices from fans.[32]

But inflation-buffeted fans accepted the higher ticket prices. By 1974 the cheapest seat cost a dollar and only the Dodgers offered a 75 cent rate for children. By 1977 the average price of a seat was $3.45 with choicer ones fetching $5.50 and more. And by 1986 a family of five reported spending $37.50 for seats and $3.50 for parking. Still, promoters could boast that baseball tickets were cheaper than those of other spectator sports. Moreover, wealthy corporations were buying up season tickets and distributing them to clients. Indeed, season tickets sold at unprecedented rates, with such windfalls ending a long-standing dependence on daily ticket sales at the parks. Some wealthy corporations also paid $20,000 and more to rent opulent suites for a season; from such lofty perches occupants relaxed in comfort, dined on gourmet foods, and watched games on closed circuit television.[33] Thus by the 1980s, all clubs hired marketing specialists to sell season tickets. In this enterprise no club matched the Dodgers's 1987 sale of over 26,000, enough to fill half the stadium for each game.[34]

As revenue from ticket sales soared, so did income from sales of concession items. Even if much of this revenue was shared by contractors and stadium authorities, this was an important windfall. By the 1980s soaring concession income contrasted sharply with 1950 sales when one owner boasted of wringing an extra dollar per spectator on such sales during a double header. Indeed, by the 1980s fans often spent more money on concession items than for tickets. Although sales of ever more costly hot dogs, beer, soft drinks and ice cream continued to lead, fans increasingly chose more expensive viands. What's more such revenues were augmented by sales of souvenirs, including yearbooks, clothing emblazoned with team logos, and other items that could also be purchased by mail order catalogs.[35] Thus, the family of five referred to above also spent $44 for concessionary items while attending a game.

Marketing experts also enticed fans with free gifts obtained at little cost to clubs since corporations often subsidized these costs as part of advertising campaigns. Called "giveaways" or "freebies," Veeck pioneered in this enterprise by giving or raffling cigars, beer, motor oil, orchids and other items. At first promoters aimed these offerings at children who by the 1960s were courted with free bat and ball days, and later by cap days, batting helmet days, T-shirt days, and the popular jacket days. By the 1970s, however, adults were targeted with women given hot pants, panty hose, halters, shorts and other personal items and men courted mainly with cheap beer dates.[36] Then as promoters learned that such events lured thousands more fans than ordinary dates, they concocted more giveaway dates. By 1983 banners, calendars, candy, seat cushions, and a host of other items were given free on announced dates. Meanwhile older promotional lures like Old Timers Days and fireworks nights continued to attract fans.[37] And by the 1980s every team had its clownish totem mascot cavorting about its park, leading cheers, teasing fans, and mocking players and umpires. Derived from children's television shows, mascots like the San Diego Chicken and the Philly Fanatic reflected the ongoing marriage of major league baseball with the television industry.[38]

Certainly television helped transform baseball into an entertainment spectacle. An instant commercial success of the early postwar era, television-viewing swiftly became the nation's most popular leisure outlet. And high on the list of the medium's most popular offerings were sports programs. As Americans embraced television and its celebrities, sports heroes also became celebrity entertainers. For baseball, television made idols of players, provided revenue which by the 1980s exceeded that of ticket sales, inspired franchise shifts and the expansion of leagues, raised the value of clubs, and sent player salaries to undreamed-of heights. Television also created new baseball fans and focused national attention on pennant races, All-Star games, championship playoff series, and World Series games. The medium also altered baseball's traditional relationship with the sporting press. Because television news services beat newspapers on fast breaking stories, a new style of journalism emerged. In baseball reporting writers now focused more on issues surrounding the game, including player unionism, salaries, racism, and player's private lives. And if some observers complained that "real" baseball fans preferred watching games on television, none could say that live attendance was affected by the medium.

By the 1980s, indeed, older forms of ball park entertainment like organ music and exploding scoreboards were being replaced by new television technology. In 1986 one popular form called "Diamond Vision" deployed large color television screens in seated areas which supplied spectators with baseball news, news of other sporting events, music, simulated fireworks and other diversions. Thus, if ball park fans still saw live players in action, their attention was being increasingly diverted by televised images of players, by replays of events on the field, by commercials, and even movie shorts. The overall aim of such entertainment was to make fans feel good even if the home team lost the game.[39] As measured by continuing high revenues and soaring attendance at games, the tendency to stage games as entertainments seemed to be working. Nevertheless, some critics are questioning the suitability of baseball's marriage to the television industry in general, and the impact of the entertainment climate on spectator behavior in particular.

CONTROLLING BALL PARK FANS

An enduring paradox faced by baseball promoters is that if one succeeds in luring a big crowd he must worry all the more about controlling crowd behavior. Recently this tension between the courting and controlling of spectators was underscored by an observer's comment that the same entertainment lures that attracted large crowds also triggered waves of violent outbursts at parks.[40] Nor was this a new phenomenon for similar warnings of "bad animal" baseball crowds had been sounded throughout the course of baseball's history.

The latest alarms of ball park violence appear to be aftershocks of the destructive urban riots of the 1960s which had social commentators invoking the "bad animal" theory to describe the violent potential of crowds. And as those episodes of crowd violence declined, observers focused attention on the violent behavior of sports crowds. By the 1970s, indeed, alarmists were citing increased episodes of sports crowd violence and were warning promoters of more to come. In response sports promoters, including baseball owners, expanded their staffs to include security experts or even "violence experts."[41] Not surprisingly, since they hosted more seasonal crowds than those of rival sports, baseball promoters were quick to respond to the problem. By the 1970s most clubs employed "security experts" and at a high-level meeting in 1972 17 of these experts denounced current baseball crowds as "unsportsmanlike, vindictively partisan, and more violence prone than any in the past."[42] An extraordinary, paranoid statement was this. Indeed, it would be difficult to find a more effusive statement of the "bad animal" theory of crowds or one more lacking in historical perspective.

Crowd Violence of Seasons Past

Although no systematic study of baseball crowd misbehavior exists, even a cursory review of the game's history bears witness to repeated acts of violence by ball park spectators of seasons long past. Even if nineteenth-century crowds were smaller and more homogeneous than today's, contemporary promoters hewed to a "bad animal" theory as they sought ways of controlling crowd

Fans at the Huntington Avenue Grounds in Boston. (Photo courtesy of the National Baseball Library, Cooperstown, N.Y.)

behavior. That they failed is evidenced by the numerous episodes of crowd misbehavior over the years.

Such incidents were reported as early as 1860 when unruly fans among a crowd of 15,000, who gathered to watch the deciding game of the championship series between the Brooklyn Excelsiors and the host Brooklyn Atlantics, goaded the Excelsior team to leave the field. The contest ended with no decision and the two teams broke off relations. Similar episodes elsewhere had club directors vainly trying to control by direct appeals or by hiring police. Alarmed by the rash of incidents, sportswriter Henry Chadwick blamed fellow reporters for encouraging misbehavior by their fulsome coverage of such incidents.[43] But reporters continued to do so. Thus, when the Cincinnati Reds ended their long winning streak by losing to the host Brooklyn Atlantics in 1870, a partisan writer gleefully told how a fan assisted the victory by jumping on the back of a Cincinnati outfielder as he attempted to field a ball. And in the game's riotous aftermath, it was noted that the Reds ran a gauntlet of abusive fans.[44]

Writers also recorded similar incidents that pockmarked the National Association era. According to Albert Spalding, gambling and liquour sales incited frequent riots at Association games.[45] Sometimes umpires were assaulted by gamblers and angry fans.[46] In 1875 repeated incidents of fans interfering with play at games played between the Boston and Philadelphia clubs prompted the directors of both clubs to issue public apologies in hopes of dampening the emotional climate.[47]

To end such abuses was one of the compelling arguments used by Hulbert in winning support for the National League in 1876. By banning liquor sales and Sunday games, by disciplining and fining rowdy players, by barring gamblers, Hulbert hoped to make NL games attractive to respectable patrons. To this end Hulbert ousted some players and teams, but his draconian measures failed to solve the problem.

By the 1880s it was apparent that most outbursts were ignited by umpires whose decisions often evoked angry protests from players and fans. But emotions were also stirred by partisanship, poor play, foul language, brawling players, long lines at ticket counters, and even by joyous victory celebrations when straw hats at times littered fields.

Indeed, victory celebrations or lamentations over defeats often inspired seat cushion battles. In 1892 one such battle at Chicago prompted the umpire to forfeit the game to the visiting Louisville team. And because promoters were unwilling to forego the revenues fetched by seat cushion rentals, such battles continued into the present century.[48] Nor could promoters muzzle swearing and cursing fans, although some vainly hoped to quell it by encouraging ladies to attend games.[49] And when a Cincinnati promoter hired bouncers to eject offensive fans from the park, he was denounced as a bully.[50]

In those years promoters regarded rare occasions when overflow crowds appeared with mixed feelings of delight and apprehension. At such times visiting teams were disadvantaged by standees ringing the playing field and interfering with play. Thus, the visiting Chicago Colts lost a game at the Polo Grounds in 1896 when a Giant hitter drove a ball into the throng which was grabbed by an absconding fan allowing the Giants to score a tainted home run.[51] Sometimes overflow crowds were impossible to control, as evidenced by the 1883 Memorial Day riot at Philadelphia. Anticipating a large holiday turnout, Athletic promoters opened ticket offices two hours early. But well before game time 14,000 fans packed the park with thousands still clamoring for admission. In the ensuing riot the crowd broke down a gate and rushed on the grounds before police could erect barricades. With fans jamming the stands and encircling the playing field, late arriving players and season ticket holders were forced to climb fences to get inside. Overall, it was a bad day for the fans whose spirits were dampened by the home team's 10–9 defeat.[52] However, there were days when boisterous, overflowing crowds caused few problems for tremulous promoters. On Memorial Day of 1888 the Giants hosted two huge crowds at separate morning and afternoon games. Each game attracted fans of all stripes, including many who could attend only on a holiday. According to a reporter, "they yelled, jumped about like colts, stamped their feet, threw their hats in the air . . . and . . . enjoyed themselves hugely," as they watched the Giants continue their successful drive toward a pennant.[53]

But umpires seldom enjoyed themselves hugely. Their decisions made them the favorite scapegoats of frustrated fans and triggered most of the mob scenes. Pity the poor umpire of this era who worked alone and could not possibly see what went on behind his back. In any game his calls incited "kicking" by players and fans, abuses promoters encouraged by paying the fines incurred by players. Thus, umpires became the manufactured villains of baseball folklore. Forced to brave the wrath of players and fans single-handedly, umpires were denied the obvious relief of safety in numbers. Although the short-lived Players League used a double umpire system in 1890, the established leagues clung to single umpires; not until 1911 did both major leagues adopt a dual-umpire system.[54]

Bullied by players and fans, umpires were often mobbed, with 10 such episodes counted during the 1882 season. That year umpire Mike Welsh was mobbed twice, once driven to the safety of President Spalding's office by a Chicago mob.[55] Likewise umpire Billy McLean was twice mobbed, once after he threw a bat at tormenting Philadelphia fans in 1884, and the following year by a Cincinnati mob.[56] Meanwhile repeated incidents of umpire mobbings at Baltimore prompted promoters to install a barbed wire barrier to keep spectators at bay.[57]

Belatedly addressing the problem, officials first empowered umpires to fine players and later tried to make club owners responsible for offending players and fans.[58] But these toothless sanctions failed to prevent umpire mobbings from becoming a chronic problem of the 1890s, nor did subsequent half-hearted measures such as bigger fines, ejections of offending players, or forbidding umpires to address spectators.[59] In truth the problem of umpire abuse was never resolved, although in the present century it was abetted by larger parks which distanced fans from playing fields, by tougher sanctions imposed by league presidents, by deploying more umpires, and by the recent unionization of umpires. Such measures virtually ended mobbings, but umpires continued to suffer verbal abuse and occasional physical abuse.

Meanwhile fans of the early years found other fish to fry as some teams aroused spectators by their aggressive, brawling style of play. In the 1880s the St. Louis Browns were targeted as dirty, foul-mouthed players. Victorious in four straight AA campaigns, the Browns provoked fans everywhere, especially in Brooklyn. In 1889 as the Brooklyn Bridegrooms threatened to end the Browns's victory skein, the final test pitted the two rivals in a decisive series at Brooklyn. One of the games erupted in a mob scene after the Browns's stalling tactics prompted the umpire to forfeit the game to the home team. When the visitors protested, a mob chased the team to the clubhouse where the players cowered behind closed doors as their attackers banged on the door and broke windows. The incident ended when the police drove off the mob and escorted the Browns to their hotel.[60]

By the 1890s this "modern . . . rowdy" style of play became the hallmark of the NL's Boston Beaneaters, Baltimore Orioles and Cleveland Spiders. Although purists scorned such tactics, others defended it as crowd-pleasing. Indeed, the "scrappy" teams drew well on the road, although their tactics provoked ugly incidents. For one, after clinching a third straight NL pennant at Pittsburgh in 1893, the coupe carrying the Boston team to their hotel was stoned by rioting fans. Pitcher Kid Nichols was struck six times about the head and outfielder Hugh Duffy was hit in the face. Later a writer blamed Boston's rowdy style of play for provoking the incident.[61]

The Beaneaters were soon upstaged by rowdier Baltimore and Cleveland teams. According to veteran umpire Tom Lynch, those teams were the worst he ever encountered, citing John McGraw of Baltimore and Pat Tebeau of Cleveland as chief offenders. Indeed, "Muggsy" McGraw was accused of inciting Baltimore fans to hurl beer glasses at rival outfielders. And Chicago manager Pop Anson lamented, "I don't see how any team can win in Baltimore."[62] But in postseason Temple Cup play in 1894 and 1895 the Baltimore Orioles got some comeuppance. In the 1894 series the Giants crushed the Orioles with the partisan New York crowd abusing the Orioles throughout the final game. The following year Cleveland hung a second defeat on the Orioles. But after winning the decisive game in Baltimore, the Spiders were mobbed twice; after being harried off the playing field by a mob, the hotel-bound victors were stoned and rotten-egged by another.[63]

Aroused by such episodes, league officials sought to curb the incendiary style of play. An 1897 edict levied fines on rowdy players and those mouthing "vulgar, indecent" language. When this failed to stop the scrappers, Cincinnati owner John T. Brush's harsh measure was adopted in 1898. This "Brush Resolution" imposed heavy fines for players using "villainously filthy language" or for brawling with expulsion and blacklisting for chronic offenders. If this edict proved to be unenforceable, at least the worst offenders were cowed by its threat.[64] Moreover, Boston's 1897 victory ended the Oriole's three-year reign as NL champions and was celebrated as a triumph of clean ball over rowdy ball. Thereafter, the rowdy ball issue declined, although it flared briefly in an ugly episode of 1898. During a game at the Polo Grounds an Oriole player called the owner of the Giants a "sheeny." That insult caused the irate owner to pull his team off the field, creating a furor among the fans and a major headache for league officials.[65]

By then falling attendance was blamed on unruly players and spectators along with the rash of fires that ravaged the wooden parks, including the 1898 conflagration at Sportsman's Park which injured a hundred fans and ended Von der Ahe's career as a promoter.[66] But the volatile atmosphere at most parks was a continuing problem, especially the foul language which prevented one fan from taking his wife to games.[67] However, promoters of the 'nineties no longer believed that the presence of ladies would improve the decorum of spectators and were cutting back on Ladies Day games.[68]

In the early years of the present century the restoration of the dual major league system burnished the game's image and boosted attendance. Still, with diminishing frequency the currents of unrest at major league parks had promoters groping for solutions to chronic problems of umpire-baiting, profanity,

The Huntington Avenue Grounds in Boston. (Photo courtesy of the National Baseball Library, Cooperstown, N.Y.)

brawling players and fans, and unsafe parks. During these years ugly episodes were traceable to all of these problems.

As ever, umpire abuse continued to head the list of problems. In 1902 manager John McGraw was driven out of the American League for umpire baiting, but he continued to plague NL umpires as manager of the Giants. As late as 1917 he was fined for slugging an umpire, one of several such episodes of those years. But bottle throwing fans were a greater menace to umpires; in 1906 umpire Billy Evans was knocked unconscious by a thrown bottle at St. Louis.[69] Bottle throwing fans also targeted players. At Brooklyn in 1907 a near miss prompted Frank Chance of the Cubs to retaliate. His return throw struck a fan, triggering a near riot. In the aftermath the Brooklyn owner halted the sale of bottled drinks for a day!

But players incited fans by brawling on the field and by responding to abusive fans with profanity, obscene gestures, and occasional assaults. In 1905 Christy Mathewson incited fans by hitting a boy for making an insulting remark. Sometimes players charged into stands to punish hecklers as did Ty Cobb on a memorable occasion in 1912. When Cobb was suspended, his teammates staged a one-day strike which ended with fines for the strikers and a continuation of Cobb's suspension. While the walkout lasted, the undermanned Tigers lost by a top-heavy score to Philadelphia.

Meanwhile increasing numbers of spectators taxed the facilities of the outmoded ball parks. In 1903 the worst ball park accident caused a panic at Philadelphia's NL park when an overhanging gallery collapsed, killing 12 spectators and injuring 282.[70] Nevertheless record numbers of fans continued to jam aging parks especially during the NL's frenzied 1908 campaign when dozens of sportswriters routinely noted the antics and misbehaviors of spectators. Some told of ladies wearing fashionable, wide-brimmed "Merry Widow" hats that blocked the vision of male fans who retaliated by tossing peanuts at the hats. Others told of seat cushion fights, of a brawl at the Polo Grounds that ended with one fan smiting another on the head with a bat, and of a brief panic at the Polo Grounds caused by a fan seizing a fire hose and spraying a section of spectators. There were incidents of fans fainting from the heat and a tragic event at Chicago where an exuberant fan, while watching the game from atop a building outside the park, lost his footing and fell to his death.[71] Still others told of organized groups of fans like the Boston Royal Rooters serenading spectators with musical instruments.

Such characters were irrepressible and usually harmless, although the Royal Rooters once caused a near-riot by staging an outfield sitdown strike at a 1912 World Series game because a clerk unwittingly sold their seats to early arrivals.[72] Over the years promoters and fans learned to co-exist with such zanies, including Brooklyn's "Sym-phoney" orchestra and the cowbell ringing, umpire-baiting Hilda Chester, Philadelphia's heckling Pete Adelis, and in recent years San Diego's "Tuba man," and "Morganna the Wild One," the notorious player-kisser. Although players and umpires complained of such characters in particular, and the raucous Philadelphia, Brooklyn and Pittsburgh fans in general, on the whole the baseball landscape was brightened by their presence.[73]

Indeed, promoters were rightly more concerned over weightier problems of umpire assaults, brawling players and fans and unsafe parks. Leading a reform movement was Ban Johnson who saw these as threats to the existence of his fledgling American League. Determined to protect his umpires, Johnson fined abusive players and orderd umpires to submit reports of each episode. Johnson also pressured owners to support umpires and at his urging the AL adopted the dual umpire system in 1909. By 1911 the NL followed suit, but NL umpires still suffered abuses. That AL umpires were better protected was evidenced by fewer incidents and a smaller turnover among umpires.

Moreover, Johnson's tough-minded policy of fining and suspending brawling players and ordering clubs to provide more police protection was working. So was his edict ordering owners to eject and arrest bottle-throwing fans which NL owners also adopted. In the 'teens the substitution of paper cups for bottles was beneficial and the passage of state and national prohibition laws lessened the numbers of drunks until the repeal of the prohibition amendment in 1933.

Combined with the opening of larger, safer ball parks, such measures significantly reduced the incidents of spectator violence. Moreover, innovations of the 1920s, such as the deployment of large electric scoreboards, efficient loudspeaker systems, and numbers placed on the backs of player uniforms, eased tensions by supplying spectators with necessary information.[74]

By the 1930s riotous episodes were rare and the occasional incidents hardly compared with old-time donnybrooks. Among these, an outburst at Detroit during the final game of the 1934 World Series posed a reminder of the persisting potential of crowd violence. The incident was triggered by Cardinal outfielder Ducky Medwick whose aggressive slide toppled the Tiger third baseman. Incensed by that play and by the big Cardinal lead, riotous spectators showered Medwick with a continuing barrage of fruits and vegetables and repeatedly drove him from his outfield position until Commissioner Landis ordered his removal from the game.

The lurking problem of crowd violence erupted in a rash of episodes during the 1940s. Three such episodes occurred in 1940, including two assaults on umpires. In one instance umpire George Magerkurth was tackled from behind by a Brooklyn fan; in the other, rioters amongst the crowd of 70,000 at Yankee Stadium pelted the umpire with missiles that littered the field, causing a 20-minute game delay. In an unrelated episode at Cleveland that year irate fans, incensed by the home team's revolt against its manager, screamed "crybabies" and hurled baby bottles at the players.

Similar outbursts occurred during the war years. In 1942 rioting fans at the Polo Grounds surged on the field, forcing the Giants to forfeit a game. Earlier that year pracice blackouts and curfews imposed by military authorities triggered ugly incidents. In a game at the Polo Grounds, a curfew ended a game just as the Giants were rallying. The ensuing uproar ended when a spotlight was shone on the American flag. In another incident repeated warnings were necessary to induce defiant smokers to respect a practice blackout.[75]

To be sure, such episodes were pale imitations of the mobbings and riots of the early years. Moreover, incidents of crowd violence declined during the postwar years and were highlighted mainly by joyous and mildly destructive victory riots like those staged by Giant fans in 1951 or by Pirate fans in 1960. But such recent incidents of crowd unrest, and especialy those of long ago, were forgotten by alarmists of recent years who reacted to the renewed surge of spectator violence.

The New Wave of Violence

According to newly ordained club security executives who met in 1972 to discuss the problem, major league baseball had never seen the likes of the recent outbreaks of crowd violence. Many sportswriters agreed, including one who counted 40 episodes during the 1970s. Most incidents involved spectators throwing missiles at players, including firecrackers, steel balls and, in one case, hot dogs and candy bars. The latter incident occurred at Yankee Stadium where thousands of opening day fans hurled their complimentary "Reggie" candy bars at its namesake, outfielder Reggie Jackson. But if Jackson's showering was a friendly gesture, Atlanta fans were more hostile in their showering of Pete Rose of the Reds with complimentary frisbees. A frequent target, the fiery Rose was assailed by firecrackers and once by a shot paper clip.[76]

Although individual acts accounted for most violent episodes of the 1970s, there was a resurgence of rioting. Most riots were "victory riots," inspired by the "Metomania" outburst of joyous New York Met fans who surged on the playing field after the team's 1969 victory snatching bases and chunks of turf as keepsakes. In 1976 Yankee fans celebrated a playoff victory in similar style, milling about like rampaging fire ants (as seen by observers in the Goodyear Blimp). The following year Yankee fans repeated by mobbing the heroic Reggie Jackson who knocked down two fans while racing for the protection of a police cordon. So frequent were the "victory riots" that promoters beefed up security forces in anticipation. However, Pittsburgh's "Big Buc Binge" riot erupted without warning after the news of the Pirates's 1971 World Series victory in Baltimore reached Pittsburgh. Upon hearing the news, 40,000 rioting fans staged the most destructive of all baseball-related riots in the city. A few fans danced in the nude and made love in public while many engaged in orgies of property destruction. In the aftermath 98 rioters were jailed.[77]

Although spared the onus for the "Big Buc Binge," baseball promoters were blamed for other riots caused by such ill-conceived lures as cheap beer nights. At Cleveland in 1974 such a stunt staged a memorable riot when drunken spectators among the crowd of 25,000 attacked players on both teams. After a Cleveland pitcher was struck by a thrown chair, the umpires forfeited the game to the visiting team. In 1977 a beer riot at Los Angeles was fueled by regular priced beer as fans in the upper deck showered spectators seated below. When the victims retaliated, the atmosphere was foamy before stadium cops, one of whom was struck in the face by a full cup, restored order. Because of such incidents, wary promoters imposed curfews on beer sales and designated some seating sections off limits to beer drinkers.[78]

But beered-up spectators were not the only rioters. At Chicago in 1979 a riot erupted over Bill Veeck's "Disco Demolition" promotional stunt. When rioting fans sailed records onto the playing field and brawled in the stands, the second game of the scheduled double header was forfeited to the visitors. In other ways well meaning promotional schemes backfired. Often items sold or given free to fans became flying missiles. Thus, scorecards were folded into paper airplanes, free bats became nerve-wracking noisemakers and sometimes were thrown, and crushed ice was formed into snowballs. And when Yankee officials ordered increased surveillance of certain seating sections as a precautionary measure, some angry spectators staged a riot that took the combined efforts of 700 stadium cops to quell.[79] Moreover, the jeering tunes that stadium organists directed at rival teams and umpires incited acts of violence as did the practice of cladding comely usherettes in tight-fitting, sexy-looking "hot pants" uniforms. And on rare occasions individual troublemakers hatched unique plots as did one who buzzed Dodger Stadium in an airplane in 1977 dropping sacks of flour and bottles which fortunately caused no injuries.[80]

Just why so many violent events were occurring, even in the new, safer, more comfortable parks of this era, confounded promoters and observers. Nor could pundits provide credible explanations. Some blamed the explosive social and political climate of the 1960s for infecting sports fans and a purblind psychologist ventured the suggestion that more women at games would upgrade the level of behavior.[81] Others supplied a smorgasbord of explanations, citing television programs for turning fans into action-obsessed maniacs, night games for cloaking misdeeds in darkness, mercenary players whose soaring salaries incited envy, and even the larger size of players, which supposedly created a monster effect.[82] Still others, drawing on popular social-biology theories of mankind's genetic-based savagery, suggested that violence was an inborn impulse.

Such armchair speculations were of little avail to promoters. Like their forebears who faced similar problems, promoters continued to rely on time-honored precautions like hiring more police, erecting barriers to playing fields, upgrading parks, and attempting to cultivate better relations with fans. In urging the latter course, Commissioner Bowie Kuhn proposed a half hour of fraternizing between players and fans before games; for their part, most clubs published and distributed informative newsletters to fans and some hired specialists to help ease tensions with neighborhood citizens.[83]

Still, scant input came from the ball park fans, although consumer advocate Ralph Nader encouraged fans to join an organization called FANS (Fight to Advance the Nation's Sports). As envisioned by its founders, FANS would lobby for reasonable ticket and concession costs and press for rule changes desired by spectators. However, lack of interest doomed FANS whose organizers clung to the dubious notion that all sports fans were alike. No doubt many balked at paying a membership fee, including (hopefully) some who might have recalled Gustav Le Bon's warning that "The power of crowds is to be dreaded, but the power of certain castes is to be dreaded yet more."[84]

But there were plenty of reasons for dreading sports crowds of the 1980s as continuing outbreaks of violent behavior plagued many such events. But the realization that they were not the only sufferers afforded small comfort to baseball promoters who saw no lessening of "crowd involvement," by now a preferred euphemism for describing spectator violence.

Not that the euphemism deterred reporters from fulsomely reporting such incidents. Such byplay made good copy even if reported events became repetitious. Thus, reporters told of abusive fans targeting players with the usual missiles. Such assaults on players were frightening enough, but Yankee outfielder Dave Winfield was terrified when an arrow struck the ground near him; so was Angel infielder Wally Joyner when a thrown knife grazed him. Both incidents occurred at Yankee Stadium and when the Yankees visited Anaheim Angel fans, recalling the Joyner assault, retaliated with macabre humor by throwing rubber knives at Yankee players. If such episodes were mercifully rare, the obscenities and racial slurs flung at players were not. As one black player, Yankee pitcher Rudy May, lamented, "There ain't no peace at all." Moreover, if harried players retaliated with curses and obscene gestures they were fined.[85] As for umpires who continued to suffer verbal abuse, at least they were no longer alone; what's more their powerful union barred promoters from showing provocative televised replays of controversial calls at parks.

Of course, many violent episodes pitted fans against fans. Midway through the 1982 season some 400 brawling spectators had been ejected from Shea Stadium while Yankee Stadium security guards at times ejected as many as 50 a night. And in one grim episode at the Shea Stadium parking lot a family was robbed and briefly kidnapped.[86]

Nor was there any lessening of victory riots during the 1980s. Although Philadelphia promoters in 1980 headed off a potential riot by cordoning off the playing field with mounted police and attack dogs after the Phillies won their first World Series, the Detroit riot of 1984 rivaled the infamous "Big Buc Binge" of 1971. After the Tigers clinched their World Series victory, an estimated 10,000 rioters milled outside the park throwing rocks, fighting and stealing—including luggage belonging to a busload of senior citizens. When it ended, one death, 82 injuries, 41 arrests and over $100,000 in property damage was reported.[87]

The continuing wave of ball park violence had pundits spewing explanations, including familiar emotional contagion and catharsis theories of crowd violence. Others cited envious "working class" fans as instigators, and one expert, invoking his "violence for power" theory, fingered hard core fans as culprits, warning that such zealots might resort to assassination of rival players to ensure their team's victory.

For their part promoters continued to cope by using pragmatic measures. Incoming spectators were routinely searched for illegal drugs, liquor or weapons and more security forces were deployed inside and outside of parks. At some parks plainclothesmen mingled with spectators looking for drug users, drunks, exhibitionists and potential troublemakers. At Fenway Park college football players were hired to perform such duties and sometimes they ousted as many as 30 culprits during a game. Similarly Yankee Stadium security forces conducted frequent "sweeps" during the course of games. And at all parks chronic offenders were identified and denied admission. Of course, such measures were costly; by the 1980s a club's annual security budget averaged $300,000.

Some tremulous promoters went even further in coping with the problem. Some eliminated liquor sales, a move that deprived Chicago promoters of $100,000 a year in lost revenues at Comiskey Park. Elsewhere promoters, hearkening to security executive warnings that "the goddamn beer" was a violence precipitator, established curfews on such sales and even considered banning them altogether.[88]

As the decade of the 1980s drew to its close, promoters continued to wrestle with the vexing problem of controlling ball park crowds. Still, when viewed from an historical perspective some comfort could be gleaned by understanding that the problem was neither a new one nor one that posed a major threat to the social order. After all, promoters of the past faced similar problems with smaller crowds accounting for outbursts that rivaled those of the present. What's more, the game survived and continued to thrive. Thus comforted, promoters of today ought not to view the problem as a new aberration, but rather as a part of a continuing human tragedy—that men still know so little of men.

To better understand the human condition has always been the goal of historians. In recent years a rising tribe of sports historians has joined the quest. Hopefully, this brief and tentative foray into the counting, courting and controlling of baseball's ball park fans will inspire others to shed light on this vital constituency of major league baseball.

NOTES

The author expresses his gratitude to his colleague at Albright College, Prof. Thomas D. Meyers, Ph.D, for his development of the graphic presentations of some of the data contained in this article.

1. David Q. Voigt, *America Through Baseball*, Chicago, 1976; *Sports Illustrated*, Jan. 16, 1989.

2. George Kirsch, "Baseball Spectators, 1855–1870," *Baseball History*, fall 1987.

3. Harry Ellard, *Baseball in Cincinnati,* Cincinnati, 1907; Henry Chadwick, Scrapbooks, I. New York Public Library; *Sporting Life,* Feb. 16, 1887; *Cincinnati Commercial,* June 15, 1870; Hy Turkin and C.S. Thompson, *The Official Baseball Encyclopedia,* New York, 1956.

4. Bill James, *The Bill James Historical Baseball Abstract,* New York, 1985; *Chicago Tribune,* January 18, 21, 22, 28, 1871; *Beadle's Dime Base Ball Player,* 1875.

5. Harry Wright, Note and Account Books, IV, New York Public Library; *Boston Daily Globe,* Oct. 1, 1879; *Boston Herald,* Aug. 26, 1883; *New York Clipper,* Oct. 6, 1883.

6. *Spalding Guide,* 1888.

7. Lowell Reidenbaugh, *Take Me Out to the Ballpark,* St. Louis, 1983; Philip J. Lowry, *Green Cathedrals,* Cooperstown, NY, 1986.

8. *Sporting Life,* Oct. 16, 1889; *New York Clipper,* Oct. 23, 1889; *Reach Guide,* 1891 cites Players League attendance figures of 980,000 to 813,000 for the NL. *Reach Guide,* 1895.

9. *Spalding Guide,* 1893.

10. *Spalding Guide,* 1895; *The Sporting News,* Dec. 25, 1897.

11. *Sporting Life,* Dec. 24, 1898.

12. *Spalding Guide,* 1900.

13. *Reach Guide,* 1901, 1902.

14. Reidenbaugh, *loc. cit.* Lowry, *loc. cit.* The remainder of this discussion is based on data provided in the accompanying charts and on chapter introductions from David Q. Voigt, *Baseball: An Illustrated History,* University Park, PA, 1987.

15. Allen Guttmann, *Sports Spectators,* New York, 1986, 145; Steven Riess, *Touching Base: Professional Baseball and American Culture in the Progressive Era,* Westport, CT, 1980, 26–39; George Kirsch, *loc. cit.,* 6. Both Guttman and Riess used photo analysis in their efforts to determine the class composition of ball park crowds. Photos showing large numbers of spectators wearing white collars impressed Riess who also cited the starting time of games, and the 50 cent basic admission price of games to support his middle class argument.

16. Guttman, *Sports Spectators,* 112–113; Riess, *Touching Base,* 39.

17. Kirsch, *loc. cit.,* 12; Guttman, *Sports Spectators,* 115.

18. G.H. Fleming, *The Unforgettable Season,* New York, 1981, *passim;* also, Charles Alexander, *John McGraw,* New York, 1988, *passim* and Roger Angell, *Season Ticket,* Boston, 1988, *passim.*

19. Brent Staples, "Where Are the Black Fans?" *New York Times Magazine,* May 17, 1987.

20. Ray Kennedy, "More Victories Equals More Fans Equals More Profits, Right? Wrong, Wrong, Wrong," *Sports Illustrated,* April 28, 1980.

21. Lonnie Wheeler, *Bleachers: A Summer at Wrigley Field,* New York, 1988, 3, 13–15, 38, 54–57, 65–66, 130–133.

22. David Q. Voigt, *American Baseball: From Gentleman's Sport to the Commissioner System,* University Park, PA, 1983; Lowry, *Green Cathedrals,* 31.

23. David Q. Voigt, *America Through Baseball,* Chicago, 1976.

24. *The Sporting News,* Dec. 11, 1886.

25. *Brooklyn Eagle,* March 30, 1889; *Philadelphia Public Ledger,* July 19, 1889; Voigt, *American Baseball: From Gentleman's Sport to the Commissioner System.*

26. David Q. Voigt, *American Baseball: From the Commissioners to Continental Expansion,* University Park, PA, 1983; Lowry, *Green Cathedrals,* 31.

27. Riess, *op. cit;* Harold Seymour, *Baseball: The Golden Age,* New York, 1971, 344; Angell, *op. cit.,* 250.

28. Voigt, *loc. cit.;* C.S. Thompson and Hy Turkin, *The Official Encyclopedia of Baseball,* New York, 1956.

29. Voigt, *loc. cit.;* Oscar Eddleton, "Under the Lights," *Baseball Research Journal,* 1980.

30. Gerald Eskenazi, *Bill Veeck: A Baseball Legend,* New York, 1988; Bill Veeck and Ed Linn, *The Hustler's Handbook,* New York, 1965; Bill Veeck and Ed Linn, *Veeck As in Wreck,* New York, 1963, 337–339.

31. *The Sporting News,* Feb. 15, 1950, Feb. 18, 1967; *New York Times,* Sept. 3, 1967 Dec. 4, 1967; *New York Post,* July 11, 1967.

32. Lowry, *Green Cathedrals,* 32.

33. *The Sporting News*, March 5, 1977; *New York Times*, June 1, 1986; *Sports Illustrated*, May 18, 1970.

34. *The Sporting News*, Sept. 20, 1987.

35. Wheeler, *Bleachers: A Summer At Wrigley Field*, 197–198; Paul Adomites, "Concessions" in John Thorn and Pete Palmer, *Total Baseball*, New York, 1989, 669–670.

36. *Baseball Digest*, July, 1959; *New York Times*, July 14, 1968, June 27, 1971; Larry Keith, "Beer is Out, Halters In," *Sports Illustrated*, July 18, 1977.

37. *New York Times*, July 8, 1983.

38. *Ibid.*, Oct. 1, 1982.

39. *Ibid.*, June 1, 1986; David Q. Voigt, *Baseball: An Illustrated History*.

40. *New York Times*, June 1, 1986.

41. Bill Gilbert and Lisa Twyman, "Violence: Out of Hand in the Stands," *Sports Illustrated*, Jan. 31, 1983.

42. *New York Times*, April 7, 1972, Aug. 14, 1972.

43. Kirsch, *loc. cit.*

44. *Cincinnati Commercial*, June 15, 1870.

45. Albert G. Spalding, *America's National Game*, New York, 1911, 189ff.

46. Henry Chadwick, Scrapbooks, I.

47. *New York Clipper*, July 10, 1875.

48. *Chicago Tribune*, Sept. 3, 1882; Paul Adomites, "The Fans," in Thorn and Palmer, *op. cit.*, 667–668.

49. *The Sporting News*, Dec. 11, 1886.

50. *Sporting Life*, May 13, 1883.

51. *New York Clipper*, Aug. 29, 1896.

52. *Philadelphia Inquirer*, June 1, 1883.

53. *New York Times*, May 21, 1888.

54. Voigt, *America Through Baseball*.

55. *New York Clipper*, Feb. 10, 1883.

56. *Philadelphia Inquirer*, April 29, 1884; *Chicago Tribune*, June 28, 1885.

57. *Sporting Life*, June 18, 1884.

58. *Spalding Guide*, 1884, 1887.

59. *Ibid.*, 1898, 1899.

60. *Brooklyn Eagle*, Oct. 9, 1889.

61. *New York Clipper*, Sept. 30, 1893; *Sporting Life*, April 22, 1893, Aug. 26, 1893.

62. *Sporting Life*, April 28, 1894, Oct. 5, 1895; Frederick G. Lieb, *The Baltimore Orioles*, New York, 1953, 34–42.

63. *Sporting Life*, Oct. 12, 1895.

64. *New York Clipper*, March 19, 1898, May 20, 1899; *Spalding Guide*, 1899.

65. *Boston Daily Globe*, Aug. 20, 1898; *Sporting Life*, Aug. 27, 1898; *Spalding Guide*, 1899.

66. *Reach Guide*, 1894, 1899; William B. Mead, *Even the Browns*, Chicago, 1978, 53.

67. *The Sporting News*, Aug. 6, 1898.

68. *Ibid.*, June 1, 1898.

69. Lowell Reidenbaugh, *100 Years of National League Baseball, 1876–1976*, St. Louis, 1976.

70. *Ibid.*; Harold Seymour, *Baseball: The Golden Age*, New York, 1971, 113–115.

71. G.H. Fleming, *The Unforgettable Season*, New York, 1981, *passim*.

72. Glenn Stout, "The Grand Exalted Ruler of Rooter's Row," *The Sox Fan News*, Aug., 1986; *The Sporting News*, Jan. 1, 1898.

73. David Q. Voigt, *Baseball: An Illustrated History*; Larry Gerlach, *The Men in Blue; Conversations With Umpires*, New York, 1980, *passim*.

74. Reidenbaugh, *op. cit.*; Eugene Murdock, *Ban Johnson, Czar of Baseball*, Westport, CT, 1982, 81–82, 106–107.

75. Reidenbaugh, *op. cit.*; Seymour, *op. cit*, 57–59; Paul Adomites, "The Fans," 665–667.

76. *The Sporting News*, June 24, 1972; Ed Linn, "Ballplayers vs. Fans," *Saturday Evening Post*, Aug. 19, 1971; Ron Fimrite, "Take Me Out to the Brawl Game," *Sports Illustrated*, June 17, 1974; *New York Times*, April 27, 1978.

77. David Q. Voigt, *American Baseball: From Postwar Expansion to the Electronic Age,* University Park, PA, 1983, 154–155.

78. *Philadelphia Inquirer,* Aug. 7, 1977; Adomites, "The Fans," *loc. cit.*

79. *New York Times,* Oct. 21, 1972.

80. *Philadelphia Inquirer,* Aug. 7, 1977.

81. *Psychology Today,* Oct. 1977.

82. Charles Einstein, "The New Breed of Baseball Fan," *Harper's,* July, 1967; R. Poe, "The Angry Fan," *ibid.,* Nov, 1975.

83. *The Sporting News,* Dec. 10, 1970; *New York Times,* Oct. 31, 1977, May 8, 1978; Veeck, *Veeck As in Wreck,* 337–339.

84. Ralph Nader and Peter Gruenstine, "Fans: The Sorry Majority," *Playboy,* March, 1978; Gustav Le Bon, *The Crowd,* New York, 1975.

85. Dave Winfield, *Winfield: A Player's Life,* New York, 1988, 268–270; *The Sporting News,* May 30, 1981.

86. Bil Gilbert and Lisa Twyman, *loc. cit.; The Sporting News,* April 18, 1981; *New York Times,* July 30, 1982, Aug. 14, 1982.

87. *Time,* Oct. 29, 1984.

88. Mark Cram, "Wild in the Seats," *Playboy,* Feb. 1982; Winfield, *op. cit.,* 266–267; *New York Times,* July 30, 1982, Aug. 14, 1982.

The Dixon Cornbelt League

W.P. KINSELLA

"Mike, I think I've found the perfect place for you to play," my agent said. His name is Justin Birdsong, and we've never met. He'd signed me up because a year ago I looked like a top prospect for the Bigs. The last time I heard from him was a few days after the college draft—a draft where I wasn't picked up. He said in spite of the lack of interest in me, he was impressed with my credentials and thought he could find me a job in minor league baseball.

Not being drafted was a particular disappointment, though not unexpected; the Expos had drafted me fourth in my junior year and I turned down a sizable bonus to sign because I wanted to finish my degree, and because I felt I needed another year of experience. Well, I got the year of experience. No injuries. Might have been better if I had been injured, then I could have had something on which to blame my decline. My average fell from .331 to .270, my stolen bases from 40 to 19, and I was caught stealing 9 times. My play at second base, which has always been just adequate, remained that way.

I don't blame the pros for not drafting me, but I also feel that if I get in a solid year of minor league ball, I'm young enough that they'll be willing to have another look.

After the draft *Baseball America* mentioned that I was the best looking second baseman not drafted. "In practice, Mike Houle is as good as anyone who's ever played the game. Perhaps with experience he'll get a second look from big league scouts."

"I can get you a contract with a team in Iowa," Justin Birdsong said. "League representative called this morning; they've got openings for all kinds of players, but they were especially interested in you. You'll be with a semi-pro club in the Dixon Cornbelt League. They play good quality baseball, close to Double A, they assure me. They also tell me that the big league scouts make regular stops at all their ballparks."

"It doesn't look as if I have much choice," I said. "Teams in organized baseball aren't exactly burning up the phone wires to either me or you, and everything I get in the mail is addressed to Occupant."

"That's the spirit," said Justin B. "I'll tell them you accept. I'll call them and they'll wire you travel money. You're to report to Grand Mound, Iowa, day after tomorrow. Oh, one other thing, since the Dixon Cornbelt League is unaffiliated, all the teams are self-supporting, what will happen is you'll get a base salary, but one of the sponsoring merchants will give you a job in the mornings. You'll have your afternoons free for practice and you play in the evenings."

The salary he named wasn't enough to pay room and board, and I told him so.

"Forgot to mention, you get free room and board with a local family. I only take commission on your baseball pay. The league representative said that since you're a business major the local insurance office will pay you to work mornings for them. You'll do fine."

"It doesn't look as if I have much choice," I repeated. "I'll be there."

***

At the Cedar Rapids Airport, I was met by a large, hearty man named Emmett Powell. The weather was hot, humid for so early in the year. Powell was in shirtsleeves, his gray suitcoat over his arm. He might have been an athlete 30 years ago, I decided. Now, his thinning hair was combed straight back off a high, ruddy forehead; his belly swelled comfortably over his belt.

"Well, Mike," he said, pumping my hand, "I'm sure you're gonna enjoy your summer in Grand Mound. And, no, before you ask, the town wasn't named for a baseball mound, though a long time ago there was a town over near Iowa City that was called Big Inning, and it was named for baseball."

We made our way to his car. I was surprised to find his wife, a pleasant, innocent-looking woman, there. In fact his whole family was there. A high school age girl and a docile brown-and-white spaniel were in the back seat. The wife was Marge, the daughter Tracy Ellen, the dog Sarge.

You'll be boarding with us this summer," Emmett Powell said. "In a small town like ours there's competition over who gets to house the ball players. Competition among families with marriageable daughters gets downright fierce," and he laughed good naturedly.

"Oh, Dad," said Tracy Ellen, exasperation in her voice. She was a pale blond with a few freckles across the bridge of her nose.

"Emmett, you behave yourself," said Marge. "Don't want to frighten this boy away."

"I just hope Mike likes cherry pie," said Emmett. "One thing we do in Grand Mound is eat well, and nobody bakes a better cherry pie than Tracy Ellen, unless of course it's her mother."

"Think you'll be able to stand all this wholesomeness?" asked Tracy Ellen.

"It'll be a change," I said. "My mom died when I was eight. My dad, my older brother and me have been baching it ever since."

"That's what we heard," said Emmett, and I wondered briefly where he had heard it. But then I supposed whoever had scouted me must have checked into my background too.

"What about my job?" I asked.

"Oh, didn't I mention? You'll be working for me. I'm the Independent Insurance Agent in Grand Mound. Got me a little office on Main Street, but end up doing most of my business from the house. Folks just drop by when the spirit moves them. It's certainly not the fast lane, but we live well. I'm planning to retire at 62, just 10 years from now. It will be a fine business for an enterprising . . . "

"Emmett, the boy hasn't even seen Grand Mound yet. Don't be trying to sell him your business. You'll have to forgive him, Mike," Mrs. Powell said, turning back to face me, "Emmett and his friends are so enthusiastic about small town life. They're worried that the small towns are going to disappear in another generation or two."

"Did you know, Mike," Emmett picked right up, "Iowa has more small towns for its size and population than any other state. They say there's a town about every half mile on every secondary highway in the state. But the farms are getting larger and the farmers fewer in number. When the farmers go the small towns die. But I guess we won't have to worry about that for a few years. Grand Mound is one of the few towns to show an increase in population. And I believe having a team in the Dixon Cornbelt League is a prime reason. You'd be surprised at how many of our players decide to become full time residents here."

The Powells lived in a two-story, white frame house on a tree-lined street. My room was on the second floor, large and bright with a huge double bed and polished hardwood floors.

They did eat well, roast pork and potatoes, three vegetables, iced tea, cherry pie. They forced seconds on me, offered thirds, insisted on a late evening snack of pie and ice cream, repeatedly pointed out that I was free to raid the refrigerator at any time.

"What teams are in the league?" I asked Emmett as I accepted another piece of pie and ice cream from Tracy Ellen. "I'm afraid my agent didn't know, or didn't tell me much."

"Not likely that you've ever heard of the teams, all small towns that sit in a row along Highway 30; there's Mount Vernon, Lisbon, Mechanicsville, Wheatland, Grand Mound, Clarence, and DeWitt."

"That's seven teams," I said. "Makes for a difficult schedule."

"Makes for three games every night of the summer," said Emmett jovially. "DeWitt's the biggest town, almost 5,000 people, Mount Vernon's next with 4,000, only us and Wheatland have less than 1,000 population. Big towns use some local talent. We had to import our whole team at first, but this year you're one of only five new players, most of the team's settled down in Grand Mound, several have married local girls." As he beamed at me his eyes moved to Tracy Ellen, who was sitting beside him on the sofa, balancing her plate on her knee. She was wearing pastel-pink shorts and top, her feet were tiny, her shoes the same pink as her clothes.

"How long has the Dixon Cornbelt League operated? I've honestly never heard of it. I took a quick glance at the *Sporting News* but couldn't find out anything about it. And how long has Grand Mound had a team?"

"Oh, the league has been around for years and years. We're unaffiliated, outside of organized baseball, which is why the *Sporting News* doesn't write us up. And Grand Mound has had a team for, oh, several years. You'll like the other players, most of them are college boys like yourself."

***

"I want to show you something," Emmett said to me later in the evening. I was sitting on the porch swing watching fireflies quivering in the tall honeysuckle. The night was silent, the heat seemed touchable, velvety. Emmett rose from a cushioned wicker chair, picked his way down the three steps to the driveway, beckoned to me in the instant before he became just another shadow amidst the moonlight-gilded leaves.

I got in the passenger side of the car and Emmett drove the few blocks to Highway 30, not turning on the lights until we were at least a block from the house. The highway was a ribbon of blackness winding between equally black fields, planting was just finished for the season.

"What you're gonna see," said Emmett, "are small town baseball fields. The other teams do their practicing at night, in fact there are exhibition games on down the line a ways. If you hadn't had such a long flight, and if it wasn't your first night here, we could have gone and scouted the opposition. Every second town we pass will have a stadium lit up like Times Square. From a distance some of them look like fire on the ocean . . . " and he trailed off unable to find the right words.

He was right to do that, for there were no words to adequately convey what we saw. Suddenly, we would take a sweeping turn into a town, and there on one side or other of the highway, like a burst of fireworks, would be the ballpark. Or, as we rolled along, the park would bloom out of the sensitive blue-black night, like a giant marigold. We would catch a glimpse of the emerald grass, perhaps a flash of white uniform before we would be gone again, the lights behind us, our future as if we were driving into ink.

The next town would be subdued, a twinkle of streetlight the only illumination, usually we could pick out the empty ballpark, huddled beside the highway like a huge, sleeping animal curled against the night. Then we pressed on, watching the horizon for the golden aura of another ballpark, another night game.

In the morning, after a breakfast offering more variety than most cafes, we headed for the office, Marge and Tracy Ellen waving goodbye from the porch as Emmett backed the car out.

Powell Real Estate and Insurance occupied half of a small yellow-painted building on Main Street. The other half housed a barbershop. The office consisted of three very old wooden desks, each one buried under a mound of papers, three, three-drawer filing cabinets, and a table holding a coffee maker. The building faced east and the window was tinted blue to keep the room cooler.

We did little work. Emmett assigned me the smallest desk in the office, explained that he had a part time secretary who came in three halfdays a week to do most of the clerical work and bookkeeping. Fifteen minutes after we arrived there were five people in the office, none of them customers, all there to look at and appraise the new second baseman. After another 15 minutes Emmett hung a small, well worn sign on the glass of the front door. It read: BACK IN 5 MINUTES. Then we all made our way across the street to the Doll House Cafe where, I suspect I met half the population of Grand Mound and vicinity before we headed home for lunch. There was a constantly rotating crowd at the cafe. A farmer in bib overalls or a townsman in shirtsleeves would come in and sit at our table for a few minutes, then exchange greetings with people at the other tables and be on his way.

The cafe owner, a large, jolly woman named Mrs. Nesbitt, offered me breakfast, then forced pie and milk on me, and tried to feed me seconds.

What puzzled me was that every person who dropped by promised to be at our practice, which was set for 2 P.M.

And they were. The Grand Mound team was called the Greenshirts, and our uniforms were a beautiful enamel-white with Kelly green trim, numbers and names. Our sweatshirts and socks were the same blazing green.

The field was picture-perfect, lovingly tended. The park was small as a button, the fence at the foul lines 298 feet, the center-field wall was 350 feet away. As we began our warmups I was amazed to see the stands filling, just as if there was a game scheduled. Behind the main grandstand the concessions were open, dispensing hot dogs, ice cream and soda.

The groundskeeper, a stoop-shouldered man named Jeremy, came around to shake hands with each player, said if we had any suggestions as to how he could improve the playing field for us, just to let him know.

I'd guess there were more than 800 people at the practice, about three-quarters of what the stands could hold. We held a routine practice and workout: calisthenics, wind sprints, stretching exercises, batting and fielding practice. The squad was larger than I would have anticipated, over 30 players, with a preponderance of pitchers.

The manager was a surprise. A name I knew, Gene Walston, a slim, graying man with a complexion like concrete. Walston had been a third base coach in the Bigs for many years, even had the nickname "Suicide" Walston, derived from his propensity to wave runners around third no matter how slim their chance of scoring. He even got to manage the final 50 games of a season after the regular manager had a heart attack. But the team blew a five game lead, lost their division, and the next season Walston was gone. He'd been away from the Bigs for over five years. It never occurred to me to wonder what had become of him.

It looked as if I was going to have competition. There was another second baseman in camp, a year or two older than me, a better fielder though he didn't appear as fast on the bases. I couldn't tell from batting practice what kind of hitter he was.

"We'll play our first intersquad game tomorrow night," the manager said, as practice was breaking up.

***

It was after that first intersquad game, after playing to a full house, that I began to suspect something unusual was going on. We were two distinct squads, half in the home team uniform, half in the visitor's uniforms of green with white trim. But I didn't have much time to worry, for immediately after the game was over a round, freckle-faced man appeared to shake my hand.

"I'm Dilly Eastwick, the sports editor," he said, his small hand damp in mine. "I make a point of covering every Greenshirt game myself. Now, Mike, I want you to know I really appreciated your play this evening, why you danced like Baryshnikov all around second base, and that backhanded stop you made in the seventh inning was one of the best plays I've ever seen."

"Thank you very much, Mr. Eastwick," I said.

"Oh, don't thank me. It was a perfect pleasure to watch you play," his eyes twinkled and his round, moon face beamed.

The line about me dancing like Baryshnikov appeared in the next edition of the *Grand Mound Leader*. Later in the week, he compared my throws to first from deep behind second and the right-field grass to a gunboat firing across the prow of a suspect ship. In the following issue he tagged me with a nickname. Mike "Gunboat" Houle, the story said, effortlessly handled six chances in the field, and turned the pivot flawlessly on three double plays.

One cannot help but be pleased with press like that.

The next week, Dilly, as he insisted all the players call him, wrote about the catcher for the Green squad, Bill Baker, a boy from Mississippi who had arrived in Grand Mound the same day I did. "He fires clotheslines to second base," Dilly Eastwick wrote, "so straight and true that the flight path remains marked in the air for innings. In fact you could hang the entire family wash on one of the throws of 'Clothesline' Baker."

And so it went. Dilly Eastwick was like an agent and press agent rolled into one. He eventually wrote up every newcomer to the team; it seemed the returning players all had nicknames. The townspeople addressed us by our nicknames when we passed on the street.

"When do they start making the cuts?" I asked one of the players who was starting his third season with the Greenshirts.

"Oh, not for a few days yet."

"But there are so many players," I insisted, "two full squads."

"Don't fret," said the player, "they carry a large roster."

***

"I can't believe how pushy my parents are," said Tracy Ellen, coming to sit beside me on the porch swing a few evenings after I arrived. At supper that evening Emmett had praised her cooking to the skies, for about the tenth meal in a row. "They're so obvious."

"I understand what they're trying to do," I said. "I think they mean well."

The moon hung heavy, the color of papaya. The leaves of the mountain ash tree in the front yard were flickering with moonlight.

"If it'll take some of the pressure off, I already have a boyfriend," said Tracy Ellen. "He doesn't play baseball."

I felt the tiniest tinge of sadness at the announcement. I suppose I'd hoped . . .

135

"They're pushing us together so hard I pretty well have to," she went on. "But I think it would be nice if we could be friends. My brothers are a lot older, went off to college, one lives in New York, one in Chicago; they have families."

"I think having you for a friend would be great," I said. "I've never had a sister; it'll be fun."

"Maybe you can ask Dad to stop trying to marry us off?"

"I'll try to be tactful," I said.

I wasn't very.

"Tracy Ellen and I have made an agreement," I said, on the way to work the next morning. "We're going to be friends, not sweethearts, so you can stop promoting a romance."

Emmett, all innocence, looked at me over the top of his glasses.

"Besides, Tracy Ellen tells me she has a boyfriend."

"Oh, yes," said Emmett, his voice full of disapproval. "A boy from Mechanicsville, built like a Clydesdale, and I might be doing a disservice to the horse to compare their intelligence."

"Sure you aren't just being a protective father?"

"His name is Shag Wilson. He chews snuff. He drives a customized half-ton truck with tractor tires about eight feet tall."

"You've made your point," I said.

***

Something is not right here in Grand Mound, but I can't put my finger on it. I have been here a month now. I have never been happier. The Dixon Cornbelt League opens play in a few days. We play an intersquad game every night, hold an informal practice in the afternoon, work at our various jobs in the morning. Our lives are busy, we fraternize little. Our *families* are there after every game; we head home with them. I am playing better than I've ever played in my life. In one way I can't wait for a Big League scout to discover me. I'll bet, the way I'm playing, I could jump straight to Triple A. But when I think of that, even when I think of the Dixon Cornbelt League opening in a few days, my back tightens, and the lump of live anxiety that has followed me all my playing days, reappears in my belly. I hoped it had gone away, but it was only lurking out in the night, on vacation perhaps.

When I think of the pressure of playing professional baseball, pressure from the fans, from the manager and coaches, from myself . . . the voices of all my coaches blend together like crows scrapping: close your shoulders; level your swing; even your stance; hit on the ground; take an outside pitch to the opposite field; cover the bag; turn the pivot; on your toes; glove on the ground; back up the base; take the cutoff; a walking lead. Eventually with all the snappish voices whirling about me I freeze, mind and body blank as snow. The baseball field becomes a bad dream, my stomach feels as if it is full of broken glass.

I remember jolting awake, standing at my position, when I should have covered first on a sacrifice play. The first baseman charged, the pitcher fielded the bunt, had no one to throw to. I remember the fans jeering, the pitcher slamming the ball into his glove, glowering at me. The manager, his eyes glowing in the dusk of the dugout, spits in my direction. I want to hide, to become invisible; I don't want to play professionally; I only want to play for fun.

***

There is something I don't like about Dilly Eastwick. For all his sincerity there is something sneaky about him, not exactly evil, but furtive; he gives the impression he is always looking over his shoulder, even while he is smiling and shaking my hand his eyes are somewhere in the corner of the room.

After practice I dropped in at the Grand Mound Library, a very old stone-pillared building, one of the original Carnegie endowments, Emmett has told me proudly.

"Well, Gunboat, how can I help you?" said Mrs. Thoman, the librarian, a sturdy woman in a blue crepe dress.

"I'd like to see the *Grand Mound Leader* for the current month but from, say, three and four years ago," I said. I found it embarrassing to be called by my nickname, especially by this cross-looking, matronly woman, but I also knew that she was one of the townspeople who never missed a game. She always sat directly behind first base, clutching a white-on-green pennant. The green-on-white pennant holders tended to sit on the third base side.

"Are you certain you want to do that?" she said, in what I'm sure, for her, was a motherly way.

"Why wouldn't I?" I said. "I'm a great fan of Dilly Eastwick, I just want to read some of his past columns."

Mrs. Thoman turned away without speaking, leaving me on the brown linoleum, the library smell of dry paper and varnish heavy in the air. She returned with an armload of papers and deposited them on a table.

As I read, I noticed that she made several phone calls. I couldn't make out any of her whispered conversation.

What I found immediately confirmed my suspicions. From a column four years earlier, Dilly wrote, "last night our second baseman, Lew "Gunboat" Driscoll, danced like Baryshnikov around second base." A day later he wrote about the new catcher, "August Marsh threw a clothesline to second base in the seventh inning to nail a runner. The flight path was so straight and true that it remained marked in the air for innings."—Dilly closed by saying, "August 'Clothesline' Marsh is going to have an outstanding season for the Greenshirts."

I didn't say anything to anyone, but I kept my eyes open. We continued to play our daily intersquad game. Twice I suggested to other players that after the game we drive to one of the other towns in the league, maybe look over some of our competition. The players looked at me strangely, each declined, saying their *families* were waiting for them.

As opening day approached Emmett announced that our opening game had been postponed; we were supposed to play Mechanicsville. "Some of their college players haven't arrived yet," Emmett said. "We'll make the games up later in the summer, wouldn't want to take advantage of them when they're shorthanded."

"You don't need a league," I said, "you get a full house for every intersquad game anyway."

I thought I heard somebody laugh.

When the postponement was announced Gil Morgenstern, a pretty good left-handed-hitting third baseman, had a fierce argument with the manager, and eventually with the third base coach and even with Emmett who went into the manager's office glancing apologetically over his shoulder. I could hear the raised voices but couldn't make out what the argument was about. The result, however, was that Gil Morgenstern packed his equipment and without a good-bye to anyone was driven to Cedar Rapids to catch a plane home to New York.

***

That evening I decided to confront Emmett.

"Emmett, Grand Mound really doesn't have a team in the Dixon Cornbelt League, do they? Be honest with me." We were sitting on the porch swing late in the evening, the sky was still indigo, a few fireflies jiggled among the honeysuckle bush closest to the porch.

"Well now . . ."

"My agent believed he'd found me a real amateur league where the Big League scouts would be looking in . . ."

"Well now, Mike, your agent's way out in California, and what he doesn't know about Iowa would fill a book or two. We may have exaggerated a bit, stretched the truth if you will . . ."

"Like lying about Grand Mound being a member of the league?"

"Now, Mike, we have the league's word that if a team drops out, or if a franchise fails, why Grand Mound gets the first opportunity to enter a team."

"For how many years?"

"Pardon?"

"How long have you been waiting?"

"Folks here in rural Iowa are set in their ways, Mike. They don't change much, and when they do they change slowly."

"How long?"

"We've . . . we've been in our present situation since just after World War II."

"But how could you do this to me, to the other players? Do you realize how unfair you are? You're ruining our chances of playing professional baseball just so you can entertain the local people with exhibition baseball, while you're trying to convince us to live here permanently."

"It's not like that at all, Mike. And I think deep down you know what I'm trying to say. You're smart, and I like you a lot, in fact I like you so much I'd be proud to have you as a son-in-law . . ."

"If things aren't the way I described, how are they? How do you see them?"

"Mike, what kind of a ball player were you in college?"

"Pretty good. You know my record."

"What did you do when the pressure was on, Mike?"

I knew what he was getting at and the force of it was like a knife twisting in my chest.

"I . . . well . . ."

"What did you do when things got tough, Mike?"

"I choked. The year I had to impress the scouts, I choked."

"We know. And we understand."

"Then everyone on the team is like me?"

"Including the manager."

" "Suicide" Walston. Of course, if anybody ever choked in the clutch . . . Do the other players know?"

"Yes. And I have to admit I've taken a little razzing from the boys down at the Doll's House Cafe. Did you believe in Santa Claus and the Tooth Fairy for a long time, too?"

"As a matter of fact, I did. And I didn't want to believe that there was anything odd going on here. Everything is so perfect . . . So everyone else knows? Is that why Morgenstern left the team so suddenly?"

"He was a denier, Mike. Claimed he'd never choked in his whole life. Didn't believe a word we told him. He'll be better off back in New York. Not happier, but better off."

"Is there something magical going on here?"

"Magical? No."

"But a team that isn't a team?"

"Mike, I think if you'll look at what we've done you'll agree that the people who originally got the idea were years ahead of their time. They saw the future, Mike, saw that the small towns were going to die, dry up and blow away like fall leaves. And they said how can we keep our town together? We can't stop our young people from going off to the cities, but maybe we could bring some folks here who, if we made life attractive for them, would stay here, marry into the community, keep the faith, so to speak. At first the plan didn't work at all; we saw baseball as the key to luring young men here, but we didn't have a team in the Dixon Cornbelt League, and there was no real possibility of us getting one. At first we brought in talented players, but when they found out what we wanted, when they found out there was no league, nothing but intersquad games, they were gone in every direction like a flock of startled birds. Then someone hit on the idea of scouting out players who didn't come through in the clutch. We had all seen hundreds of them, some of us had been there ourselves: pretty fair amateur ballplayers until the crunch came.

"In Grand Mound we gave those players a place to play baseball, a way to play so they were never in a situation where they had a chance to choke."

"But didn't they run off, too, when they realized what the situation was?"

"Oh, the first few years were pretty rough, but you know, Mike, deep in his heart, every player who is a choker knows it. Even now the odd one won't admit it, but to most it's such an immense relief to know the pressure's off, that they make a real effort to fit right in here in Grand Mound."

"Everyone on the squad knows but me?"

"Some are slower to catch on than others, Mike. Your teammates are just bursting to tell you, but I think it's been over 10 years since any player spilled the beans, so to speak. We only bring in four or five players a season now, and soon, we hope, there's going to be a season when the whole squad will return intact."

"And Marge and Tracy Ellen? They know everything?"

"Can't live around Grand Mound for long without knowing. Marge and I have been married 27 years, even back then I had to compete with a ball player who was courting her. That was a real dilemma for the folks who managed the ball club. If she married the ball player Grand Mound gained a citizen. They'd have been a lot happier if I went off to Iowa City or Ames to find me a wife, but they decided to let nature take its course, and happily, Marge chose me."

"And you chose me for Tracy Ellen?"

"I scouted you myself, Mike. Actually the whole family scouted you. I took my annual holidays and the three of us flew down to U.C., Davis, watched seven home games. We even sat at the next table in a restaurant called the Blue . . . something-or-other."

"Blue Parrot."

"Right. You never noticed us, of course. You were with a dark-haired girl and another couple; you ordered roast beef and cherry pie a la mode."

"Tracy Ellen scouted me, too?"

"You were her choice for second base."

"What about this boyfriend with the truck? Somebody's been lying to me."

"Not lying, Mike, just being a little devious. But I'd say it worked pretty well, for everybody concerned."

"And Shag Wilson?"

"A lot nicer boy than I let on. If you check the files you'll find he got his truck insurance at a whopping discount."

"That's more than devious."

"Mike, are you happy?"

I considered for a few seconds before nodding.

"What more can I say? You sleep on it, son. I honestly think you could catch on with a Triple A ball club, and if your heart's set on giving it a try, no one in Grand Mound will stand in your way."

I lay awake for a long time. Tracy Ellen was out on a date, and I mentally tracked every vehicle that turned off the highway until the customized truck rumbled down the street and turned sharply into the driveway. Tracy Ellen kept her goodbyes mercifully short.

When she came in I was waiting on the landing. "You don't have to do that anymore," I said. "Unless you want to."

"You've realized what's going on?"

"Yes."

"I was hoping you would, soon. And I was afraid, too, that you'd leave, like Morgenstern. You're not going to leave, are you? You're not mad?"

"How can I be mad? I can't be mad at people who mean well, who know me better than I know myself. There's only one thing that can make me leave, and that's if you want to keep up this brother-sister arrangement."

Tracy Ellen sighed audibly.

I took her in my arms then, tentatively at first, for she was light and fragile against me, but there was a tenacity to the way she held the hair at the back of my neck as she pressed her mouth into mine. We tiptoed down the stairs and out onto the moonlight and honeysuckle-drenched porch. We sat on the swing, Tracy Ellen with her legs curled under her, an arm around me, her head on my shoulder, her pale hair turned silver by the moon.

"Memorial Day is coming up," said Tracy Ellen.

"We play a double header."

"Fireworks afterward."

"Fireworks are only fun if you can watch them with someone you like a lot, someone you can hold hands with and maybe kiss once or twice."

"When did you know you were going to stay?"

"I think I decided a long time ago. There's something about the way you wave goodbye in the mornings, as if you really mean it, as if you'll truly miss me, that just breaks my heart."

BOOK REVIEWS

INTRODUCTION TO REVIEWS

The following review section does not pretend to cover all the significant baseball books and movies that appeared between this and last year's *Annual*. A book review editor soon learns that even if he aims to be comprehensive, a host of obstacles face him: publishers' publicity departments seemingly intent on avoiding publicity for their authors, books that no reviewer appears interested in, reviewers' busy schedules that require long lead-times (thus eliminating books that are right off the presses) and, of course, the book review editor's own shortcomings.

However, the reviews in this year's *Annual* are certainly representative of the broad scope of baseball history literature and the extraordinary variety of scholars dedicated to the national pastime. The books reviewed range from serious scholarly tomes to slick "coffee table" picture books. The reviewers come from fields as diverse as economics, cultural anthropology, and public administration, as well as from history.

One thing these reviewers have in common is a passion for the game that is reflected in the character of their reviews. The reader will find few wishy-washy, middle-of-the-road critiques. The strong feelings of the baseball fan are reflected in the reviewers' powerful responses (both positive and negative) to what they read or saw. Many of you, who have read or will read the books reviewed, may find yourself as provoked by the reviews as by their subjects. If so, I think the reviewers have done their job and also remained within the tradition of American baseball—where debate and dispute are endemic and a large part of the fun.

This year the reviews have been ordered roughly by category: Biographies & Autobiographies; Oral Histories & Histories; Studies of Teams and Their Cities; Aspects of the Game (e.g., Spring Training); Beyond the Field (e.g., Broadcasting); "Coffee Table Books"; and Fiction and Movies. I hope that this will allow readers a chance to compare new or recent offerings in the different genres of baseball history literature.

Finally, I hope you will have as much fun reading the reviews as I had putting them together. For in addition to a shared passion for the game, all of the reviewers were wonderful people with whom to work. Maybe it says something profound about baseball that it attracts scholars who are just nice people.

Fred Roberts
Michigan State University

McLain, Denny, with Mike Nahrstedt. *Strikeout: The Story of Denny McLain*. St. Louis: The Sporting News Publishing Company, 1988. 288 pp. $16.95.

Niekro, Phil and Joe, with Ken Picking. *The Niekro Files*. Chicago: Contemporary Books, 1988. 227 pp. $16.95.

Smith, Ozzie, with Rob Raines. *Wizard*. Chicago: Contemporary Books, 1988. 187 pp. $16.95.

On average, baseball autobiographies, whether they cover a season or a career, offer much more substantial fare than they used to. Brosnan's *The Long Season* (1960) and Bouton's *Ball Four* (1970) set standards that forever changed the genre. B&B were frank, funny, insightful, moving, and the stories were well written. A generation later, these two are still the best; they have never been surpassed, although they have been occasionally approached and perhaps even equalled (by Pat Jordan, Sadaharu Oh, and Bill Veeck, for example). At the other end of the scale, however, many sports autobiographies are still being published that are no better than the bland porridge that used to be served in pre-B&B days.

Ozzie Smith's *Wizard*, for example, is a generation or two behind its time; it would fit most comfortably on a shelf among baseball books that appeared 40 or 50 years ago. On the other hand, *Strikeout: The Story of Denny McLain*, is an engrossing book that, for better and also for worse, could hardly have been written before the eighties; much of its action takes place in foul territory—but come to think of it, that's true of all the really good ones.

While Denny McLain's is among the most candid of baseball books, Ozzie Smith's is one of the *least* revealing. It is disappointing because after finishing it we know Osborne Earl Smith no better than we did before we started. He grew up in Mobile and Los Angeles, had four brothers and a sister, parents who separated when he was an adolescent, went to college (and graduated, according to the *Baseball Register*), married soon after he became a big leaguer, and apparently has two sons. That sentence just about equals the total amount of attention he devotes to those human interest subjects. The rest of the book—99 percent of it—records in exhausting detail what happened on the baseball diamond season by season. Sooner or later, even Cardinal fans are likely to get bored. A good editor would have returned the manuscript to the authors as a serviceable first draft but unacceptable final copy.

The Niekro Files purportedly consists of exchanges of letters from one brother to the other during the 1987 season. This is an awkward format because it's hard to believe that Phil and Joe actually sat down once or twice a week and wrote two-to-three-page letters to each other. Tape-recorded cassettes, yes, but letters?

In any event, the "letters," if that's what they are, start slowly. They get livelier around the time when the brothers win their 530th victory, passing Jim and Gaylord Perry to become the winningest pitching brothers of all time. Things become even more interesting when Joe tries to explain an emery board that falls out of his pocket during a game—at precisely the moment when four umpires are closing in on the pitching mound to examine Mr. Niekro's glove and uniform for possible contraband. The book ends at an emotional point that all but overwhelms the reader—when Joe pitches in the 1987 World Series—the first time in their long careers that either made it past the league playoffs.

The book has a false and misleading subtitle: "The Uncensored Letters of Baseball's Most Notorious Brothers"—no doubt some zealous marketing executive's bright idea. There is nothing here that anyone could consider censoring, and certainly nothing even remotely "notorious" about the Niekro brothers. (A typical closing line: "I'm going to have some chocolate-chip cookies and cold milk and hit the sack.")

About the only "secrets" a reader will discover is that Phil has worn a toupee for years and that both brothers love polka dancing and fishing almost as much as baseball. Above all, though, they love their families and each other, and indeed it is their willingness to express this love that elevates their book into something quite extraordinary. Athletes all too often seem to be emotional cripples, but the Niekro brothers are refreshingly different: "I love you," they say, matter-of-factly, without discomfort or embarrassment. What the publisher's subtitle really means is that some people at Contemporary Books can't recognize a class act even when they practically trip over it.

Denny McLain's *Strikeout* is less a baseball book than a book about the criminal justice system and the pitfalls, paradoxes and perfidies inherent in human relationships. The only pitcher in more than half a century to win 30 games in a season, McLain's fall from stardom was as rapid as his rise. He won 31 games in 1968, 24 in 1969, and three years later, at the ripe old age of 28, was all washed up.

Thereafter, with no particular skills and a wife and four children to support, he tried to hustle a buck in any way he could. But it was hard to earn enough to stay on the fast track he had grown accustomed to without now and again encountering some less-than-savory characters. As a result, with the passage of time Dennis Dale McLain inevitably got into trouble. In 1985, he was railroaded into a 23-year sentence in federal prison, of which he served an interminable 2½ years before his conviction was thrown out on appeal.

Is it possible for an innocent man to wind up spending hard time in prison? Well, Denny McLain is a scary case in point. He was certainly no babe in the woods, but he deserved 23 years in jail—or even 2½ years, for that matter— about as much as Iran's late Ayatollah Khomeini deserves the Nobel Peace Prize. McLain comes across as self-centered and gullible, not a very good judge of people, someone who all too often, and not entirely by accident, winds up in the wrong place at the wrong time. These aren't admirable qualities, to be sure, but they aren't exactly federal crimes, either.

In McLain's case, the American judicial system failed to administer justice fairly and impartially and the result almost cost him his life; except for the emotional support of his wife, Sharyn (nee Boudreau), he might never have survived the experience. ("On New Year's Eve, 1963, I made the smartest move of my life and she made the dumbest. I asked her to marry me, and she said yes.")

Strikeout is exciting and spellbinding from beginning to end, both because the events described are inherently mind-boggling and because the writing is outstanding. McLain and co-author Mike Nahrstedt have combined to produce a stimulating, fast-paced, and yet thoughtful story that rivals an Elmore Leonard or John D. MacDonald tale of adventure and intrigue. Not to be missed: the chapters on daily life in prison and the description of an unbelievable softball game played in the summer of 1987 on the grounds of the Federal Correctional Institution at Talladega, Alabama.

One final note: none of these three books has an index. Maybe it doesn't much matter with *Wizard,* but readers of *The Niekro Files* and *Strikeout* deserve at least an index of names and probably something more detailed than that.

Lawrence S. Ritter
New York University

Greenberg, Hank. *The Story of My Life.* New York: Times Books, 1989. Edited and with an introduction by Ira Berkow. 311 pp. Illustrations. $19.95.

Hank Greenberg's credentials as baseball star are impeccable. A perennial American League All-Star, "Hammerin Hank" batted a lifetime .313 in a 13-year career spent almost entirely with the Detroit Tigers. Four times the right-handed first baseman led the American League in home runs and in runs batted in. Four times he led the Tigers into the World Series. In 1935 he won the league's Most Valuable Player award. Three years later he hit 58 home runs in a furious chase to catch the Babe. Greenberg's career totals place him among the lifetime leaders in batting average, home runs, slugging percentage, and the ratios of home runs and RBI's to times at bat. The first player ever to earn $100,000 for a single season's play, in 1956 he won election to Baseball's Hall of Fame. No less impressive were his achievements off the field as baseball executive, businessman, and as cultural hero to Jewish-Americans in the 1930s and 1940s. All this and more is captured in this fine autobiography, edited and with an introduction by Ira Berkow.

Greenberg died of cancer in 1986 before he had a chance to finish this book. At the family's request, Berkow completed the task by editing Greenberg's own notes and by introducing material gleaned from interviews with many people who knew the man. At times, the result is choppy. Transitions between Hank's own prose and Berkow's attempt to offer context or to fill in gaps in the story line don't always work. But this is a minor quibble. For the most part, Berkow's intrusions, along with his sensitive introduction, enhance Greenberg's rich story.

Several significant themes move this book well beyond the typical sports autobiography. In his own words, Greenberg offers a vivid picture of the game he played—including the excitement of being on his own as an 18-year-old Bronx boy with minor league teams in North Carolina and Texas, his rise to the Tigers, the wonderful success he enjoyed in Detroit, and his not-always-pleasant contract negotiations with the club's owner Frank Navin. No less interesting are his reminiscences about his teammates and his opponents.

Enmeshed in this unabashed love story of the game is Greenberg's appreciation of his position as both a Jewish and an American hero in the midst of Depression and World War. His well-known decision in 1934 to play on Rosh Hashanah, the Jewish New Year, but not on Yom Kippur, the holiest and most solemn day for Jews everywhere; his conscious efforts to stand up to the barrage of anti-Semitic taunts and gestures he received from other ball players; his important role as an unofficial advisor to other Jewish players such as Henry Eisenstat and Al Rosen; and the affinity he felt and the advice he offered Jackie Robinson, who broke the color line in the major leagues while Greenberg played out his career in Pittsburgh in 1947, are all well-detailed. Despite his own disinterest in formal religion, this second-generation Jewish-American understood the role he played. As he poignantly put it:

> Being Jewish did carry with it a special responsibility. After all, I was representing a couple of million Jews among a hundred million gentiles, and I was always in the spotlight. I was big—six foot four. . . . I was there every day, and if I had a bad day, every son of a bitch was calling me names so that I had to make good. I don't know why I was doing it, but I just had to show them that a Jew could play ball. . . . as time went by, I came to feel that if I, as a Jew, hit a home run, I was hitting one against Hitler (pp. 116–117).

In simplest terms, Greenberg and other highly visible Jewish athletes of his times, regardless of the depth of their religious convictions or ethnic sensibilities, were appropriated as symbols by other American Jews. As symbols, they demonstrated their ability to succeed in America, even in the midst of economic hardship, and showed themselves to be tough, strong Jews capable of resisting oppression—be it in the form of a Father Coughlin or Nazi Germany—in order to survive.

Far more subtle, but no less important, Greenberg's success in the quintessential American game, his willingness to risk his life in military combat in order to defend the country he loved, and his successful career as baseball magnate and financier confirmed the promise of assimilation for many of his generation. For children of immigrants like himself who came of age between the world wars, Greenberg represented the possibility that one could fully appreciate and enjoy what America offered without giving up attachments to an ethnic past. His children's recollections of their father also suggest how historical circumstances and the passage of time made such perceptions less relevant for the next generation. Ironically, the eldest son of perhaps the greatest Jewish American folk hero of the 1930s and 1940s tells us that he grew up in a family so devoid of formal Jewish content that as a Yale college student he believed his religion to be Congregationalist.

Such concerns about the dilution of Jewish identity are at the heart of current debates among Jewish scholars who are less than sanguine about the future of American Jewry. Although hardly intended for that audience, they too will find much richness in this wonderful story of a baseball giant who was also a decent and interesting human being.

Peter Levine
Michigan State University

Ritter, Lawrence S. and Mark Rucker. *The Babe: A Life in Pictures.* New York: Ticknor & Fields, 1988. 282 pp. $40.

Pirone, Dorothy Ruth and Chris Martens. *My Dad, The Babe: Growing Up with an American Hero.* Boston: Quinlan Press, 1988. 251 pp. $17.95.

Babe Ruth has, not surprisingly, been the subject of more than 25 biographies, more than any other baseball player, and probably more than any other American athlete. Among the best are Robert W. Creamer, *Babe: The Legend Comes to Life* (1974) and Marshall Smelser, *The House That Ruth Built* (1975), both written at the time when Hank Aaron was breaking the Babe's home run record. The reasons for the great interest in Ruth are not hard to discern. He was, unquestionably, the greatest player in the history of the national pastime. During his 22-year career he hit 714 home runs, or one every 11.8 times at bat; had a batting average of .342, and a slugging percentage of .690. (Ted Williams is second at a distant .634.) But he was not only the most powerful slugger in baseball history. Ruth was also the best left-handed pitcher of the late 1910s, establishing a record for consecutive World Series innings pitched without yielding a run, a lifetime 2.28 ERA, and a winning percentage of .671 topped by just a couple of men in the Hall of Fame. Babe Ruth changed the nature of major league baseball. Scientific baseball, characterized by stealing, the hit and run, and guile, was replaced by power baseball. He put the home run into the lexicon of baseball and brought out the fans to see this new style of play.

But the Babe was not merely a superstar who was the dominant player in the first Yankee dynasty. In the 1920s (the Golden Age of Sport) when each sport had its leading hero, Ruth shone above them all. Most sports heroes in the 1920s seemed to certify that such traditional American values like hard work and rugged individualism were still relevant even though the United States had become a predominantly urban nation. Actually, while Ruth was an athlete with great prowess, his skills seemed to be more natural rather than the product of hard work, such as an earlier hero like Ty Cobb. Cobb played baseball as serious work, while for Ruth playing baseball was play. Ruth was admired for his achievements accomplished in spite of himself. He was renowned for his sexual and culinary appetites which would have worn out lesser men, but didn't seem to faze him. He was admired for his money-making ability which enabled him to earn a salary in excess of the President of the United States (but then he usually had a better year). He was a hero in a consumer society who spent freely, lived royally, and enjoyed the good life that average Americans could only dream of. And at the same time, this man-child continued to perform superhuman feats such as hitting home runs for invalid boys bedridden in hospitals, or supposedly calling his shots. In the words of Marshall Smelser "he is our Hercules, our Samson, Beowulf, Siegfried." Like the heroes of mythology he stirred the public imagination and earned its affection and respect.

Each of the two latest additions to the Babe Ruth bibliography, Lawrence S. Ritter and Mark Rucker's *The Babe: A Life in Pictures* (1988) and Dorothy Ruth Pirone's *My Dad: The Babe* (1988) has its own particular niche to fill. As the title suggests, *The Babe: A Life in Pictures,* is a visual survey of the life of the Bambino. The text is by Ritter, the noted author of *The Glory of Their Times,* and is a very good summary of the life and career of Ruth, although one should not expect any great new revelations. He does not, for example, take a particular stand on such controversial events as Ruth's illness in 1925 or his "calling" his home run off Charley Root in the 1932 World Series. Rucker assembled the graphics. He is identified by the publisher in a blurb as "the game's greatest pictorial archivist," and if this book is any evidence, that was not an exaggeration.

Following a brief introduction, the text is divided into eight sections. The first section, "St. Mary's Industrial School for Boys," follows the Babe as a child through his leaving school for professional baseball. There are some marvelous pictures of young George Herman Ruth, Jr., including a family photo from 1896 when he was just 18 months old (p.15), several shots of Ruth at St. Mary's, and one of Ruth and his father at the family saloon in 1915 (pp.20–21). The next chapter examines his hurling career in Boston when he was "the best left-handed pitcher in baseball," followed by five chapters on his great career with the Yankees. The last chapter, "Final Innings," covers his life from 1935 when he retired from baseball up to his death. The graphics were collected from more than 40 sources, principally the National Baseball Library at Cooperstown, New York, private collections, particularly Barry Halper's, historical societies, the Babe Ruth Museum, and various commercial archives. In addition to the hundreds of black and white photographs, there are 16 pages of color visuals consisting of magazine covers, advertisements, posters and memorabilia. In all, this is as attractive and comprehensive a graphic biography as I can possibly imagine.

Dorothy Pirone's biography of her father is, not unexpectedly, a very different, highly personalized account of a great American sports hero. Her goal is to set the record straight about her father and family, and has some of the earmarks of a "Daddy Dearest" tale. Dorothy was born in 1921, but not to Mrs. Helen Ruth, and was not publicly identified until 16 months later when she moved in with her father. Her family life was a disaster. She lived with Helen who separated from the Babe in 1925 until her death in a fire in 1929 and, shortly after her father married Claire Hodgson, moved in with them. The Babe loved his little girl, but was away from home a lot, and Dorothy was badly treated by her stepmother, who saw her as just so much excess baggage. While her stepsister got the best schooling and fanciest clothes, Dorothy, like Cinderella, wore hand-me-downs, had a small room, and was left home on family trips. Dorothy left home when she turned 18, and soon got married, looking for the family life she never had at home. Not surprisingly, she is very critical of Claire Ruth, who she felt manipulated her father in deleterious ways.

The chief contribution of this book is the information we get about Ruth as the private man. The rest of the book tells us little about Ruth the celebrity and sports hero that we don't already know. The chief revelation is Dorothy's recent discovery that Juanita Ellias, the wife of Ruth's accountant, and an old family friend that Dorothy cared for between 1965 and 1980, was actually her natural mother. Ruth and Juanita had an affair in 1920, and Dorothy was the product. In sum, these reminiscenses would have made a fine magazine article or two, but don't really provide enough for a book.

Steven A. Riess
Northeastern Illinois University

Snider, Duke with Bill Gilbert. *The Duke of Flatbush.* New York: Zebra Books, 1988. 288 pp. introduction; photos.

In *Portnoy's Complaint,* Phillip Roth has Alex discuss the beauty and control gained from playing center field and he has his hero revel in his imitation of "Duke" Snider returning to the dugout after making the final putout of an inning. Roth's fond remembrance of the Duke is one shared by many boys who grew up in Brooklyn in the decade following World War II. Elected to Baseball's Hall of Fame in 1980, Edwin "Duke" Snider batted .295 and had over 400 home runs during his 18-year career, 1947–1964. From 1953 through 1957 he annually hit over 40 home runs and six times during his career he drove in more than 100 rbis. The Duke hit 10 World Series homers and is the only player to hit four homers in two different World Series. While some have questioned whether Snider's credentials rightfully entitle him to Hall status, he was compared favorably to Mickey Mantle and Willie Mays during the years when they roamed the outfields for New York's three different teams.

Snider's autobiography, written with former sportswriter Bill Gilbert, looks at his baseball career from his high school days in Compton, California until his election to the Hall of Fame. However, most of the book, as the title intimates, focuses on his years with the Brooklyn Dodgers. Snider seeks to provide insights not only into himself—his frustrations and successes—but into his teammates as well.

What Snider and Gilbert offer us is a boring book. The work is of little utility to the professional historian of baseball and the afficionado of the sport will uncover virtually no new insights. The book is essentially an attempt to capitalize on the nostalgia movement, and it is one of a growing number of autobiographies being published on luminaries of New York's golden age of baseball. In fact, Snider recognizes in the concluding paragraph that "It says something about the Dodgers, especially the Brooklyn Dodgers, that to so many people we remain a symbol of baseball, and of America itself in the 1940s and 1950s. Those of us lucky enough to be young in that special time can still see that special team—. . .Ebbets Field still stands. The Brooklyn Dodgers still live." (p. 288)

Snider's biography would have been more insightful and valuable if he had reflected on this statement rather than simply articulating it. It would have been interesting if a former player speculated on why the Brooklyn Dodgers continue to have such a hold on our sense of time and place. This kind of analysis might be too much to ask from this kind of book, but even within the context of this genre of work Snider's biography leaves something to be desired. One need not be a supporter of the kiss-and-tell books which now can be found in the sports section of our local bookstores, but this work is far too much of a throwback to an earlier and more romantic period of baseball biographies. As a result, Snider presents his teammates simply as a great bunch of guys, although he admits that Leo Durocher was not the most lovable person on the diamond. The day-to-day tensions which naturally are created among players during the lengthy season seem to have been forgotten. Even more distressing is the absence of virtually any new insights into these players. There are some interesting comments, such as the claim that Jackie Robinson "made us better because of his ability and he made us closer because of his suffering." (p. 56) Unfortunately, they are far too few and even where they do exist are insufficiently analyzed.

Snider pushes all the right buttons in his effort to evoke the memory of better days, when players performed for the love of the game rather than money. He never proclaims that the players of his era were better than today's (he never raises this point), but he does state that "Today's players have a lot more money, but they'll never have what we had, and what we still have." (p. 20) While Snider admits that the lengthy train rides teams often took resulted in sleepless nights, he remarks that it created greater cohesion and comradeship among the players. In a similar vein, Snider concedes that the new stadiums are beautiful structures and offer big improvements in fan comfort, but he insists that "for atmosphere and the sheer joy of baseball in God's fresh air and the thrill of feeling a part of it all as a player or even as a fan, give me Tiger Stadium or Wrigley Field or Fenway Park. Better yet, give me Ebbets Field." (pp. 64–65)

Despite its many problems, Snider's autobiography does have its moments. In a book designed to take you back to those thrilling days of yesteryear, Snider evoked such a memory for me. He reminisced about the fifth game of the 1952 World Series, a game I attended with my father and brother. Snider also provides some interesting insights into how he became increasingly obsessed with being elected to the Hall of Fame. The most interesting story in the book is Snider's discussion of how Walter Alston blew the final game of the 1962 playoff by not bringing in Don Drysdale and by incorrectly positioning his infielders in the final inning.

There is no doubt that Edwin "Duke" Snider was an important component of the great Brooklyn Dodger ball clubs in the decade following World War II. Yet his own story adds little to our understanding of these teams, its members, and its significance that cannot be already gleaned from Roger Kahn's *The Boys of Summer* or Peter Golenbock's *Bums*.

Melvin L. Adelman
Ohio State University

Langford, Walter M., *Legends of Baseball: An Oral History of The Game's Golden Age*. South Bend, IN: Diamond Communications, 1987. 227 pp. $8.95 (pbk.).

Broeg, Bob and William J. Miller, Jr. *Baseball from a Different Angle*. South Bend, IN: Diamond Communications, 1988. 269 pp. $12.95 (pbk.).

Baseball "histories," once proferred exclusively in the form of traditional chronological narrative, now appear in many guises ranging from collections of photographs and anecdotes to anthologies of recorded interviews and topical essays. The two volumes under review here are excellent examples of the latter two genre.

Walter Langford, former professor of Modern Languages and erstwhile tennis and fencing coach at the University of Notre Dame, is an avid student of baseball and indefatigable interviewer of the game's "old-timers." 'Tis a pleasurable pastime, but how does Langford justify yet another "oral history" when library shelves are beginning to groan under the weight of such books? (Collectively, never have so many been asked to say so much about so little of consequence.) Let him speak for himself: "The preparation of this book responds to a twofold motivation. For one thing, I feel the need to emphasize further the greatness of the pre-1950 period in the development of baseball by having some of the representative figures of that epoch recount many of their memories and experiences. Besides this, there is the intention to reveal in some detail the numerous differences in the playing conditions and circumstances of that era in contrast to the present." (p. xii) Unlike many comparable volumes, *Legends* delivers on its promises with style, sophistication, and substance.

To accomplish his objectives, Langford "set forth with tape recorder in hand to visit [16 'old-time stars' from the 1920s to the 1940s] where they live across the land—in Table-of-Contents order Joe Sewell, Glenn Wright, Carl Hubbell, Charlie Grimm, Mel Harder, Larry French, Travis Jackson, Joe Moore, George Uhle, Luke Sewell, Babe Herman, Dutch Leonard, Terry Moore, Johnny Vander Meer, Marty Marion, and Al Lopez. Although one might reasonably argue that the terms "stars" and "legends" do not apply to all of these players, the result is a series of absorbing and highly informative *conversations*. The term "conversation" is critical as the format is that of a printed interview (Langford's questions with the subject's responses) instead of the more common autobiographical account or collage of recollections. We have "heard" from some of these persons before—e.g., Lopez, the Sewell brothers, and Vander Meer appear in various of Don Honig's "oral histories" and Herman appears in Lawrence Ritter's pioneering *Glory of Their Times*. Despite some inevitable overlap and slightly different accounts of the same incidents, such material is complementary rather than repetitive. And, to my mind, in each case Langford's is the better "interview" because of his more acute historical consciousness.

The "scholar" in Langford made sure *Legends* would not be another run-of-the-mill collection of oral interviews wherein editors are content simply to transcribe often superficial reminiscences. An introductory chapter provides context for the interviews by identifying the major differences between "Baseball's Golden Age" and today's unabashedly commercialized era. Moreover, he takes pains to draw from the interviewees comparisons between the game past and present; notwithstanding the predictable distortion produced by the rose-colored glasses of nostalgia, their observations and opinions give special poignancy and depth to our understanding of baseball in "the good old days." And, unlike many who produce essentially scissors-and-paste "oral histories," Langford enhances the value of the book by bracketing each interview with a concise biographical sketch, personal commentary, and statistical career profile.

Legends is a model of the "oral history" genre. Regrettably, the publisher did Langford and his readers an inexcusable disservice. Because both serious students and the casually curious will want to know what one or another interviewee had to say about a particular person or event, the inexplicable absence of an index severely compromises the utility of this otherwise excellent book.

Bob Broeg, veteran sportswriter for the *St. Louis Post-Dispatch,* and William Miller, associate professor of Asian and European history at Saint Louis University, have combined their distinctive talents and perspectives to produce a look at baseball from, well, a different angle. At first blush the book appears to be a topical treatment of the historical evolution of 14 aspects of the game including ball parks, rules, equipment, franchise moves, journalists, broadcasters, playing managers, relief pitchers, scandals, and even umpires. But early into the brief introduction, the reader is fully aware that this is no conventional "history." *Baseball from a Different Angle,* as underscored by the book's titular emphasis, is a unique volume—an utterly charming, captivating, lively, insightful, provocative, and instructive freewheeling blend of baseball lore, anecdotes, fact, fancy, and personal opinion. Dedicated to "the Baseball curious," the book is less a history than a celebratory chronicle emphasizing the "who did whats," "what ifs," "firsts," and "how comes" of baseball's past. Those interested in substantive discussions of monopolistic economics, race and ethnicity, administrative politics, and a host of cultural matters central to baseball history will have to look elsewhere.

For the reviewer, the book is the equivalent of a Hoyt Wilhelm knuckler. The contribution of each author is unclear, but the prose, approach, and content suggest that the book rests primarily on the writing, wit, and expertise of Broeg, one of the most skillful and knowledgeable sport journalists in American history. (Indeed, the best portions of the book are those where Broeg draws upon his vast personal experiences, especially the section on writers and broadcasters.) Although the book makes no pretense to be a scholarly work and instead is directed toward a general audience, only readers well-versed in baseball history will be able to appreciate or even understand many of the references and assessments. The informal, almost "chatty" style makes for a delightful and entertaining "read," but an excessive penchant for alliteration (Bill Veeck is a "colorful, collarless character"), literary cuteness (Mike Kelly is "the tippling Mick from Troy"), and "in-group" vernacular (Frank and Brooks Robinson are "F. Robby" and "B. Robby") become annoying. Informed opinion and speculation on controversial issues are refreshing and welcomed, but ahistorical conjecture (e.g., a second Abner Doubleday might have invented baseball, if Judge Landis had ruled Ty Cobb and Tris Speaker guilty of fixing a game there might have been no Hall of Fame, "most" major league umpires "would have taken the same opportunity" and worked as "scabs" during the 1979 strike) and interpretation (blamed for the Black Sox scandal is "Old Roman Comiskey, the Irishman whose niggardly pay created temptation") are neither.

Authors deserve to be critiqued on the basis of the book written, not the book reviewers feel they could or should have written. The difficulty here is that Broeg and Miller in a self-assessment of their work admit to writing two different books: "What they've done, hopefully, is write a baseball textbook for Bill Miller's class at St. Louis University and other sports history classes elsewhere and, just as hopefully, strung together enough entertaining facts and viewpoints that . . . reviewing publications might consider it to have trade-book quality." (p.x) I'll score it a "K" on the first effort and an inside-the-park home run on the second. Just as I cannot fathom the book serving as a textbook for history courses (supplementary reading, yes), I cannot imagine any baseball aficionado failing to read it time and again for pleasure and profit.

As this highly personal, even personalized, "history" is likely to become a minor classic in baseball literature, it is unfortunate that the authors and publisher were not more attentive to production details. Typical of the careless editing and proofreading is the unintentionally erroneous statement: "Jackie Robinson wasn't the first big league black in 1947." The index is simply atrocious—e.g., there is no entry for "umpires" or "umpiring" despite an entire chapter and numerous scattered references about arbiters, 16 of the umpires mentioned in the chapter are not indexed, and the page numbers for some of those entered are incorrect or incomplete. Apparently the authors are responsible for the absence of a bibliography and footnotes, as they quote approvingly John Barrymore's famous non sequitur: "Going down the page to read a footnote is like going downstairs to answer the doorbell on the first night of your honeymoon." (p.xi) Pardon my disciplinary bias, but those who profess to write history had best not screw around with the canon: at a minimum, references— endnotes are fine—should have been provided for controversial statements and the considerable amount of new information that was derived from personal observation or private sources.

Larry R. Gerlach
University of Utah

Kirsch, George. *The Creation of American Team Sports: Baseball & Cricket, 1838–72*. Urbana and Chicago: University of Illinois Press, 1989. 277 pp. $27.50.

Okrent, Daniel and Steve Wulf. *Baseball Anecdotes*. New York and Oxford: Oxford University Press, 1989. 356 pp. $18.95.

"The whole history of baseball has the quality of mythology."
Bernard Malamud
"What do they know of cricket who only cricket know?"
C.L.R. James *(Beyond a Boundary)*

Both of these histories are published by a major university press and address a central issue: Why did baseball become the American national pastime? The two present interesting and paradoxical contrasts in their styles of baseball history research and writing.

On the surface, Kirsch's book, with its weighty academic title, careful scholarly notes at the end of each chapter, and concluding comments on methodology and bibliography, seems much less appealing to a wide audience than Okrent and Wulf's pithily titled volume. Kirsch has chosen to explore baseball's rise within a carefully circumscribed and seemingly exotic subject: baseball's triumph over cricket in the U.S. in the period from 1838 through 1872. Kirsch relates his analyses to the work of other leading academic baseball scholars (e.g., Adelman, Goldstein, Hardy, and Tyrrell). He refers to abstract concepts like modernization, industrialization, social class and, above all, urbanization. Kirsch presents statistical tables with titles like "Birthplace, Age, Occupation, Wealth, and Residence of Members of Newark Cricket and Baseball Clubs, 1855–60."

Okrent and Wulf, on the other hand, simply acknowledge their debt to "countless clubhouse raconteurs . . . and . . . countless writers who have written down the words of other tale-tellers," as well as the oral and written history collection of the National Baseball Library. Okrent and Wulf do not distract the reader with a bibliography, footnotes, or most other specific forms of scholarly acknowledgment of the work of other authors and raconteurs.

Okrent and Wulf's anecdotes range from Abner Doubleday's supposed invention of the game to Buckner's "error of the century." They confine their conclusions to a page-long "ENVOI" at the end of their book, where they find "no reason to think that the game's color would fade entirely," despite the frequent replacement of real grass by plastic turf, flannel by polyester and "the rough-and-ready, outside-the-mainstream sort" of player by "a more conventional character type."

This assessment is based on "the persistence of improbability, of the game's incredible ability to present something new on the fan's every visit to the ballpark"; "the rich irony that inevitably flourishes wherever people pursue the same task day after day"; and "those blessedly rare individuals who somehow found their way into the game's embrace." Couldn't we expect something more insightful from the authors of this book of 340-plus pages? After all, the same observations might be made about many other American sports.

This weak finish is a late inning tip-off that Okrent and Wulf shed little light on the mythological quality of baseball history they invoke in their Malamud epigraph (quoted above) and discuss in their preface. There Okrent and Wulf acknowledge their responsibility to evaluate the reliability of the chosen stories, for "the very act of repeating a tale is part of the mythifying process." The mythological theme is highlighted by the title of Part 1 of *Baseball Anecdotes*, "THE BOOK OF GENESIS: From Cartright's Code to Delahanty's Death." But Okrent and Wulf fail to follow through with this motif. If there is a continuity with the allusion to *Genesis*, it is that, in plowing through baseball anecdote after anecdote, many are likely to be reminded of reading the long lists of who begot whom found in parts of that first of the Five Books of Moses.

While Okrent and Wulf take on the task of evaluating the reliability of anecdotes, all too often their specific sources are not revealed. Even when a particular author or book is cited, there are no page references or other bibliographic data provided. It is interesting that, in contrast to *Baseball Anecdotes* from Oxford University Press, *The Oxford Book of American Literary Anecdotes* and *The Oxford Book of British Political Anecdotes* include extensive lists of specific source acknowledgments.

These criticisms may seem academic quibbles; but they are not. One of the great pleasures of writing baseball history is your audience. Readers include many nonacademic baseball scholars who want to be able to draw independent judgments or to follow up on interesting leads. It would have helped these readers immeasurably if (like *The Oxford Book of American Literary Anecdotes*) this book included an index of topics in addition to a name index. Without the former, the critical and inquiring reader will find it difficult to explore continuing or unifying themes in this mass of undigested anecdotes. It would have been nice to look up such subjects as no-hitters, contract disputes, fights, alcohol, women, and gambling.

Even more important, *Baseball Anecdotes* purportedly relies upon the rich tradition of "oral history" that has become an important part of baseball literature. But in recent years baseball books that claim to be oral histories often combine indiscriminately written sources and primary oral ones. The reader is left wondering: Am I hearing the actual player's voice or a ghostwriter's version? Is this a contemporary account or one influenced by years of hindsight and innumerable retellings? All too often these questions are left unanswered and unexamined by Okrent and Wulf. As it is, *Baseball Anecdotes* is entertaining when read in short doses but does not fulfill its potential promise to academic or scholarly baseball fans.

Paradoxically, if serious "nonacademic" baseball scholars were to give Kirsch's book a chance, they would find it a far more exciting, engaging, and even mythological reading experience than *Baseball Anecdotes*. While Kirsch is an exacting researcher, he is also a highly skilled storyteller. The American saga of cricket's failure and baseball's triumphant, if sometimes troubled, evolution from the amateur era to commercialism and professionalism comes to life as Kirsch interweaves his analyses with memorable quotes from contemporary observers. Often Kirsch begins chapters by describing events or happenings that epitomize the trends to be analyzed in the following sections. For example, in a chapter stressing the importance of spectators in determining the relative success of the two team sports, he starts by comparing the "respectable and orderly assemblage" that witnessed the matches between the All-England cricket 11 and an all-star American team of 22 at Hoboken's Elysian Fields in October 1859 to "the riotous scene at the Putnam Base Ball Club's ground" in Brooklyn in August 1860.

Kirsch has unearthed striking excerpts from newspaper reports and editorials that cover both games (matches) and organizational meetings or conventions. These latter are crucial to Kirsch, who argues that off-the-field developments were as important as on-the-field events in determining the very different fortunes of baseball and cricket in the U.S. Because of the relatively underdeveloped state of baseball as a sport in the beginning of the nineteenth century, the early linkage of the game to nationalist sentiments, and the relatively diverse social backgrounds of baseball players and fans, baseball clubs and associations were willing and able to adapt the game's rules and structure to changing American conditions (e.g., social, political, economic realities). By contrast, cricket's adaptability was limited by its relatively advanced state of development, the continuing dominance of English-born players (except in Philadelphia), and the unquestioned role of England's Maryebone Cricket Club as *the* supreme international cricket authority.

Of course, the question that many readers may ask is: why bother with cricket at all? Even very serious American sports fans know little and care less about cricket. At best they have a vague impression of long, boring contests. Baseball's triumph would seem self-evident to virtually any American. In fact, Kirsch does suggest that baseball won, at least in part, because it was far more attuned than cricket to the quick tempo of American life. It was also easier to learn to play and to appreciate as a spectator than the more developed and demanding "scientific" English game. However, Kirsch also shows that cricket was a serious rival of baseball in America, at least until mid-century. If there is a flaw in Kirsch's book, it is that while he explores the differences among the rival sets of baseball rules (e.g., the New York game versus the Massachusetts variety), he provides the reader with very little information about cricket *as a game* played in the 1850s, 60s, and 70s.

In *Beyond a Boundary,* the late C.L.R. James used his memories of playing and writing about cricket in the West Indies and the United Kingdom as the framework for telling the story of his very political life. Like Kirsch, James recognized that social life and sports are closely linked. Analysis of popular culture is not intellectual slumming, but can reflect a serious respect for the interests, enthusiasms, and intelligence of the masses. Perhaps that is the reason for James's comment: *"What do they know of cricket who only cricket know?"* In reading Kirsch on cricket and thinking about the probable knowledge of the game by Kirsch's readers, I sometimes wondered: "What do they know of cricket who only baseball know?"

For the many readers with little interest in or knowledge of cricket, the most fascinating part of this book will be the final chapters. These focus on the debates aroused by baseball's transition from its pre-Civil War amateur era to its postwar era of commercialization and professionalization. Many baseball lovers raised serious moral and ethical challenges to the changes of the late 1860s. The traditionalists' fears included the monopolization of the best players by a few teams, the transformation of baseball from a healthy recreation for many into serious work for a few, and the loss of any sense of true loyalty between player and club. Some amateur organizations attempted to return baseball to what they viewed as the golden era of the 1850s and early 60s.

Although this "revival" was doomed to failure, it is fascinating that many of the same moral and ethical issues raised by the nineteenth-century traditionalists can be seen as underlying more recent purist critiques of baseball (e.g., of free agency and franchise hopping). These newer critics also appeal to an almost sacred golden age, though usually the 1950s and not the 1850s. If the Okrent and Wulf book fails to live up to its Malamud epigraph, Kirsch's description of baseball's period of transition confirms the view that "The whole history of baseball has the quality of mythology." Although the period traditionalist baseball fans identify as a golden age may change through time, the continuity in values associated with that idyllic period suggest that, like myth-ology, baseball history deals with eternal human quandaries and recurring moral dilemmas at the heart of a particular culture.

The keys to understanding the mythological quality of baseball's history lie in the painstaking research of social historians like George Kirsch rather than in the simple repetition of tales. If more academics would learn to write as well as Kirsch, maybe more publishers would be willing to produce serious sports studies and our better understanding of the nation's pastime would help produce a better understanding of our nation's culture.

Fred Roberts
Michigan State University

Colletti, Ned. *You Gotta Have Heart: Dallas Green's Rebuilding of the Cubs*. South Bend, IN: Diamond Communications, 1985.

Langford, Jim. *Runs, Hits & Errors: A Treasury of Cub History and Humor*. South Bend, IN: Diamond Communications, 1987.

Talley, Rick. *The Cubs of '69: Recollections of the Team That Should Have Been*. Chicago: Contemporary Books, 1989.

Wheeler, Lonnie. *Bleachers: A Summer in Wrigley Field*. Chicago: Contempo-rary Books, 1988.

"Do they still play the Blues in Chicago,
when baseball season rolls around? . . ."
Steve Goodman, "A Dying Cub Fan's Last Request"

There is something altogether charming and yet inexplicable about the Chicago Cubs. If one lives in or around the city of Chicago, or perhaps receives cable transmissions from the nation's second great superstation, WGN, it is almost impossible not to be bombarded with superhype suggesting that the Cubs are truly America's foremost baseball passion. Columnists George Will and Mike Royko carry on the *cause celebre* with their huge syndicated audiences, drawing lessons for every turn in life's path from the misfortunes and failures of baseball's most glorious year-in and year-out losers. The popular myth is that no sports franchise (perhaps no American institution) is as widely beloved as the hapless Cubbies. The Cubs, we are often told, have all that most appeals to the nostalgic whims of the nation's massive baseball audience: long and glorious baseball tradition, with its poignant mixture of ancient championship heritage and con-temporary humanizing defeat; the land's most beautiful and memory-strewn ballpark, with its ivy-covered red-brick outfield walls, its decades of baseball memories, its friendliest of intimate baseball confines, and (until this past season) its anachronistic tradition of sunshine daytime baseball. And for the modern-era fan, there is also a television network that beams each and every home and road game into family dens from Chicago's suburbs to Denver, Wichita, and L.A. To hear Cubs supporters tell it, there is no team that can rival the Cubbies in the fervor of fan support, in the richness of baseball tradition, or in the blessing of possessing baseball's most beautiful cathedral ball field.

Indeed, a considerable fan-cult has grown up around the Cubs since 1984, as well as around their WGN superstation media star, charismatic announcer Harry Caray, who is every bit as much the icon for Cubs fans of the late 1980s that Mel Allen was for Yankee rooters of the 1950s, that Bob Prince was for Pirates boosters of the 1960s, or that Ernie Harwell and Vin Scully have been for Tigers and Dodgers fans over the past three full decades. Yet such blind baseball fandom is always somewhat provincial in its purview, and numerous baseball purists would argue that much-celebrated Cubs-mania of the 1980s is no more impressive than other ongoing love affairs between local fans and several of the nation's older baseball franchises. These are always teams which boast both history-laden ball parks and memorable baseball traditions—traditions blending glorious (almost mythic) superstars with years of heart-rending late season defeats and cherished pennants lost. The Tigers of Detroit and the Red Sox of Boston have been described in this fashion by baseball's poet-laureate Roger Angell. The Dodgers of Brooklyn sprouted an incomparable nostalgic tradition which has indeed lasted almost three decades after the team departed for L.A. and thus took on a different personality altogether. In short, the Cubs have no exclusive title to the claim of being America's special team; nor is the phenomenon of Cub mania as exclusive and unprecedented a phenomenon as those supporters in the Windy City and its environs would have you or themselves believe. This compels one to search further for explanations of the special aura attached to the Cubs, especially for so many fans residing thousands of miles from Chicago's North Side, fans who have never even set foot inside Wrigley's ivy-covered confines.

One predictable spin-off of the furor surrounding the favorite ball club of Chicago's affluent North Side has been the considerable market for Cubs literature—especially for Chicago-based publishing houses keenly aware of the potential gold mine of sales in an era already marked by an explosion of sports books, especially baseball books. It should be pointed out, however, that Cubs books are of a particular strain, and differ radically from the poorly ghostwritten ball player biographies and locker-room diaries penned in seemingly endless numbers for the New York baseball market. While the latter venue has witnessed popular player-promotion books featuring almost every member of the Yankees and Mets roster, Cubs books tend to find their subject in the heart-breaking history of Cubs fandom itself. They are aimed at the nostalgic appeal of Cubs teams from past decades—not the personality cult of contemporary play-ers—and in this sense Cub literature is immediately of greater interest to the serious baseball reader—wherever his own sympathies lie. Especially delightful to the tradition-oriented fan-reader are books exploring what it means to suffer season after season with the hapless Cubbies—*viz.,* to have each spring's fond hopes dashed by predictable late-season tragic collapses, to live out each agonizing baseball season with the cry of "wait until next year!" This is the stuff any baseball fan can identify with—the very essence of the best of baseball's rich literature. From novels like Malamud's *The Natural* to biographies like Creamer's *Babe,* baseball is always the essential stuff of tragedy and defeat. Baseball is always more life-metaphor than pure athletic contest, and it is this cult of defeat and hopeless mediocrity which is seemingly the repository for our answer to the riddle of the Chicago Cubs.

Perhaps the best among vintage Cubs books have been Jim Langford's *The Game is Never Over* and Barry Gifford's *The Neighborhood of Baseball,* books which focus most on the plight of lifelong Chicago Cubs fandom. Together these fan-diaries provide intimate personal histories devoted to watching the Cubs throughout a seemingly endless saga of defeat in the 1950s and early 1960s. Gifford's 1985 book has the added benefit of setting this nostalgic period of Ernie Banks and Billy Williams against a revival of Cubs glory during the thrilling divisional title in 1984. It was the 1984 season, of course, which seemed to launch the current furor surrounding the Cubs, and the last several summers have witnessed a spate of important new titles exploring both the phenomenon of Cubs fandom and the onfield traditions of Cubs baseball history. What the most recent books offer—when taken as a whole—are the beginnings of an explanation for precisely what it is that draws tens of thousands to Wrigley Field fandom—through the miracle of television or through personal pilgrimages to the quaint North Side ball park. One explanation for the Cubs' special appeal must lie in the preoccupation of the baseball fan (unlike the football or basketball fan) with teams married to perennial and inevitable defeat. Recent books by Rick Talley and Jim Langford explore this phenomenon for the Cubs perhaps as well as it has been documented for any single club within the venerable tradition of baseball literature. A competing explanation, however, lies in the phenomenon of televised sport itself, as well as in the powerful effects of present-day marketing techniques. Lonnie Wheeler and Ned Colletti—while setting out ostensibly to write books dealing with bleacher fandom and front-office baseball management, respectively—provide books that are especially revealing concerning the promotion of Cubs baseball as a multimillion-dollar entertainment spectacle aimed at a voracious Midwestern and national audience of television sports fanatics.

Rick Talley's *The Cubs of '69* is a standard baseball book on the surface: a personal reminiscence about a great team of our baseball past which blends accounts of past summers' heroics with intimate portraits of yesterday's heroes in the light of life's subsequent events. It is a book squarely in the tradition of Roger Kahn's *The Boys of Summer* or Dom Forker's recent *The Men of Autumn.* Unlike Kahn's often self-indulgent treatment of his own personal autobiography, however, or his labored accounts of life's expected bitter blows upon teammates who once together reached baseball's pinnacle, this book is more about the bitter moments of on-field defeat surrounding the fiasco of one of baseball's most poignant summers. Talley focuses on how the baseball defeats of a single season have subsequently shaped the lives of a couple dozen players, as well as those of thousands of fans who lived and ultimately died with that most infamous of all Cubs teams. Nineteen sixty-nine—with its moon-walks, Woodstock, and Vietnam—is a hard year to forget, Talley reminds us; but perhaps 1969 dies hardest in the memories of Chicago ball fans who are doomed to remember that the best Cubs team of all time brought only the bitterest conclusion to decades of "seasons that might have been."

Langford's book provides the larger backdrop against which the disasters of September 1969 can be best read (for the newcomer) or remembered (for the veteran Cubs watcher). Here the acceptance of baseball defeat is a philosophical counterpoint, and the treatment in *Runs, Hits & Errors* is on the whole more lighthearted and humorous. This book is more a pastiche and scrapbook than a thematically structured text, and here lie both its strength and weakness. The weakness is only that this is more a book to jog the memory of the insider than one which will unfold the wonders of Cubs history for newcomers to Chicago baseball; this is definitely a book for the lifelong Cubs fan. The strength is an incomparable collection of baseball memories set forth in anecdote, contemporary journalistic account, photographs, and classic newspaper cartoons. The joy of this book is also found in the inevitable humor which surrounds baseball's most inept teams, players, and moments. There is little funny about football; there is boundless humor in baseball's shared moments of ignominy and inept play. And much of that humor oozes from the pages of Langford's delightful small book.

Colletti is an original "bleacher bum refugee" from the 1960s who subsequently took a job as public relations assistant with the North Enders "to participate first-hand in the rebuilding of the Cubs under Dallas Green." That rebuilding effort is the subject of *You Gotta Have Heart,* which aims to provide a spirit-lifting, inspirational account of the Dallas Green years of Cubs resurgence. These were, after all, the new glory seasons, destined to bring long-awaited Cubs successes to baseball's most patient of downtrodden fans. What actually confronts the reader of Colletti's book, however, is a between-the-lines tale of all that is most disarming and distasteful about present-day baseball front-office management. Green's successes were short-lived and on-field victories in 1984 (a division title, but still no trip to the October Classic) were purchased at a price which in retrospect has once again bankrupted the Cubs slim talent reserves. Colletti's rendering of Green's egocentric tenure ends with words which today drip with cruel irony: "Our job here isn't finished yet!" What is most evident in Colletti's account is that, for good or bad, the Dallas Green era was an inescapable changing of the guard for what had heretofore been an amazingly consistent saga of Cubs baseball history under Philip K. Wrigley and his successors.

Nowhere is the changing of the old order surrounding Cubs baseball better portrayed than in Lonnie Wheeler's excellent book *Bleachers,* one of the most unusual and insightful baseball books of recent years. Wheeler sets out to discover the true nature of Cubs fandom, and to unlock explanations for Cubs magnetism and for the joys surrounding sunshine baseball within the game's most venerable and idealized park. What he finds through his own daily bleacher experience is largely a disappointment for both Wheeler and the reader: the old-time bleacher fan is gone, replaced by yuppies and college students who come to the bleachers of Wrigley not for the baseball so much as for the media event—to be seen on television in all their shirtless beer-guzzling glory. This is perhaps the most insidious of all the ways that television has spoiled our greatest sporting national treasure of big league baseball.

Wheeler launches his summer in Wrigley Field with lofty expectations: "I thought of the bleachers as a window on baseball . . . I thought of them as a balcony over baseball's summer serenade . . . I was going to spend the season there, and I thought it would be baseball heaven." But of course Wheeler never finds quite what he came looking for, and the losses of old style "bleacher culture" which he encounters instead are as poignantly painful as any on-field losses which mark the eight decades of Cubs Wrigley Field play. Wheeler's account of this shift in the game's aura and audience is insightful and poignantly told. One can feel an old order fading and a new one emerging, and Wrigley Field is only a single stark example of a universal baseball phenomenon. The game will survive and even grow in its popularity, but it will never be the same again. And at the heart of Wheeler's book is the final irony surrounding the marketing of the Chicago Cubs. The tradition which is hyped endlessly by Harry Caray and WGN—the ivy and sunlight of Wrigley—is ultimately a frail myth which is rapidly being destroyed by the very commercialism which spreads the message. Night ball came to Wrigley in the summer of 1988; skyboxes and a huge football-style press box appeared for Opening Day 1989; and while the Cubs have artfully concealed the announcement to date, a Diamond Vision scoreboard is currently under construction outside Boston which will replace Wrigley's hand-operated centerfield scoreboard in time for 1990 season play. Wheeler's book in the end reveals the ultimate paradox surrounding the Chicago Cubs. Nostalgia for 1950s baseball—best symbolized by the flamboyant Harry Caray—is the lure with which WGN draws its huge TV baseball audience; yet the anachronistic charms of Wrigley Field are inevitably being destroyed by the very superstation monster which of recent years has best sustained the myth itself.

Peter C. Bjarkman
West Lafayette, Indiana

Lawson, Earl. *Cincinnati Seasons.* South Bend, IN: Diamond Communications, 1987. 218 pp. $16.95.

Walker, Robert Harris. *Cincinnati and the Big Red Machine.* Bloomington: Indiana University Press, 1988. 158 pp. $19.95 (hardcover), $8.95 (pbk.).

Wheeler, Lonnie and John Baskin. *The Cincinnati Game.* Wilmington, OH: Orange Frazer Press, 1988. 271 pp. $29.95.

Earl Lawson, a Baseball Hall of Fame writer, has published an excellent autobiography of a 34-year career (1951–84) during which he covered some 6,800 games and wrote about 10 million words about the Cincinnati Reds.

Rich in diamond anecdotes, Lawson's work covers a period of enormous change in sports and society. The game has moved from an era of train travel to the jet age. The National League has seen the westward movement of the Giants and Dodgers, the switch of the Braves from Milwaukee to Atlanta and the birth of new franchises in San Diego, Houston, Montreal and an expansion team in New York, the Mets.

It was also an era of desegregation in baseball. Jackie Robinson and Branch Rickey's Brooklyn Dodgers had erased the racial barrier in 1947, but Lawson notes that as late as the mid-1950s Reds' outfielder Bob Thurman slept in the basement of a black funeral home as the team broke spring training camp in Tampa, Florida, and toured southern cities en route home. Thurman's slumber was less than sound, as he was convinced that dead bodies were nearby.

Lawson focuses not only on the glory years of the Big Red Machine, but also on the comparatively lean years of the 1950s and 60s. Although the Reds won little (except the 1961 National League pennant) in those two decades, they had some individual stars and colorful characters. Lawson details the exploits of Big Ted Kluszewski, Johnny Temple, Roy McMillan, Vada Pinson and Frank Robinson, among others.

He traces in detail his experiences of being physically assaulted by Temple in June 1957 and Pinson in June 1962. In Pinson's case he signed a warrant for assault and battery after the outfielder "sucker punched" him following some stories which criticized his defensive play and failure to develop bunting skills. Lawson dropped charges after a jury was unable to reach a verdict, feeling that he had made his point, that players could not attack writers with impunity.

In a sentimental chapter, "He Showed Us How to Die," Lawson recounts how the late Fred Hutchinson waged a gallant battle against cancer. Hutch, who brought the Reds their first pennant in 21 years in 1961, saw his team almost win it again in 1964. Tied for first place on the last day of the season, the Reds, playing under Coach Dick Sisler, were shut out by Cincinnati native Jim Bunning and the Phillies, 10–0, giving St. Louis a winning one-game edge.

Much of Lawson's book is about sportswriting and managers. Without question, he considers Rogers Hornsby one of the great right-handed hitters and worst managers in major league history. Lawson also writes about other Reds managers—Birdie Tebbetts, Jimmy Dykes, Mayo Smith, Hutchinson, Sisler, Don Heffner, Dave Bristol and Sparky Anderson.

Despite two world's companionships and the great players of the 1970s—Johnny Bench, Pete Rose, Tony Perez, Joe Morgan and others—Lawson says that the greatest player in his 34 years on the Reds beat was Frank Robinson. He applauds Robinson's competitive drive and natural ability, his absolute fearlessness at the plate. But his off-the-field adventures were another story and the Reds traded him after the 1965 season. Let go in one of the club's worst trades ever, Robby proceeded to lead Baltimore to the American League pennant, hitting .316 with 49 homers and 122 RBI's. His arrest on a concealed weapons charge at a late-night Cincinnati fast food hamburger chain was followed by a guilty plea and a court-imposed fine. The Reds didn't like that kind of publicity nor his "bad influence" on star prospect Pinson. Robinson was described by the Reds as an "old 30" when traded.

To this day, Lawson writes, Robinson is angry with the Reds. They sent no one to Cooperstown in August 1982, when their former star was inducted into the Hall of Fame. They also refused to retire his number 20, a standard practice of clubs whose former players make the Hall.

Looking back on his 34 years, Lawson concludes that today's players and writers never again will have the kind of close relationship that he enjoyed. Why not?

"It's a matter of economics," he writes. "With baseball salaries as they are today, the lifestyles of the players and writers are completely different. Away from the ball park, the two live in completely different worlds . . ."

Some of today's "New Breed" of sportswriters inevitably will ask if old-time writers lost their objectivity by being "too close" to players and managers, if writers should play intermediary between player and club, and if writers really should "care" whether the team they cover wins or loses.

Lawson clearly belongs to the old school of sportswriters, and during his time he was one of the best. His book is a "great read," not only for Cincinnati fans, but for all National League followers.

***

Walker, a professor of American Civilization at George Washington University, focuses on the intimate relationship between the Reds, the city and its citizens. He traces the evolution of the game from the "Town Ball" of 1860 to the current day. But the heart of the book is the story of a love affair—between the city, its citizens and the Big Red Machine of the 1970s.

In an age of social turmoil, the Reds featured not only a lineup of All-Stars, but also black shoes, high socks and clean shaves. None of the anti-establishment stuff for General Manager Bob Howsam and Manager Sparky Anderson. Anderson says: ". . .We have gone through at least three eras in the last 15 years, and still the Reds to me are the only ones that look like a major-league team. They look major league. And they never change. And that to me is the best legacy Howsam left our game." Howsam insisted, Walker writes, that Reds players reflect community values—clean-cut, conservative in appearance and hardworking.

A native of the Hyde Park area of Cincinnati, Walker writes affectionately of his home town and its ball club. He gives former Mayor Eugene P. Ruehlmann enormous credit for leading the move to a new Riverfront Stadium in 1970. The rebirth of downtown followed the prosperity of the 1970s Reds.

Walker's book is solid scholarship, based on primary source documents and interviews with public officials, civic leaders, former Reds players, managers and club officials, as well as major media figures. It is an entertaining and most readable book.

***

Wheeler, a former Cincinnati *Enquirer* columnist and Baskin, an Ohio author, have produced a work rich in local history. They contend that no other city has been more significant to baseball than Cincinnati. There, in 1869, a band of mustachioed fellows led by cricketeer Harry Wright formed the Red Stockings and revolutionized the sport by making it truly professional.

After that famous 64–0 season, the Red Stockings fell on hard times. They were expelled from the National League for selling beer at the ball park, and became the movers behind the American Association, baseball's first insurgent professional league.

When, in 1901, the American League became "major," its leader was Ban Johnson, a former Cincinnati sportswriter whose position had been arranged by Charlie Comiskey, a former Reds' manager. Another Reds' manager was Clark Griffith, eventual owner of the Washington Senators.

All but the most knowledgeable fan will learn a good deal from this book. How much salary could a player command in 1989 if he could hit .518, score 339 runs and hit 59 home runs? Shortstop George Wright did this for the 1869 Reds. His salary was $1,400 and the payroll for the entire 10-man roster was $9,300.

It was, of course, a different game. Pitchers were forbidden to bend their elbows—except after the games—until 1872 when they first were permitted to snap their wrists. Fielding gloves were introduced in 1875. The mound was 50 feet from home plate until 1893 when the present 60 feet, six inches was mandated. Debate raged over how many bad pitches should constitute a walk. The rule varied from nine in 1879 to four in 1889.

The Reds played baseball's first night game at old Crosley Field on May 24, 1935, when President Franklin D. Roosevelt lit the lamps by throwing a switch at the White House. Reds Pitcher Paul Derringer then bested the Phillies, 2–1.

The authors are lavish in their praise of Cincinnati's amateur baseball program which has produced more than 20 major leaguers. Four from one high school—Western Hills—went on to become big league managers—Pete Rose, Don Zimmer, Jim Frey and Russ Nixon.

Lawson's book could best be characterized as richly anecdotal. Both Walker and Wheeler-Baskin are historical, with the former strong on the interrelationship between baseball and local culture.

These emphases may well be reflected in their treatments of Pete Rose, threatened in early summer 1989 with suspension from baseball for a year or for life, respectively, if he bet on baseball games or on his own team.

Lawson, in a chapter entitled "This Rose Will Never Die," focuses not only on Pete Rose, ball player, but on his relationship with him. On the occasion of Lawson's retirement, Rose presented him with a 14-carat gold Omega watch, engraved: "Scoops, thanks for all your great baseball years and your friendship. Pete Rose."

Perhaps with some irony, Lawson quotes Joe Reichler, then of the baseball commissioner's office. . . . "Pete's the best advertisement baseball has."

Walker's prologue features "Rose Rounding Third," and bowling over Cleveland Indians Catcher Ray Fosse, to score the winning run for the National League in the 1970 All-Star Game.

Walker quotes Reds' Hall of Fame Catcher Johnny Bench on Rose: ". . . with Pete there have been mega different things—I mean between divorce and paternity suits and all that—and still he is the guy they name streets after."

Wheeler and Baskin noted that conservative Cincinnati could forgive Rose's divorce and paternity suit and other mischievous wonts that it wouldn't tolerate in others. It was, they wrote, almost a "boys will be boys" approach.

Clearly, baseball always seemed to come first to Rose. When Pete tired of his second-place Reds making excuses for slumps in 1987, he called a meeting and assailed them. He ordered them to keep their minds on the game, pointing out that despite divorce and paternity suits filed against him, he went 17 for 28 at the time.

John Molloy
Michigan State University

Buege, Bob. *The Milwaukee Braves: A Baseball Eulogy.* Milwaukee, WI: Douglas American Sports Publications, 1988. 415pp. $12.95 (pbk.).

Baseball has long been unchallenged as our most literary game, and baseball books are unprecedentedly hot in the 1980s. There has been no shortage of tomes on all aspects of the national pastime in recent years, with more than 100 novels exploiting baseball for setting or theme during the past decade or so alone. Countless team histories, Horatio-Alger-style biographies, and soul-baring tell-all confessionals by our favorite diamond heroes have spiced up our recent Hot Stove League seasons. Yet too many baseball confessionals and autobiographies of current vintage are seemingly conceived solely for the mass-market audiences of New York and the eastern seaboard; hence we suffer through an almost endless supply of ultimately uninteresting and usually poorly ghostwritten books featuring virtually every player holding a spot on the New York Yankees and New York Mets rosters. Against this backdrop of exploitation baseball books it is refreshing to find a true gem like the one offered here by veteran Milwaukee sportswriter Bob Buege, a book which captures the thematic essence of all that is best in baseball—and thus all that is best in baseball books to boot.

Mr. Buege's loving eulogy on the short-lived franchise (1953–1966) which brought big-league baseball to Milwaukee offers far more than straightforward history of the glory years for a single successful expansion team; it is also a vividly drawn portrait of the best that was baseball in those golden summers of the 1950s—before the grass was plastic, the ball parks were covered with inflatable domes, and the baseball heroes of our youth transformed into the distant media-stars and insufferable millionaire-athletes of the sound-bite electronic era. This is truly a book in the finest tradition of successful baseball books, one with a solid focus on the true nostalgia of the game, and one which brings to life a significant historical epoch from within the most nostalgic and historical of all our national games.

Buege recounts the story of 13 seasons of Braves baseball in Milwaukee, doing so with the rich historical detail of the astute scholar, the gripping narrative style of the accomplished journalist, and the balanced perspective of the proficient social critic. The tale begins with a brief history of minor league baseball in Wisconsin; it details the excitement of the first arrival of Lou Perini's inept Braves from Boston in 1953; it follows season-by-season accounts of unsurpassed on-field successes in the late 1950s, and then chronicles the corporate greed and front-office bungling which only a few short seasons later were to transplant one of baseball's most lucrative franchises into the potentially open-ended Atlanta television market of the exploding new southland. Buege's treatment brings to life such past diamond greats as Henry Aaron, Eddie Mathews and Warren Spahn and captures the grip they held on this city for an all-too-brief decade which was witness to one of baseball's truly great love affairs.

The success of this book is its delicate balance of on-field baseball excitement with the carefully detailed story of front-office corporate baseball management. The text is illustrated with dozens of excellent black and white photographs which successfully complement Buege's historical narrative. This volume is a must for any fan of baseball in the 1950s and any student of baseball's coast-to-coast expansion. It is also recommended reading for non-fans with even the mildest curiosity about why baseball still reigns unchallenged as America's foremost national passion.

Peter C. Bjarkman
West Lafayette, Indiana

Cohen, Stanley. *A Magic Summer: The '69 Mets.* New York: Harcourt Brace Jovanovich, 1988. 352pp. $16.95.

This baseball season represents the twentieth anniversary of one of the celebrated championships of the game. In 1969, the first year of divisional play, the New York Mets won the Eastern Division of the National League by eight games over the second place Chicago Cubs; the Mets then took the National League pennant with a three-game sweep of the Atlanta Braves. This most improbable season culminated with New York winning the World Series from the Baltimore Orioles in five games.

Within the charmingly encapsulated world of baseball, the Mets' season is memorable enough. The team had been lovingly notorious in its early years by losing often in every conceivable way and by offering New Yorkers a nostalgic collection of former Dodgers, Giants and Yankees. When the Mets shot from a ninth place finish in 1968 to the World Championship the following year, the accepted explanation was that a miracle had occurred.

As Stanley Cohen points out in his splendid book, *A Magic Season,* the Mets rise to glory was not so much a miracle as the plausible result of good management. Gil Hodges had been hired from Washington to pilot the Mets not because he had been a popular player with the Brooklyn Dodgers but because he had brought the Senators some respectability. Tom Seaver, Jerry Koosman, Tug McGraw and Nolan Ryan were part of a young pitching staff that showed that George Weiss, the Mets general manager from 1962 through 1966, could still spot and sign talent as he had when building the Yankee dynasty.

Cohen interviewed almost all of the members of the 1969 Mets about their recollections of that season. A sad and recurring theme is the importance of Gil Hodges' managing. Players recalled his considerate but serious manner in pressing for the best in his charges. He could insist on high standards while also nurturing the confidence of his players—an impressive ability in any organization. One suspects that had he lived, Hodges' managerial record would have guaranteed his inclusion at Cooperstown.

The Mets' principal competition down the stretch came from Leo Durocher's Chicago Cubs. The strategic battles between Durocher and Hodges are a great example of how baseball sustains its appeal. One can easily imagine the conversations between generations of fans about those two managers' playing days during the glory years of New York baseball.

A refreshing aspect of the book is that it offers an inside perspective of how a championship season is played without gratuitous personal information. Cohen has generally avoided what Red Smith called, ". . . the customary scatological references that young writers confuse with realism."

To his greater credit, the author has also spared us hard core social science, but he does effectively place the Mets' season in its time. In 1969, men first landed on the moon, and it was also a year sandwiched between the assassinations of 1968 and tragedies like Kent State that were to come. The boost that the Mets' triumph lent John Lindsay's re-election campaign is established, and so is the atmosphere of the turbulent Vietnam era.

The 1969 season reflected the Mets' real emergence as a team with its own character. When they swept the Dodgers and Giants in consecutive series at Shea about Memorial Day, nostalgia gave way to excitement. The early Mets of Casey Stengel had let National League fans in New York laugh lest they cry. The new Mets restored what had been missing for a decade—dreams about the future.

A Magic Summer makes no pretense of duplicating *The Boys of Summer*. The interviews with former Mets focus primarily on that one season rather than the vicissitudes of life. Cohen has written a lively account of one of the memorable seasons of the modern game.

Neil Sullivan
New York

Zinsser, William. *Spring Training.* New York: Harper & Row, 1989. 197 pp. $16.95.

One would probably enjoy anything written by this noted author, editor, and teacher—his best known work, *On Writing Well,* has sold nearly half a million copies—but the fact that William Zinsser is also a lifelong baseball fan makes him more than a reporter at spring training who happens to write superbly. It lets him, "a pilgrim on an old American pilgrimage," bring his own memory of the game to *Spring Training;* and memory "is the glue that held baseball together as the continuing American epic."

While the charm of memory enriches this book, especially as seen in the "codgers" who frequent spring training games and the longtime residents of Bradenton, Florida, whose annual six-week love affair with major league baseball has been renewed since the 1920s, this is not a nostalgia piece. Nor is it primarily a paean to the old days, the old ball parks, or even the game itself, though Zinsser's veneration of all is evident. Instead, *Spring Training* is the patient study of a town (Bradenton), a team (Pittsburgh Pirates), a system (the thorough approach of since-fired general manager Syd Thrift and field manager Jim Leyland), a process (spring training), and their interaction and symbiosis in the February/March rites of anticipation and renewal.

Zinsser approaches spring training with the interest of a well-informed fan and the methodology of a veteran educator. He has a good reporter's knack for asking deceptively simple, no-nonsense questions: "What does spring training mean to you?" "How do you teach the fundamentals of that particular skill?" Perhaps because the questions are so forthright, perhaps because his subjects can relate to the teacher in Zinsser, their answers are remarkably sincere and direct. They bypass the platitudes of most spring training interviews and cut to the essence of their craft. Players see it as a refresher course, a time to work on problems from the previous season, an opportunity to develop confidence as they follow the timetable to Opening Day. The coaches and manager stress the time needed to teach the younger players, who now reach the major leagues with less experience than ever before. An umpire speaks for the entire enterprise, belying the easygoing facade of exhibition baseball: "The thing about spring training is that the more you work, the better off you are."

All of these comments are like spokes on the wheel whose hub is Thrift and Leyland. Their patient, disciplined approach to baseball resuscitated a moribund Pittsburgh franchise and won back the city's despairing fans. The general manager's philosophy, "The Gospel According to Thrift," as Chapter Three is called, focuses on knowledge and preparation. Leyland emerges as the ideal man to implement that philosophy. His practices are characterized by discipline, orderliness, and organization. "Preparation," writes Zinsser, "was at the heart of his character."

The deliberate nature of these men is reflected in the approach of their staff. Batting instructor Milt May, for instance, concentrates on five "absolutes for every hitter," while pitching coach Ray Miller puts his basic principles onto a T-shirt for each of his charges: "WE WORK FAST, THROW STRIKES, CHANGE SPEEDS." The succinct summaries of each speciality, along with the admiring portrait of Thrift, are the highlights of the book, but there are several other delightful gems—a cameo appearance by the crotchety Hall of Famer Edd Roush, a brief history of Bradenton, and a loving portrait of old McKechnie Field—which make it a rewarding entree to the world of spring training.

Allen E. Hye
Wright State University

Waggonner, Glenn, Kathleen Moloney and Hugh Howard. *Baseball by the Rules: Pine Tar, Spitballs and Midgets; An Anecdotal Guide to America's Oldest and Most Complex Sport*. Dallas, TX: Taylor Publishing Company, 1987. $12.95.

I must admit that the idea of a book about the rules of baseball, albeit an "anecdotal" one, did not stimulate my enthusiastic juices. Then again, I didn't think that the Dodgers had a chance against the A's in the 1988 World Series. *Baseball by the Rules* is the proverbial triple-threat of books: reference, history, and entertainment assembled in one tight package. Even the most knowledgeable of fans will find enlightenment on almost every page.

Authors Glen Waggonner, Kathleen Moloney, and Hugh Howard "intended to explicate the 'rulebook' to take each of the dry as toast rules and illuminate them with real-life stories," a task which they approach with great wit and charm. And, as they "think that a knowledge of the evolution of the game enhances our understanding of it," the book is spiced with the game's history: the trivial, the substantial, and the analytical.

Baseball by the Rules is organized along the lines of the *Official Baseball Rules,* with 10 chapters, each devoted to a different facet of the game ("Objectives of Game," "Definition of Terms," "The Batter," "The Runner," "The Pitcher," etc.). There, however, the similarity ends. While the official rules would fail to entertain even the greatest lover of legalistic prose, Waggonner et al. cavort blithely through game situations, rule changes, interpretations and exceptions.

Take for example their discussion of "The Ball." After stating the official specifications ("The baseball must be spherical. It must be composed of a cork core, followed by a layer of rubber, woolen and cotton yarn. . . . Its weight is to be between 5¼ ounces . . .; the circumference must be 9 to 9¼ inches"), the authors discuss the evolution of its weight (from 3 ounces in 1845 to 5½ to 6⅕ ounces in 1854, to its current standards as early as 1872), offer a history of lively ball controversies, provide a wonderful picture of Baseball Commissioner Kenesaw Mountain Landis and League Presidents Will Harridge and Warren Giles examining "reclaimed" cork and rubber centers used during World War II, recall a remarkable June 29, 1929 game when the Cubs and Reds used only one ball, and close with a section on Charlie Finley's "orange ball" proposal, all in the brief space of five pages.

Waggonner et al. have a wonderful eye for photos and quotations. Casey Stengel opens the chapter on "Starting and Ending the Game" with the observation, "Now there's three things you can do in a baseball game. You can win, or you can lose, or it can rain." On the same subject, radio announcer Dizzy Dean, barred from reporting weather conditions due to wartime censorship, explained a game delay as follows: "I can't tell you folks why this here game has been stopped by the umpires, but if you'll be kind enough to stick your heads outta the windows, you kin see for yerselves. And you'd better hold an umbrella over your head when you do."

Baseball by the Rules serves as a reference book as well. At the end of each chapter there is a list of major modifications covered therein. Appendices include a glossary of key terms and a chronology of rule changes.

Where *Baseball by the Rules* errs, it is often in the direction of cuteness. One tires quickly of the reverential reference to "The Book" when referring to the *Official Baseball Rules* and, at times, the quotations, while always entertaining, bear scant relationship to the rule discussed. Several anecdotes lack dates and whoever proofread the photo captions (a youthful Casey Stengel in a Giants uniform is ejected from a 1960 game, among other errors) should be returned to the minors. These small irritations aside, *Baseball by the Rules* should find a comfortable place on your baseball shelf, among the books you turn to most often.

Jules Tygiel
San Francisco State

Smith, Curt. *Voices of the Game: The First Full-Scale Overview of Baseball Broadcasting, 1921 to the Present.* South Bend, IN: Diamond Communications, 1987. 594 pp. $22.95.

The significance of the mass media to post-industrial sport has been long acknowledged, but apart from broad surveys and autobiographical accounts, little has been done to probe the leading personalities and processes of sports broadcasting. Curt Smith has taken an important first step by sketching the history of baseball on radio and television, and despite some shortcomings, his book is an important contribution to the history of sportscasting. A native of New York and graduate of Allegheny College, Smith has written for the *Saturday Evening Post* and has been a speech writer for John Connally and Ronald Reagan. His previous foray into baseball history was a biography of pitcher/broadcaster Dizzy Dean in 1978, and he has also written radio/TV columns for *Baseball Bulletin* and *Baseball* magazine.

The book follows a roughly chronological order from the earliest days of radio, 1921–1933, to 1987. Interspersed are four chapters featuring famous calls and typical descriptions by various announcers and two attractive photograph sections which present the leading men behind the microphone from a conservatively attired Graham McNamee, to barechested Harry Caray. A page and one-half bibliography, five page chronology and useful index close the volume. The reader meets all the principal team and network announcers, from radio pioneers such as Pittsburgh's Harold Arlin and St. Louis' France Laux to television contemporaries like Al Michaels and Tim McCarver, and the book ranges from major personalities such as Mel Allen and Vin Scully to lesser known figures such as Hal Totten and Loel Passe.

Smith includes extensive detail and a wealth of illustrative quotations, some familiar and some not. From the text and acknowledgments it is evident that he has employed an impressive array of sources, including at least 38 interviews with announcers and broadcast executives as well as materials from the National Baseball Library. Unfortunately, historians will be disappointed at the absence of footnotes, and the skimpy bibliography which contains no list of interviews, no articles, and a sadly incomplete list of books. Missing are several helpful autobiographical accounts and many important books including Benjamin Rader's *In Its Own Image,* the second and third volumes of David Voigt's *American Baseball,* and Dick Crepeau's *Baseball: America's Diamond Mind.* These missing works would have given Smith's account needed perspective, conceptual sharpness, and broader meaning.

Stylistically *Voices of the Game* reminds one of a former sportswriter who entitled his column "Hanging Out the Morning Wash." Interesting details are strung together in short choppy paragraphs, loosely organized around time periods and teams. Smith seems more interested in nostalgia than in a search for meaning and explanation. For example, the reader is advised that Bill White was the first black broadcaster, but no attempt is made to describe or assess the efforts of blacks to integrate the sportscast booth. Efforts to relate developments in sport to other events in society can be a valuable technique, but *Voices'* digressions into the social and political scene fail to hang well with the rest of the work. Often the reader feels as if someone is switching the radio or television dials from sports events to news programs without any attempt to relate the two.

Despite these weaknesses, students owe a debt to Smith for identifying the broadcast crews and for the wealth of information he provides about baseball broadcasting. Despite his emphasis on the entertainment value of his material, Smith offers some interesting insights. For instance he suggests that Tony Kubek's puritanical view of the game and distaste for distractions such as the Chicken and ball girls arose from the former Yankee's need to reaffirm the professionalism of the game he had played. Smith also re-enforces the impression that broadcast executives need to cater to a variety of sports audiences from the knowledgeable cable fans who follow baseball closely all season long, to the more general viewers who equate baseball solely with the playoffs and World Series.

Many of the book's shortcomings may result from its treating a relatively untouched subject, and on balance there is much to recommend it. Baseball fans will welcome the trip down memory lane and the evocation of faded voices and moments. Historians will welcome Smith's new material and view it as a starting point for refined judgments about broadcasters and the relationship between the game and its communicators.

Jim Harper
Texas Tech University

Wimmer, Dick. *Baseball Fathers, Baseball Sons.* New York: Morrow, 1988. 192 pp. $15.95.

Try as I might, ultimately, I have difficulty liking *Baseball Fathers, Baseball Sons.* This situation is not prompted by a lack of rich metaphors for baseball or fatherhood (i.e., baseball as socialization or as rite of passage, fatherhood and herohood fused in an odyssey of life and sport), because the book evokes many such fertile metaphors. My uneasiness is prompted by the awkwardness and loose construction with which these metaphors are juxtaposed.

Wimmer apparently presumes that the stature of the baseball "greats" interviewed will carry the book, and gives correspondingly little attention to structuring the text. His personal odyssey with his two sons while collecting the interviews leaves him untransformed, the journey being less of an occasion for gaining new insight and more of an exercise in awe. Synthesis of the admittedly rich interviews with the likes of Ted Williams, Ozzie Smith, Sandy Koufax, et al.

171

is almost totally absent, with the exception of a single comment about the commonness of an obsessive dedication to the game (which often makes pro baseball fathers distant and inaccessible figures to their sons). Approaching his baseball heroes with the same hushed reverence that a boy might direct to a father who functions more as an idol than as a person, Wimmer sidesteps the responsibility to integrate or interpret what his heroes say, using their greatness as a tacit excuse for not doing so.

The structuring of chapters also reflects the nonsynthetic nature of the book. Short chapters detailing action on the home high school baseball team are interspersed with longer chapters composed of travelogue and interviews with pro heroes. The two sets of chapters meet only once at the end of the book, one highly satisfying hit which doesn't do much to relieve the frustrations of several other failures to connect in previous chapters.

Readers who share Wimmer's strong hero-worship principle will not share my dissatisfaction. There is pleasure to derive in witnessing Wimmer's enjoyment in traveling to collect the material for the book. It seems overwrought, however, to claim that sports stars are the "true American royalty." Americans also honestly dislike the notion of royalty. In the quintessentially American game, our heroes are rightfully worshipped, but they are in another sense not at all unlike ourselves. This latter point is the one that Wimmer ostensibly comes so close to, but in fact so cleanly misses. His sons appear to be more sanguine on this score, less in awe of the heroes and more likely simply to take practical benefit from their coaching.

My final misgiving about the book is with the sublimation of the game itself to the ego dynamics of the father-son relationship. The role of the son as a potential threat to the father's ego, "adolescent rebellion," and Dad's sensitivity to being called "lame," are foregrounded in such a way as to detract from the commonality of playing baseball as a potential way of building truly shared experiences for fathers and sons. If Wimmer had repented at all of this highly hierarchical, Oedipal model, he could have written a much more interesting book, in which hero-worship and father-son competition were given their due, without putting a stranglehold on the creative impulse of the book.

If Wimmer's sons had figured more substantially as co-authors rather than being presented as playful, pesky, and pride-inducing offspring, the text might have come alive. Virtually no attention is given to sons as active shapers and inspirers of their fathers, to complement the reverse perspective. For example, in the discussion of Roy Hobbs (in the film *The Natural*, another text on baseball as odyssey, but an odyssey which does result in personal transformation), any reference to Hobbs' son and his effect on his father is noticeably lacking.

The unrelenting dualism in Wimmer's structuring of father-son and hero-fan relations renders the book, which on the basis of its subject matter had the potentiality of being truly excellent, essentially a mundane although still readable volume. Wimmer's sentimentalism in claiming that sharing baseball with his sons is like a second childhood (of which he would "not trade a moment for the world") raises an uneasy specter of baseball player as eternal adolescent, rather than as someone involved in a process of development to maturity—

maturity which accepts with grace the inevitability of the father's ultimate transformation from hero to teacher.

Karen Larson
Gustavus Adolphus College

Honig, Donald. *The Greatest Pitchers of all Time*. New York: Crown Publishers, Inc., 1988. 144 pp. $14.95.

Honig, Donald. *The Greatest First Basemen of all Time*. New York: Crown Publishers, Inc., 1988. 144 pp. $14.95.

Honig, Donald. *Baseball in the Thirties: A Decade of Survival*. New York: Crown Publishers, Inc., 1989. 240 pp. $24.95.

These three works on baseball by Donald Honig and published by Crown Publishers, Inc. definitely fit the category of "coffee table" books. Slick, glossy covers, lavish pictures, and a "folksy" writing style all contribute to the image of books meant to be selectively leafed through in one's leisure moments. Certainly they are attractive and provide a quick reference to many of the former greats of professional baseball.

In *The Greatest Pitchers of All Time*, Honig has selected 22 pitchers beginning with Cy Young, Rube Waddell and Dizzy Dean, and concluding with such modern mound heroes as Jim Palmer, Steve Carlton and Tom Seaver. Certainly one cannot quarrel with the author's selections but one wonders why not have the top 25 pitchers of all time. This would then allow the inclusion of Ferguson Jenkins which would help to "integrate" Honig's list. Also, a recent study by Theodore Hindson of Southwest Texas State University listed Nolan Ryan as the fifth best pitcher of all time. (Hindson used a rather complicated point system, i.e., 100 points for pitching 600 games, 100 points for having 2,000 strikeouts, etc.) Honig acknowledges that Ryan holds numerous records but states that "on the dark side of Ryan's ledger, the thing that has kept him from scaling pitching's ultimate heights, is his wildness. . . . This liberality has held the otherwise nearly unhittable Ryan to a lifetime 261–242 record" (after the 1987 season). This seems entirely too subjective and makes as much sense as not including someone as a great hitter who hit over 40 home runs a season for 10 seasons because he had a lot of strikeouts.

The basic format is to simply introduce the pitcher and provide a number of pictures which reflect various stages of the player's career. Many of these are very rare photos and the author should be congratulated for his efforts in this endeavor. The text is liberally sprinkled with quotes from contemporaries which lends a nice authenticity to the vignettes. Sometimes, however, the author's penchant for purple prose is almost overwhelming. For example, in referring to Walter Johnson, Honig states, "He was in his way more representative of his country than anyone else in that city of elected representatives, a genuine embodiment of the bruited American ethos."

The Greatest First Basemen of All Time follows the same format. It has only 19 players on the list and includes such fan favorites as George Sisler, Lou Gehrig, Jimmie Foxx, and Hank Greenberg as well as modern era stars such as Steve Garvey, Keith Hernandez, Eddie Murray, and Don Mattingly. Those chosen had to play the position exclusively which is why the author argues, rather logically, that he left out such stars as Stan Musial and Ernie Banks. Lifetime records of the "chosen" are included at the end of the work (this was true of the *The Greatest Pitchers* also).

Baseball in the Thirties: A Decade of Survival promises more than it delivers. Those readers expecting baseball in the thirties to be put within the perspective of the Great Depression will be disappointed. Honig follows a pattern of a year-by-year chronology replete with numerous pictures and a special feature on one outstanding player of that year. Sometimes Honig's folksy characterizations work very well. In describing Washington owner Clark Griffith as a "man who left pressure marks on every dollar he touched" and of whom it was said, "that he would sell his own mother if the price was right," Honig noted that it wasn't his mother he sold but "his manager, shortstop, and son-in-law Joe Cronin." Certainly this is both humorous and informative. However, as a history this is merely chronology. Even an extended essay on the impact of baseball on such cities as Detroit, Chicago, and St. Louis, hard hit by the depression, the development of a "new breed" of cocky players that fans could identify with and steps that major league baseball took to ensure popularity such as the return to a livelier ball, and the introduction in 1933 of the All-Star game would have been useful.

In summary, these works by Honig are attractive, picture-filled volumes, which will be of interest to casual and younger fans, and can provide some quick points of reference to serious scholars of the game. For interpretive and analytical discussion, the serious scholar and fan will have to look elsewhere.

Lawrence E. Ziewacz
Michigan State University

Kinsella, W.P. *The Further Adventures of Slugger McBatt*. New York: Houghton Mifflin Co., 1988. 179 pp. $7.95 (pbk.).

After two highly successful novels, *Shoeless Joe* and *The Iowa Baseball Confederacy* (the former was also the basis for a film, *Field of Dreams*), W.P. Kinsella is back in his favorite genre, the short story. The 10 stories in *The Further Adventures of Slugger McBatt,* several of which have already appeared individually elsewhere, comprise his second collection of baseball stories (the first was *The Thrill of the Grass*), and a splendid collection it is.

Those familiar with Kinsella's novels will recognize old friends in some of the stories. Gideon Clarke, the narrator of *The Iowa Baseball Confederacy,* returns with two more tales which add to the magic lore of Johnson County, Iowa, where things are still "out of kilter." There is also a spin-off from *Shoeless Joe,* "The Eddie Scissons Syndrome," a quasi-scientific look at the imposters who claim to be former major leaguers in order to bask vicariously in the fame they never achieved themselves.

Individually, the stories in *Slugger McBatt* range on a spectrum from the delicate and simple "Frank Pierce, Iowa" to the intense and complex "K Mart." "K Mart" explores childhood as "the best days of our lives" but dwells on the haunting adult sense of "what-might-have-been" if only we had acted in time. The suicide of an old friend dredges up regret for youthful betrayal and the feeling of having contributed to the death of "real flesh and blood with a heart that breaks and a soul full of human longings."

"Frank Pierce, Iowa" describes the silent, mysterious disappearance of a small town through a "crack in time." Significantly, this happens at the juncture of two American religions, i.e., the end of a church service and the beginning of a baseball game. With the angelic boy who leads the town into the next dimension and the promise that "What is about to happen to us will not be death," it is a localized version of what is sometimes termed the "rapture," the calling away of believers in Christian eschatology. In something of a departure from Kinsella's novels, only this story among the 10 in *Slugger McBatt* makes significant reference to religion.

Collectively, the tales fall between the dreamy fantasy of *Shoeless Joe* and the apocalyptic churning of the floodwaters in *The Iowa Baseball Confederacy*, though they are perhaps closer to the latter. The result is the lovely mix of whimsy and melancholy which characterizes Kinsella's writing and consistently makes it much more than "just" about baseball. Baseball does indeed provide the common thread which links the characters and the stories in *Slugger McBatt,* but there are fewer game sequences and "Baseball is . . ." discourses than in the other works. The author makes this point by having one narrator declare, "this is not a story about baseball," though he goes on to advise the reader, "Perhaps I should let you be the judge of that."

What the stories are about is the "soul full of human longings," even in the panicked extraterrestrial being in "Reports Concerning the Death of the Seattle Albatross are Somewhat Exaggerated." Beyond their easy humor, the tales depict the poignant trials and struggles of life—loneliness, rejection, intimidation, sexual longing, the search for an identity under social pressure to conform—and mankind's attempts to come to grips with them. Sometimes the strategies are successful, as in the title story where the narrator uses his artistic talents, first as a refuge then as revenge, to cope with the neighborhood bully. At other times, it is evident that Kinsella's characters are walking a fine line between sanity and madness, life and death. We see that human equilibrium is fragile and all too often yields irrational responses to stressful situations. This gives the stories an inner tension, which complements the structural tension created by key questions in most of the tales: "Will the town really disappear?", "What shall we do with Herky's ashes?", "Will I ever find Freddy?" The result is a rich kaleidoscope of stories which will take its rightful place alongside Kinsella's other great works of baseball fiction.

Allen E. Hye
Wright State University

An Essay Film Review of *Eight Men Out,*
Bull Durham, and *Major League*

Since the success of Barry Levinson's *The Natural* (1984), baseball films have turned from "box-office poison" (a term that Robert Cantwell used to describe sports films in a 1969 *Sports Illustrated* article) to box-office bonanza and video rental mainstay. Films about baseball have always been subjected to close scrutiny by reviewers who have felt obligated to protect the purity of the national game from contamination or exploitation by the movie medium. More often than not (and certainly not without justification or reason), reviewers have found fault with the historical inaccuracies and misrepresentations in baseball films, with the inevitable love story tie-in, with the badly staged action scenes, with the inability of writers and directors to characterize baseball players accurately, or with any other miscue or error that could be entered on the film review scorecard. Commentators have even ridiculed sports films for being stupidly or embarrassingly sentimental when they try to be serious or tragic.

Actually the turning point for baseball films occurred with the release of *Bang the Drum Slowly* (1973) and *The Bingo Long Traveling All-Stars and Motor Kings* (1976). *Bang the Drum Slowly,* with its screenplay written by Mark Harris based on his novel, showed that the drama of life and death and the meaning of friendship formed with a knowledge of the certainty of death could be poignantly captured in the ritual of baseball. The film showed that what happened to the New York Mammoths and to Henry Wiggen and Bruce Pearson off the diamond was important to the bonds that made a group of men a human community as well as a team. *Bingo Long* dramatized the developing solidarity of a group of Negro National League renegades who want to be "their own men" and to share the profits of their work equally. The emotional truth of this film resides in the pride of these remarkable players and in their determination to be free agents as men and ball players. While the eventual demise of the Negro Leagues is signalled with Esquire Joe Callaway's signing to a minor league contract, Bingo Long and Leon Carter, who are considered too old to make the white major leagues, will play out their days in their renovated St. Louis park and see their stardom eclipsed by those taken in past the "color line."

The power of baseball films, then, is concentrated in their ability to dramatize and incorporate emotional truths, their capacity for revising baseball history or our sense of it, their visual power of capturing the meanings of the sport as ritual and secular religion, and their potential for focusing on national themes and a creed of faith as these are centered in baseball. Current filmmakers like John Sayles, Ron Shelton, and David Ward clearly understand this power as the "heart of the order," and they have produced films that are rich in thematic meanings and visual images. While baseball appeals to the statisticians and quantifiers as well as those who worship its inherent beauty of numerology, the sport also speaks untold volumes to the American spirit and to that side of our national psyche that knows that human drama is more than the statistical record and that character (or the lack of it or failure of it) is the litmus test of greatness or legendary status.

John Sayles offers a revisionist view of the Black Sox Scandal in *Eight Men Out* as well as an analysis of America coming of age in the postwar era in 1919–1920. The conspiring players are not condemned outright as their act is placed in the larger context of the stinginess of Charles Comiskey, the greed and amorality of the underworld fixers, the corruption of the postwar period that baseball was not immune from, the highly individualized motives of each player, the seductive power of temptation when one allows oneself into its presence. As Sayles has said, this film offers insight into why the players would have done it, making the fix understandable but not justifiable. *Eight Men Out* is an American tragedy of manipulation as the players become successive pawns in the hands of their owner, the gamblers, and the league officials who wanted this "single sin" (as David Q. Voigt has called it) removed with all taint. Sayles has dramatize the complex series of events with bribes, cross-bribes, double-crosses, treachery, and confusions with skillfully developed tension. Like all great tragedies, this is a study of character and its responses to the forces of pride, greed, desire for revenge, sense of being wronged, and other motivating factors.

As Sayles has also said, this is a "film about growing up," and America's coming of age is not without its price or costs. The players are victimized by external forces as well as by the limitations of their backgrounds, temperaments, and personalities. One senses from watching this remarkably rich film that something significant happened in this sad episode beyond the eventual expelling of the players. One is astounded at the cynicism of the gamblers and their contempt for the national pastime as well as their low views of human nature. The underside of the American dream is fully exposed as self-interest proves to be the cornerstone of entrepreneurship. Baseball is a business opportunity to those who control it, and monetary concerns dominate. When the players try to take a larger share, they jeopardize everything and become the villains and corrupters. Sayles tells a complex story in *Eight Men Out,* and he refuses to simplify the developments, making the viewer deal with the complexities. The film is a triumph of storytelling and narrative, and it takes its place with Arthur Miller's *Death of a Salesman* and *All My Sons* as great American tragedies and insights into the American soul.

Ron Shelton directed *Bull Durham* and wrote its rich and quirky screenplay. It is a baseball film that affirms America's belief in baseball and in its magical qualities and emotional satisfactions. For Annie Savoy, baseball is a church, a religion without guilt, and an opportunity to share her unusual wisdom with her annually chosen player on the Durham Bulls minor league team. Annie makes her projects feel "confident" and helps them "expand their minds," and they make her "feel safe. And pretty." It is an exchange that works well for her, and for Nuke LaLoosh, the young pither with an arm that is a gift of the gods, whom she takes as a lover only after she has read Whitman to him all night on the first night of their relationship.

While the minor leagues may be, for a few, the steppingstone, for Crash Davis the Carolinas League is another step down in the organization and another level closer to the end of his almost exclusively minor league career (with only 21 days in "The Show"). He has been sent to Durham to teach Nuke what is required to be a major leaguer. In the process of making Nuke respect his talent, taking the signs the catcher gives him, and learning how to pitch without thinking, Crash Davis has his best season in baseball. Nuke is called up to the "Big Show" as the big club expands its roster at the end of the season, and Crash is cut loose as an expendable commodity. He finds a job with the Asheville Tourists, hits his 247th home run, and decides it is time to quit.

Crash's compensation for this disappointment is the love that he discovers for Annie Savoy. At first, both of them are reluctant to admit that they could establish a committed and permanent relationship. Annie's "boys," like Nuke, make her feel young and "pretty" as well as "safe," and her relationship with Crash involves risks. Eventually Annie trades Nuke for Crash, who speaks Annie's language of passion combined with intelligence and who respects the game of baseball as a way of life and belief. When Crash is told of his outright release from the Bulls, he goes to Annie's house, and she takes him into the inner sanctum of her private shrine to baseball. Her sanctuary (which she did not allow Nuke to see or share) is replete with historical pictures (including one of a woman's baseball team), gloves, candles, memorabilia, and a color photograph of Thurman Munson with a newspaper about his death in an airplane crash. While she loses Crash briefly as he finishes his career with the Asheville club, he returns to her and indicates that he may become a minor league manager in the organization. He has the brains, patience, and knowledge to manage. For Annie and Crash, baseball is a way of life. In the voice-over of the closing sequence Annie quotes Walt Whitman: "I see great things in baseball. It's our game, the American game. It will repair our losses and be a blessing to us." Baseball, then, repairs the losses of middle age and blesses us with its ritual of renewal, its confirmation of the gifted gods who are chosen to play it at its highest level, and its integrity as a simple sport that rewards us with joy and satisfaction. Baseball is a national resource where talent and class combine to produce a much needed show of meaningful action and secular ritual. It is also a world of natural actions and a world where any kind of theory can be applied, regardless of how wild or outrageous. It is the Dionysian spirit incorporated, and as one of the Durham Bulls' coaches says, it sure "beats working at Sears." *Bull Durham* shows how the spirit of play, the magical and unexpected, and the sublime and the ridiculous all are kept alive in baseball. It is not the religion of our forefathers but the religion created out of the magical origins of games and play. Baseball is the closest thing to a natural religion that we have.

Major League, written and directed by David Ward, is another in the long line of film comedies about baseball and starts out looking like an extended Cleveland joke. However, the underlying themes of the film are directly relevant to the modern situation of baseball as a profitable business and lucrative profession.

As the new owner of the Cleveland Indians franchise, former showgirl Rachel Phelps has inherited a team that she wants to fail so she can move it to Miami. There she has been promised a new stadium, with high revenue producing luxury private boxes, as well as a "sweetheart" deal that includes a new condominium for her. In order to utilize an escape clause in her contract with the city, she sets out to put together a team of aging or over-the-hill veterans and no-name, inexperienced rookies that will fail to draw over 800,000 fans for the season. Mrs. Phelps views the franchise as a business commodity and personal plaything, not as a team with tradition or identification with the city of Cleveland.

The players invited to spring training are a diverse group that seems well suited to fulfilling their planned futile and dismal season. However, what the scheming owner does not realize is that the older players, including Jake Taylor, the central character and a catcher, are determined to hold on longer in the majors. The younger players like "Wild Thing" Rickie Vaughan and Willie Mays Hayes are determined to prove themselves with this opportunity, and even a high paid star who is only concerned about his upcoming free agency and his handsome face as a marketable commodity can be persuaded by his manager and fellow players to play serious ball again.

The working-class theme is central to the appeal of *Major League*. When the team learns of the owner's plan, revealed to them by the manager, they become committed to try to win the pennant even though they know that their effort will mean that they will all be gone after the season. When the owner realizes that the team is making an effort to improve and is beginning to get the attention of the fans, she employs a negative incentive system by taking away the comforts and privileges of major league status. She arranges for them to travel in an antiquated turboprop plane and then in an aging bus. They are reduced to minor league status, but as the "perqs" are taken away, they become more determined to play with pride and to win. They realize that being a major leaguer means performing with professional pride, with dedication to the game and an appreciation for its personal rewards, and with team solidarity. The long buried pride of Cleveland in its team re-emerges as the Indians go from a 60–61 team to tie the Yankees for the division and force a dramatic one-game playoff that is one of the best action sequences in any baseball film.

In the playoff game the wily old veteran pitcher, who is a Gaylord Perry type that doctors baseballs with anything from Vaseline to snoot, holds the team in the game and is relieved in the ninth by "Wild Thing" Rickie Vaughan, who strikes out the triple-crown Yankee slugger on three fast balls. With the game tied 2–2 Willie Mays Hayes, the black outfielder and speed merchant base stealer, beats out a grounder to first, steals second, and scores from second on a squeeze bunt by Jake Taylor. Bad knees and all, Taylor beats the throw to first and Hayes streaks home. The Indians have won by being scrappy, determined, and united. They have shown that they can be major leaguers by trying harder and by being united in a common cause. Overcoming the humiliations and deprivations imposed by their owner, they show that high-priced ball players do not guarantee success.

While David Ward's *Major League* is clearly a comedy and has some great comic sequences (the individual arrivals of the team members at the spring training site, the manager's urinating on Roger Dorn's high-priced contract that says he does not have to do calisthenics, and the radio broadcasting sequences with Bob Uecker), the underlying theme is a serious one and one that strikes a responsive cord in audiences tired of pampered and spoiled superstars and conniving owners. Baseball may well be the only source of miracles or the place where players can still define the values and meanings of the game in spite of the efforts of others to treat it as a business commodity. This film is closer to David Anspach's *Hoosiers* than it is to the *Rocky* formula because *Major League* is rooted in an American value system and set of attitudes about work and effort. Popular fictions and fantasies contain real truths and emotions, and underneath its comic surface, *Major League* is an expression of many feelings of working-class America.

These three recent baseball films reveal the skill of the directors/writers (and in all three instances the director also wrote the screenplay) to show how baseball remains our national game, how we can still see "great things" in it, and how it repairs our losses and is a blessing to us (to rephrase Annie Savoy, who is quoting Whitman).*

Douglas A. Noverr
Michigan State University

---

*Note: This review was written before *Field of Dreams* was released.

CONTRIBUTORS

Robert Barney is a professor of physical education at the University of Western Ontario where he teaches and writes sport history. A college athlete at the University of New Mexico he has been a "blood red" Bosox fan since 1939.

Bill Felber, editor of the *Manhattan Mercury,* in Manhattan, Kansas, is a frequent contributor to *Baseball History.*

W.P. Kinsella has published 14 books and over 200 short stories. He is best known for his multi-award winning novel *Shoeless Joe.* Other books include *The Iowa Baseball Confederacy, The Thrill of the Grass, Dance Me Outside,* and *The Fencepost Chronicles.* This past spring, the movie *Field of Dreams,* based on *Shoeless Joe* and starring Kevin Costner and James Earl Jones, captured the hearts of many who saw it, whether they were baseball fans or not.

Walter Langford's interviews have been a regular feature since *Baseball History* first appeared. He is the author of *Legends of Baseball* and is a retired Notre Dame professor of modern languages.

Norman Macht, a former general manager in the minor leagues, is the co-author, along with Dick Bartell, of *Rowdy Richard.* He is currently working on a biography of Connie Mack.

Debra Shattuck is a captain in the United States Air Force and currently teaches American history at the United States Air Force Academy at Colorado Springs. Her work on women and baseball has also appeared in *Total Baseball.*

Wayne Stewart's writings on baseball have appeared in *Baseball Digest,* the SABR *Research Journal,* and the official publications of a number of major league baseball clubs. He also writes a regular column for *Baseball Bulletin.*

A.D. Suehsdorf has been writing baseball history since he retired as editorial director of Ridge Press. His work has appeared in *Baseball History,* numerous SABR publications and in the recently published *Total Baseball.*

David Voigt is a professor of sociology at Albright College. He is the author of *American Baseball,* a three volume history of the game and most recently of *Baseball: An Illustrated History.*